COGNITIVE NEUROPSYCHOLOGY

Volume 23 • Issue 5 • July 2006

Special issue: Selective deficits in developmental cognitive neuropsychology

Guest editor: Bradley C. Duchaine

Contents

COGNITIVE NEUROPSYCHOLOGY

The journal aims to promote the study of cognitive processes from a neuropsychological perspective. Cognition is understood broadly as including perception, attention, object recognition, planning, language, thinking, memory, and action. It covers neuropsychological work bearing on our understanding of normal and pathological cognitive processes at any stage of lifespan. It also covers neuroimaging and computational modeling research that is informed by consideration of neuropsychological phenomena.

Cognitive Neuropsychology is of interest to cognitive scientists and neuroscientists, neuropsychologists, neurologists, psycholinguists, speech pathologists, physiotherapists, and psychiatrists.

Notes for contributors are available from the publisher on request and manuscript submission guidelines are given on the inside back cover of most issues.

Subscription information

Cognitive Neuropsychology is published by Psychology Press Ltd, an imprint of the Taylor & Francis Group, an Informa business.

New subscriptions and changes of address should be sent to: Psychology Press, c/o T&F Customer Services, Informa UK Ltd, Sheepen Place, Colchester, Essex, CO3 3LP, UK. Telephone: + 44 (0)20 7017 5544; Fax: + 44 (0)20 7017 5198; Email: tf.enquiries@tfinforma.com

Send change of address notices at least six weeks in advance, and include both old and new addresses.
Subscription rates to Volume 23, 2006 (8 issues) are as follows (prices inclusive of postage and packing):
To individuals: £290.00 (UK); $478.00 (Rest of world)
To institutions: £900.00 (UK); $1,485.00 (Rest of world)
Cognitive Neuropsychology (**USPS permit number 016265**) is published eight times per year in February, March, May, June, July, September, October, and December. The 2006 US Institutional subscription price is $1,485.00. Periodicals postage paid at Jamaica, NY by US Mailing Agent Air Business Ltd, c/o Priority Airfreight NY Ltd, 147-29 182nd Street, Jamaica, NY 11413, USA. **US Postmaster**: Please send address changes to pCGN, Air Business Ltd, c/o Priority Airfreight NY Ltd, 147-29 182nd Street, Jamaica, NY 11413, USA.

Back issues: Taylor & Francis retains a 3-year back issue stock of journals. Older volumes are held by our official stockists: Periodicals Service Company, 11 Main Street, Germantown, NY 12526, USA to whom all orders and enquiries should be addressed. Tel: + 1 518 537 4700; Fax: + 1 518 537 5899; Email: psc@periodicals.com; URL: http://www.periodicals.com/tandf.html

Information about Psychology Press journals and other publications is available from http://www.psypress.co.uk

Go to www.psypress.com/cogneuropsychology for current information about this journal, including how to access the online version or to register for the free table of contents alerting service.

Cognitive Neuropsychology is covered by the following abstracting, indexing, and citation services: Current Contents (ISI); ASSIA; APA PsycINFO; Sociological Abstracts; Biosciences Information Service; MLA International Bibliography; EMBASE; LLBA; Neuroscience Citation Index (ISI); Research Alerts (ISI); Social SciSearch (ISI); Social Science Citation Index (ISI); Social Services Abstracts; SciSearch (ISI); CDAB; UnCover; Linguistics Abstracts; SCOPUS.

Typeset in the United Kingdom by Techset Composition Limited, Salisbury, Wiltshire.

COGNITIVE NEUROPSYCHOLOGY, 2006, 23 (5), 675–679

Psychology Press
Taylor & Francis Group

Selective deficits in developmental cognitive neuropsychology: An introduction

Bradley C. Duchaine
Institute of Cognitive Neuroscience, University College London, UK

Traditionally, neuropsychologists have studied selective impairments in patients who suffered brain damage as adults. These selective impairments have revealed much about cognitive organization in normal brains (Shallice, 1988; Zeki, 1993) and have initiated major research programmes (Forde & Humphreys, 2002; Milner & Goodale, 1995; Shallice, 1988; Yin, 1969; Zeki, 1993). In addition, analysis of lesion location in patients with selective deficits has been critical for the localization of cognitive mechanisms (Broca, 1861; Milner & Goodale, 1995; Scoville & Milner, 1957).

Although most documented selective impairments were caused by brain damage in adulthood, selective impairments can also result from developmental disorders. Rather than suffering damage to particular mature cognitive mechanisms, individuals with selective developmental disorders fail to develop certain cognitive mechanisms. A number of developmental disorders have been investigated using a cognitive neuropsychology approach (Baron-Cohen, Leslie, & Frith, 1985; Butterworth, 1999; Coltheart, Masterson, Byng, Prior, & Riddoch, 1983; Temple, 1989, 1997), and recent years have seen growing interest in selective developmental disorders (Blair, 2005; Duchaine & Nakayama, 2005; Klein, Cosmides, Murray, & Tooby, 2004; Nijboer, van Zandvoort, & de Haan, in press; Peretz & Hyde, 2003; Temple & Richardson, 2004). Selective developmental deficits have also generated considerable discussion in recent years (see Thomas & Karmiloff-Smith, 2002, and the commentaries), with some even suggesting that such deficits are unlikely to exist (Karmiloff-Smith, Scerif, & Ansari, 2003; Thomas & Karmiloff-Smith, 2002).

SUMMARY OF THE PAPERS

This special issue presents four papers that showcase the power and promise of cognitive neuropsychology approaches to selective developmental disorders. Collectively the papers demonstrate that developmental disorders can contribute to a range of research areas and address varied questions within an area. The papers investigate selective developmental deficits affecting four abilities: spatial perception, face perception, reading, and memory. They also differ in their aims. Three papers attempt to determine the nature of the impaired mechanisms giving rise to the disorder (Duchaine, Yovel, Butterworth, & Nakayama, 2006; Temple & Richardson, 2006; White, Frith, Milne, Rosen, Swettenham, & Ramus, 2006), and White et al. (2006) also test a hypothesis about the etiology of dyslexia. In contrast, McCloskey, Valtonen, and Sherman (2006) use the pattern of errors made in spatial tasks to

Correspondence should be addressed to Bradley C. Duchaine, Institute of Cognitive Neuroscience, University College London, Alexandra House, 17 Queen Square, London WC1 N 3AR, UK (Email: b.duchaine@ucl.ac.uk).

http://www.psypress.com/cogneuropsychology
DOI:10.1080/02643290600631515

develop a theory of how object orientation is represented. Despite their differences, all the papers interpret their results within standard cognitive models or, in the case of McCloskey et al., propose a cognitive model to account for their results. Each paper also discusses the issues that researchers face when making inferences from selective developmental deficits.

In a series of papers, McCloskey and colleagues (McCloskey & Palmer, 1996; McCloskey & Rapp, 2000a, 2000b; McCloskey et al., 1995) have documented the severe visual localization deficits experienced by a young woman, AH, with no history of neurological damage and many normal visual abilities. On tasks requiring AH to point to the location at which an object appeared, she pointed to the opposite side of the display on half of the trials. Amazingly, even though she was unable to judge the side on which the object was presented, she accurately indicated the distance of the object from the centre of the display. Her pattern of errors led to the proposal that object location is represented by separately specifying the distance of the object and the direction of the object from a reference point in a spatial coordinate system (McCloskey et al., 1995). In this issue, McCloskey, Valtonen, and Sherman (2006) extend their coordinate-system hypothesis to the representation of object orientation. They report results from three subjects with object-orientation deficits and demonstrate that their extension of the coordinate-system hypothesis can account for the subjects' striking errors.

In the second article, my colleagues and I (Duchaine, Yovel, Butterworth, & Nakayama, 2006) take a new approach to prosopagnosia. For years, cognitive neuroscientists have debated whether face processing involves content-specific mechanisms specialized for faces. To address this issue with a more systematic approach than past case studies of prosopagnosia, we tested the predictions of each alternative to the face-specific account. Our results were inconsistent with each alternative hypothesis and thus implicate impairments to face-specific mechanisms. In addition, the results indicate that the construction of face-specific mechanisms involves a developmental process not involved in the development of other visual recognition mechanisms.

The sensorimotor hypothesis of developmental dyslexia proposes that the phonological deficits underlying reading problems in dyslexia arise due to preexisting sensorimotor impairments. In the third article, White, Frith, Milne, Rosen, Swettenham, and Ramus (2006) test the predictions of the sensorimotor hypothesis with a powerful combination of approaches. First, they examined whether developmental dyslexia is invariably accompanied by sensorimotor impairments. Consistent with other results (Ramus et al., 2003), many children with dyslexia were normal with sensorimotor tasks. However, because the dyslexic children were more likely to have sensorimotor impairments than control children, sensorimotor impairments may be a sufficient but not a necessary cause of reading impairments. If so, sensorimotor impairments should lead to reading impairments. Autistic children have higher rates of sensorimotor impairments than normal children, so the authors assessed the sensorimotor and reading abilities of a group of autistic children. The autistic children showed a mixture of normal and impaired performance on both the sensorimotor measures and the reading measures. Critically, many autistic children with sensorimotor impairments had normal reading skills, and the occurrence of sensorimotor impairments within the autistic group was entirely independent of the occurrence of reading impairments. Hence, the combination of results from dyslexic and autistic subjects reveals a double dissociation between sensorimotor ability and reading ability, which strongly suggests that developmental dyslexia is not caused by sensorimotor impairments.

Cognitive theories of memory propose the existence of multiple memory systems that carry out different functions (Schacter & Tulving, 1994). Past work has found that some of these systems are developmentally dissociable (Temple & Richardson, 2004; Vargha-Khadem et al., 1997). Temple and Richardson (2006) extend this work by demonstrating a new set of dissociations. In particular, they studied the case of MM, a nine-year-old boy without any history of brain damage. MM's results showed intact visual episodic memory and normal learning over repeated trials. In contrast, he had deficits with verbal episodic memory, autobiographical episodic memory, and semantic memory.

DEVELOPMENTAL DEFICITS AND THE TRANSPARENCY ASSUMPTION

Some researchers have argued that developmental disorders, unlike acquired disorders, are unlikely to be properly described within standard cognitive theories and should not be used to draw inferences about normal cognition or normal cognitive development (Karmiloff-Smith et al., 2003; Thomas & Karmiloff-Smith, 2002). Neuropsychological inferences are based on a number of assumptions (Caramazza, 1986; Shallice, 1988), one of which is the transparency assumption,[1] which maintains that overall cognitive organization in cases with neuropsychological impairments is normal except for the impaired mechanisms and their outputs (Caramazza, 1986, 1992). Violation of the transparency assumption is argued to be especially likely in developmental disorders, because plasticity in developing brains is likely to lead to atypical cognitive mechanisms and overall organization (Thomas & Karmiloff-Smith, 2002).

Because cognitive reorganization may occur after brain damage, similar concerns also apply to studies with acquired disorders. Shallice (1988) suggests two defences against misleading dissociations due to reorganization after brain damage, and these are also applicable to developmental disorders. First, inferences should be based on classical dissociations, which contrast normal performance on one task with impaired performance on another task, rather than dissociations in which performance on neither task is normal. Classical dissociations are stronger evidence for dissociability, because they suggest that the mechanism carrying out the task performed normally is not impaired. The second defence against spurious dissociations is the double dissociation. Spurious double dissociations could arise only if damage to a mechanism or a failure to develop it led to opposite dissociations in different individuals. While possible, such an outcome seems unlikely.

The fit between normal models of cognition and results from acquired cases indicates that the transparency assumption is not violated after brain damage. Similarly, past studies (Temple, 1997) and the papers in this issue suggest that normal cognitive models effectively account for selective impairments in developmental disorders, but undoubtedly this issue will continue to be an important topic in developmental cognitive neuropsychology.

DEVELOPMENTAL DISORDERS AND DEVELOPMENTAL MODULARITY

The preceding discussion suggests that developmental disorders, like acquired disorders, can contribute to models of normal cognition. However, developmental disorders also can provide additional information not supplied by acquired disorders. Dissociations in developmental disorders are not only functional dissociations, but also reveal dissociations between developmental processes (Temple, 1997).

For example, if a subject with a developmental disorder is normal with tasks measuring Ability A and severely impaired with tasks for Ability B, this dissociation suggests that the cognitive mechanisms underlying Ability A developed normally while those underlying Ability B did not. This developmental dissociation indicates that the development of the cognitive mechanisms for Ability A rely on different developmental

[1] The transparency assumption is similar to Shallice's subtractivity assumption (1988) and Thomas and Karmiloff-Smith's assumption of residual normality (2002).

processes than do the mechanisms giving rise to Ability B. A double dissociation, like that seen in White et al. (2006), would indicate that the mechanisms for both abilities involve different developmental processes. Note, however, that the developmental dissociability of two cognitive mechanisms does not imply that their construction does not involve any of the same developmental processes, but only that they involve at least some different processes.[2]

FUTURE DIRECTIONS

Although the investigations of selective developmental deficits in this issue utilize behavioural measures to address cognitive and developmental issues, the study of selective developmental impairments also holds great promise for other research issues. Our understanding of the genetic basis of cognition is certain to increase enormously in the near future, and research into selective developmental disorders will contribute much to this exciting area (Fisher & DeFries, 2002; MacDermot et al., 2005; Meyer-Lindenberg et al., 2004). Selective developmental disorders, like selective acquired disorders, also provide a means to determine the location of cognitive functions (Meyer-Lindenberg et al., 2004; Molko et al., 2003). Research is also likely to uncover procedures that ameliorate selective deficits and lessen the difficulties created by these deficits (Merzenich et al., 1996; Temple et al., 2003).

Many questions can be addressed through these disorders, and the most powerful approaches will combine cognitive, neural, and genetic analyses in longitudinal studies (Ramus, 2004; Temple, 2003). Multi-faceted approaches will be demanding, but a deep understanding of these fascinating conditions will be an exceptional scientific achievement.

PrEview proof published online 30 March 2006

REFERENCES

Baron-Cohen, S., Leslie, A. M., & Frith, U. (1985). Does the autistic child have a "theory of mind"? *Cognition, 21*, 37–46.

Blair, R. J. R. (2005). Applying a cognitive neuroscience perspective to the disorder of psychopathology. *Developmental Psychopathology, 17*, 865–891.

Broca, P. (1861). Remarques sur le siege de la faculte de langage articule, suivies d'une observation d'aphemie. *Bulletin de la Societe Anatomique, 6*, 330–357.

Butterworth, B. (1999). *The mathematical brain.* London: Macmillan.

Caramazza, A. (1986). On drawing inferences about the structure of normal cognitive systems from the analysis of patterns of impaired performance: The case for single-patient studies. *Brain & Cognition, 5*, 41–66.

Caramazza, A. (1992). Is cognitive neuropsychology possible? *Journal of Cognitive Neuroscience, 4*, 80–95.

Coltheart, M., Masterson, J., Byng, S., Prior, M., & Riddoch, M. J. (1983). Surface dyslexia. *Quarterly Journal of Experimental Psychology, 35*, 469–495.

Duchaine, B., & Nakayama, K. (2005). Dissociations of face and object recognition in developmental prosopagnosia. *Journal of Cognitive Neuroscience, 17*, 249–261.

Duchaine, B., Yovel, G., Butterworth, E.J., & Nakayama, K. (2006). Prosopagnosia as an impairment to face-specific mechanisms: Elimination of the alternative hypotheses in a developmental case. *Cognitive Neuropsychology, 23*, 714–747.

Fisher, S., & DeFries, J. C. (2002). Developmental dyslexia: Genetic dissection of a complex cognitive trait. *Nature Neuroscience Reviews, 3*, 767–780.

Forde, E. M. E., & Humphreys, G. W. (2002). *Category-specificity in mind and brain.* Hove, UK: Psychology Press.

Karmiloff-Smith, A., Scerif, G., & Ansari, D. (2003). Double dissociations in developmental disorders? Theoretically misconceived, empirically dubious. *Cortex, 39*, 161–163.

Klein, S., Cosmides, L., Murray, E., & Tooby, J. (2004). On the acquisition of knowledge about personality traits: Does learning about the self engage different mechanisms than learning about others? *Social Cognition, 22*, 367–390.

MacDermot, K. D., Bonora, E., Sykes, N., Coupe, A.-M., Lai, C., Vernes, S. C., Vargha-Khadem, F., McKenzie,

[2] In fact, given that the entire brain develops from a single cell, the construction of all cognitive mechanisms involves many shared developmental processes.

F., Smith, R. L., Monaco, A. P., & Fisher, S. E. (2005). Identification of FOXP2 truncation as a novel cause of developmental speech and language deficits. *American Journal of Human Genetics*, *76*, 1074–1080.

McCloskey, M., & Palmer, E. (1996). Visual representation of object location: Insights from localization impairments. *Current Directions in Psychological Science*, *5*, 25–28.

McCloskey, M., & Rapp, B. (2000a). A visually based developmental reading deficit. *Journal of Memory and Language*, *43*, 157–181.

McCloskey, M., & Rapp, B. (2000b). Attention-referenced visual representations: Evidence from impaired visual localization. *Journal of Experimental Psychology: Human Perception and Performance*, *26*, 917–933.

McCloskey, M., Rapp, B., Yantis, S., Rubin, G., Bacon, W. F., Dagnelie, G., Gordon, B., Aliminosa, D., Boatman, D. F., Badecker, W., Johnson, D. N., Tusa, R. J., & Palmer, E. (1995). A developmental deficit in localizing objects from vision. *Psychological Science*, *6*, 112–117.

McCloskey, M., Valtonen, J., & Sherman, J. (2006). Representing orientation: A coordinate-system hypothesis, and evidence from developmental deficits. *Cognitive Neuropsychology*, *23*, 680–713.

Merzenich, M. M., Jenkins, W. M., Johnston, P., Schreiner, C., Miller, S. L., & Tallal, P. (1996). Temporal processing deficits of language-learning impaired children ameliorated by training. *Science*, *271*, 77–81.

Meyer-Lindenberg, A., Kohn, P., Mervis, C. B., Kippenhan, J. S., Olsen, R. K., Morris, C. A., Berman, K. F. (2004). Neural basis of genetically determined visuospatial construction deficit in Williams syndrome. *Neuron*, *43*, 623–631.

Milner, A. D., & Goodale, M. A. (1995). *The visual brain in action*. New York: Oxford University Press.

Molko, N., Cachia, A., Riviere, D., Mangin, J. F., Bruandet, M., Le Bihan, D., et al. (2003). Functional and structural alterations of the intraparietal sulcus in a developmental dyscalculia of genetic origin. *Neuron*, *40*, 847–858.

Nijboer, T. C. W., van Zandvoort, M. J. E., & de Haan, E. H. F. (in press). Covert colour processing in colour agnosia. *Neuropsychologia*.

Peretz, I., & Hyde, K. L. (2003). What is specific to music processing? Insights from congenital amusia. *Trends in Cognitive Sciences*, *7*, 362–367.

Ramus, F. (2004). Neurobiology of dyslexia: A reinterpretation of the data. *Trends in Neurosciences*, *27*, 720–726.

Ramus, F., Rosen, S., Dakin, S. C., Day, B. L., Castellote, J. M., White, S., & Frith, U. (2003). Theories of developmental dyslexia: Insights from a multiple case study of dyslexic adults. *Brain*, *126*, 841–865.

Schacter, D. L., & Tulving, E. (1994). *Memory systems*. Cambridge, MA: MIT Press.

Scoville, W. B., & Milner, B. (1957). Loss of recent memory after bilateral hippocampal lesions. *Journal of Neurology, Neurosurgery & Psychiatry*, *20*, 11–21.

Shallice, T. (1988). *From neuropsychology to mental structure*. Cambridge, UK: Cambridge University Press.

Temple, C. M. (1989). Digit dyslexia: A category-specific disorder in developmental dyscalculia. *Cognitive Neuropsychology*, *6*, 93–116.

Temple, C. M. (1997). *Developmental cognitive neuropsychology*. Hove, UK: Psychology Press.

Temple, C. M., & Clahsen, H. (2002). How connectionist simulations fail to account for developmental disorders in children. *Behavioral and Brain Sciences*, *25*, 769–770.

Temple, C. M., & Richardson, P. (2004). Developmental amnesia: A new pattern of dissociation with intact episodic memory. *Neuropsychologia*, *42*, 764–781.

Temple, C. M., & Richardson, P. (2006). Developmental amnesia: Fractionation of developing memory systems. *Cognitive Neuropsychology*, *23*, 762–788.

Temple, E., Deutsch, G. K., Poldrack, R. A., Miller, S. L., Tallal, P., Merzenich, M. M., & Gabrieli, J. D. E. (2003). Neural deficits in children with dyslexia ameliorated by behavioural remediation: Evidence from fMRI. *Proceedings of the National Academy of Sciences*, *100*, 2860–2865.

Thomas, M., & Karmiloff-Smith, A. (2002). Are developmental disorders like cases of adult brain damage? Implications from connectionist modelling. *Behavioral and Brain Sciences*, *25*, 727–788.

Vargha-Khadem, F., Gadian, D. G., Watkins, K. E., Connelly, A., Van Paesschen, W. V., & Mishkin, M. (1997). Differential effects on early hippocampal pathology on episodic and semantic memory. *Science*, *277*, 376–380.

White, S., Frith, U., Milne, E., Rosen, S., Swettenham, J., & Ramus, F. (2006). A double dissociation between sensorimotor impairments and reading disability: A comparison of autistic and dyslexic children. *Cognitive Neuropsychology*, *23*, 748–761.

Yin, R.K. (1969). Looking at upside-down faces. *Journal of Experimental Psychology*, *81*, 141–145.

Zeki, S. (1993). *A vision of the brain*. Oxford: Blackwell.

Psychology Press
Taylor & Francis Group

Representing orientation: A coordinate-system hypothesis and evidence from developmental deficits

Michael McCloskey
Johns Hopkins University, Baltimore, MD, USA

Jussi Valtonen
Johns Hopkins University, Baltimore, MD, USA, and University of Helsinki, Helsinki, Finland

Janet Cohen Sherman
Harvard Medical School, Massachusetts General Hospital, Boston, MA, USA

This article concerns how the orientations of objects are represented in the human brain. We propose a coordinate-system hypothesis of orientation representation (COR) and show that the hypothesis provides an explicit basis for interpreting orientation errors. Next, we report results from three studies of individuals with developmental deficits in the processing of orientation information, demonstrating that the COR hypothesis can interpret the error patterns in each study. We conclude by discussing several issues concerning the interpretation of our results, the COR hypothesis, and the use of developmental deficits as a basis for inferences about normal cognition.

Representing the orientation of objects in the visual field is important for a variety of reasons. For example, perceiving the direction in which predators or potential prey are facing is a life-or-death matter for many creatures, and a person reaching out to grasp an object must apprehend how that object is oriented in order to position her hand appropriately. Even in circumstances not involving direct interaction with objects, information about orientation may be crucial for interpreting a visual scene. The significance of a scene may, for instance, be quite different depending upon whether two people in the scene are facing toward or away from one another. Orientation is also important in processing visual symbols, such as arrows on street signs, or letters of the alphabet (e.g., *b*, *d*, *n*, *u*).

Despite the importance of orientation information, little attention has been directed toward questions concerning how the orientation of objects is represented in the visual system (or elsewhere in the brain). Neurophysiological research has identified cells in primary visual cortex that are sensitive to the orientation of edges (e.g., Hubel & Wiesel, 1968). However, encoding the orientation of an entire object presumably implicates higher order representations at more central levels of the visual system, and the available

Correspondence should be addressed to Michael McCloskey, Department of Cognitive Science, Krieger Hall, Johns Hopkins University, 3400 N. Charles St., Baltimore, MD 21218, USA (Email: michael.mccloskey@jhu.edu).

We thank Daniel Dilks, Uyen Le, and Emma Gregory for helpful comments, Lucila Halperin and Sara Shavel-Jessop for help in preparation of figures, Cary Savage and Daniel Dilks for their assistance with the studies of T.M. and B.C., respectively, and B.C., T.M., and A.H. for their cooperation in the studies.

http://www.psypress.com/cogneuropsychology

DOI:10.1080/02643290500538356

neurophysiological evidence does not speak to the nature of such representations.

A substantial body of behavioural research explores orientation processing in normal and impaired children and adults, as well as in nonhuman species. In addition to clarifying the concept of orientation (Howard, 1982; Howard & Templeton, 1966) this research documents a variety of interesting phenomena, including difficulties in processing oblique orientations (for reviews, see Appelle, 1972; Rudel, 1982) and problems in mirror-image discrimination (for reviews, see Bornstein, 1982; Corballis & Beale, 1976; see also Davidoff & Warrington, 2001; Harris, Harris, & Caine, 2001; Turnbull, 1997; Turnbull, Beschin, & Della Salla, 1997; Turnbull, Della Salla, & Beschin, 2002; Turnbull, Laws, & McCarthy, 1995; Turnbull & McCarthy, 1996). In the context of these phenomena some general suggestions about representation of orientation have been offered. For example, several researchers have suggested that difficulties in discriminating left–right mirror images (e.g., b and d, → and ←) are a consequence of *reduction coding*, in which the internal representation of a stimulus (somehow) fails to represent the difference between the two mirror-image orientations, or *duplication coding*, in which representations of both orientations are generated regardless of the actual orientation of the stimulus (see, e.g., Corballis & Beale, 1976; Deregowski, McGeorge, & Wynn, 2000; Noble, 1968). However, these suggestions say nothing about how an object's orientation is represented.

We suggest that progress in understanding normal and impaired processing of object orientation requires the formulation of specific hypotheses concerning the nature of orientation representations. Our aim in this article is to present one such hypothesis. The hypothesis builds upon assumptions proposed by McCloskey and colleagues (McCloskey, 2004; McCloskey & Rapp, 2000b; McCloskey et al., 1995) concerning the representation of location in the visual system. These assumptions were motivated by the visual localization errors observed in A.H., a young woman with a developmental deficit in perceiving the location (and orientation) of visual stimuli. Accordingly, we first describe A.H.'s pattern of localization errors and the location-representation assumptions suggested by this pattern. We then present our hypothesis of orientation representation. Next, we describe results from three individuals with developmental deficits in orientation perception (including A.H.) and show that the orientation hypothesis provides a basis for interpreting the results. We conclude with a brief discussion of several issues concerning the proposed hypothesis, the interpretation of the reported results, and the use of developmental deficits as a basis for inferences about normal cognition.

A.H. AND VISUAL LOCATION REPRESENTATIONS

A.H., a right-handed woman with normal visual acuity and visual fields, was studied at Johns Hopkins University for a period of nearly four years, during which time she was 18–21 years old and an undergraduate university student (McCloskey, 2004; McCloskey & Palmer, 1996; McCloskey & Rapp, 2000a, 2000b; McCloskey et al., 1995). A.H. has no history of neurological injury or disease, and neurological examination, electroencephalogram, and structural magnetic resonance imaging conducted during the study revealed no abnormalities.

A.H.'s visual localization errors

A.H. exhibited systematic error patterns in tasks requiring her to perceive and respond to the location of visual stimuli. For example, in one task (McCloskey & Rapp, 2000b) an X was presented for 1 s on a computer monitor at a far left, near left, near right, or far right location while A.H. fixated a central point (see Figure 1A). Upon stimulus offset A.H. indicated where the X had appeared by touching the screen. On over half of the trials she touched the wrong side of the screen, and all of her errors were left–right reflections across the midline (e.g., touching the near right position for a target

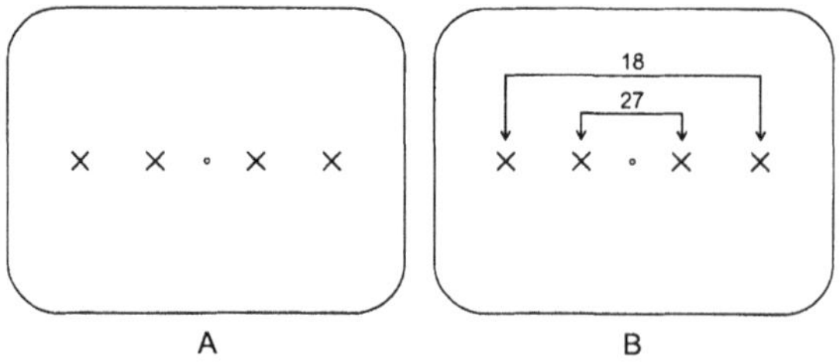

Figure 1. *A. The four locations on a computer monitor at which target Xs were presented one at a time. B. A.H.'s pattern of localization errors. The number above each arrow indicates the number of errors in which a stimulus presented at one of the connected positions was localized to the other position. For example, A.H. made 18 errors in which a target presented at the far left position was localized to the far right position, or vice versa.*

on the near left; see Figure 1B). Tasks requiring up–down localization of visual stimuli yielded analogous patterns of up–down reflection errors (McCloskey et al., 1995).

Coordinate-system location representations

On the basis of A.H.'s visual localization errors—left–right and up–down reflections—McCloskey and colleagues (McCloskey, 2004; McCloskey & Rapp, 2000b; McCloskey et al., 1995) proposed that at the level(s) of the visual system where her errors arise, locations of objects are represented in a spatial coordinate system defined by a reference point that serves as the origin and orthogonal axes through that point.

According to this hypothesis, an object's location is represented by specifying its distance and direction of displacement from the origin along each reference axis. For example, given a visual display involving a fixation point and a target stimulus (Figure 2A), a coordinate system might be defined by horizontal and vertical axes through the fixation point (Figure 2B). Assuming for convenience that polarity is assigned to the axes such that right and up are the positive

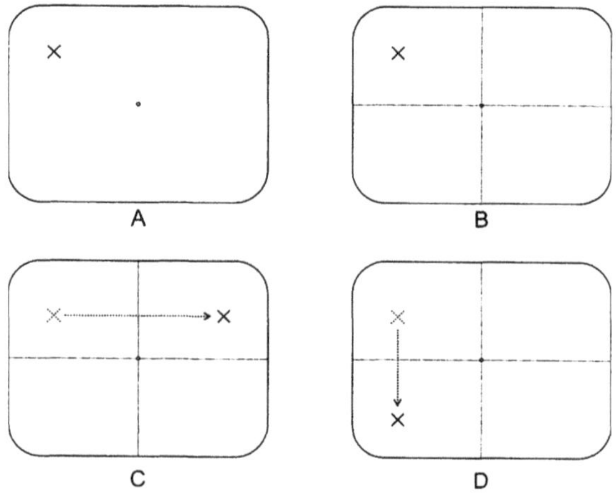

Figure 2. *A. Fixation point and X displayed on a computer monitor. B. Horizontal and vertical reference axes through the fixation point. C. Localization error that would result from specifying + rather than − as the direction of displacement along the horizontal reference axis. D. Localization error that would result from specifying − rather than + as the direction of displacement along the vertical reference axis.*

directions, whereas left and down are negative, the location of the target might be represented as follows (with distance in arbitrary units):

DISPLACEMENT FROM ORIGIN ON HORIZONTAL AXIS
  DIRECTION −
  DISTANCE 50

DISPLACEMENT FROM ORIGIN ON VERTICAL AXIS
  DIRECTION +
  DISTANCE 30

The crucial assumptions of this hypothesis are (a) that location is represented with respect to orthogonal reference axes, and (b) that distance and direction of displacement along an axis are represented separately (see McCloskey, 2000, for further discussion of coordinate system representations).[1]

[1] For expository convenience we have stated the hypothesis in terms of two-dimensional spatial representations; however, it generalizes straightforwardly to three-dimensional representations. Also for convenience we have characterized the coordinate system in Cartesian terms. Coordinate systems involving angular displacements—for example, a spherical coordinate system specifying azimuth (horizontal angular displacement), elevation (vertical angular displacement), and radial distance—could also provide a basis for interpreting A.H.'s errors. For present purposes the important assumption is that direction and magnitude of displacement are specified separately.

Given these assumptions, A.H.'s reflection errors may be interpreted by positing a selective visual deficit in which distance along reference axes is represented accurately, but direction of displacement is frequently misrepresented. For example, if direction of displacement along the horizontal axis were mistakenly specified as "+" for the X in Figure 2 the result would be a reflection across the vertical axis (see Figure 2C). Similarly, if direction of displacement along the vertical axis were specified as "−" a reflection across the horizontal axis would result (Figure 2D).

Although cognitive scientists and neuroscientists often refer to hypothesized spatial representations with terms like *coordinates*, *coordinate system*, and *coordinate frame*, in most instances the intended meaning is rather nonspecific; the terms are not intended to imply that location representations specify distances or angular displacements from reference points along reference axes. However, some researchers have posited explicit coordinate system representations on the basis of behavioural or neurophysiological evidence (e.g., Lacquaniti, Guigon, Bianchi, Ferraina, & Caminiti, 1995; O'Keefe, 1993; O'Keefe & Nadel, 1978; Soechting & Flanders, 1989, 1992). For example, Soechting and Flanders (1989, 1992) assessed people's accuracy in pointing to visually specified targets under several conditions, and they argued from the results that targeted arm movements require a transformation from an extrinsic coordinate system that represents target location in terms of azimuth, elevation, and radial distance from the shoulder to an intrinsic coordinate system specifying location in terms of yaw and elevation of the upper arm and forearm. A.H.'s error pattern converges with the results of these previous studies to support the conclusion that the brain implements coordinate systems at some levels of spatial representation.

Representing orientation

The coordinate-system hypothesis can be extended to encompass representations of orientation. However, the extension is not entirely trivial. Orientation representations are somewhat more complex than location representations, because representations of orientation involve (we suggest) not a single reference frame, but rather relationships between reference frames. Furthermore, in representing the relationship of one reference frame to another multiple parameters must be specified. For most of these parameters various alternative forms of representation can be envisioned, and in some cases we had no firm basis for choosing one form over another. We nevertheless opted to make a specific, albeit somewhat arbitrary, choice in these cases, believing that an erroneous but specific hypothesis is preferable to a vague proposal that does not allow clear predictions or interpretations. (In several such cases we mention potential variants of, or alternatives to, our assumptions.) Hence, our hypothesis should be viewed as a preliminary proposal. A number of researchers have previously discussed orientation in terms of relationships between reference frames (e.g., Davidoff & Warrington, 2001; Harris, Harris, & Caine, 2001; Howard, 1982; Ittelson, Mowafy, & Magid, 1991; Priftis, Rusconi, Umiltà, & Zorzi, 2003; Riddoch & Humphreys, 1988; Turnbull & McCarthy, 1996), but have not developed the notion into specific hypotheses about the nature of orientation representations in the brain.

In the following sections we first lay out the assumptions of our coordinate-system hypothesis of orientation representation and then discuss the various forms of orientation error that could arise in constructing or using the posited representations. For convenience of expression we refer to our proposal as the COR (coordinate-system orientation representation) hypothesis.

Relating object-centred and external frames of reference

We assume that at some level or levels of representation—in the visual system and perhaps also in other perceptual, cognitive, or motor systems—the orientation of an object is represented as a relationship between an object-centred frame of reference and a second frame of reference external to the object. For the sake of simplicity we consider only two-dimensional objects and reference frames; the framework we develop could, however, be extended straightforwardly to three dimensions.

Consider the simple stimulus in Figure 3A, which has a particular orientation relative to the external frame of reference indicated by the dashed lines. The external frame (in this example or in any instance of orientation representation) could be defined by the axes of the observer's body, or on some nonegocentric basis (e.g., the direction of the gravitational force, the walls of a room). For present purposes we simply assume an external coordinate system with orthogonal axes (which we refer to as vertical and horizontal), without concerning ourselves with how the axes were defined. We further assume that each axis has a polarity, with one end designated positive (+) and the other negative (−). Finally, we assume that the external reference frame need not be centred on the object; the centring in the figure is merely for illustrative convenience.

Figure 3B depicts an object-centred representation of the stimulus object. We assume that the representation specifies the arrangement of object parts within a coordinate system defined by the object's principal axis of elongation and a secondary axis orthogonal to the principal axis. The representation might look something like the following:

BAR
  LOCATION (0, 0)
  TILT (0°)

CIRCLE
  LOCATION (+20, −5)

SQUARE
  LOCATION (−20, +10)
  TILT (0°)

The TILT component indicates how the part is tilted with respect to the principal object axis, and LOCATION(x, y) is a shorthand for

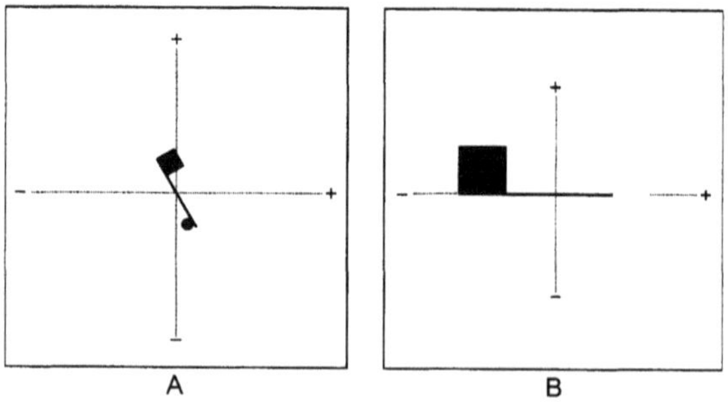

Figure 3. *A. Stimulus object in an external reference frame defined by horizontal and vertical axes. B. Object-centred representation, with principal axis defined by the object's major axis of elongation and secondary axis perpendicular to the principal axis.*

representations of displacement distance and direction along the principal and secondary axes. For example, LOCATION (+20, −5) indicates that the circle is displaced from the origin 20 units in the positive direction along the principal axis and 5 units in the negative direction along the secondary axis.

The representation as described is highly incomplete—for example, it says nothing about the sizes of the parts—and none of the details are intended as serious proposals about the form of object-centred representations. Our intent is merely to illustrate the general assumption that the object-centred representation specifies how the parts of the object are arranged within an object-based coordinate system. Note that the object-centred representation is orientation-invariant—that is, the representation carries no information about how the object or any of its parts is tilted or otherwise arranged relative to any external reference frame. For example, even though the bar is tilted relative to the axes of the external reference frame, the object-centred representation specifies a 0° tilt because the bar is aligned with the principal axis of the object-centred frame; the bar's tilt relative to the external axes is simply not addressed. (Hence, in any illustration of an object-centred representation, such as that in Figure 3B, the depicted orientation is arbitrary. Any other orientation could have been

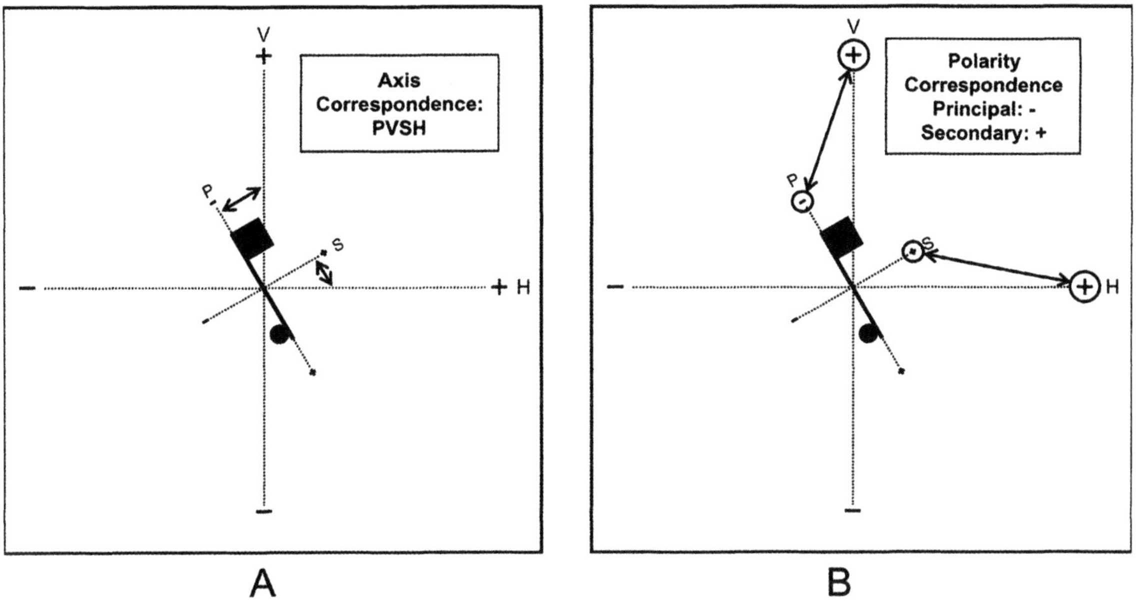

Figure 4. *A. Establishing axis correspondences. The principal axis of the object-centred reference frame is mapped onto the vertical axis of the external frame, and the secondary object axis is mapped onto the horizontal external axis. B. Establishing polarity correspondences. The positive pole of the object's principal axis is mapped onto the negative pole of the corresponding (vertical) external axis (negative polarity correspondence), and the positive pole of the object's secondary axis is mapped onto the positive pole of the corresponding (horizontal) external axis (positive polarity correspondence). V = vertical axis; H = horizontal axis; P = principal axis; S = secondary axis.*

used, as long as the relationships between axes and object parts were maintained.[2])

Given an object-centred representation, the object's orientation relative to an external reference frame may be represented by specifying the relationship between the object-based frame and the external frame. We assume that the orientation representation specifies (a) a correspondence between object axes and external axes, (b) the tilt of the object axes relative to the external axes, and (c) the relationship between the polarity of the object axes and the polarity of the external axes. We consider each of these components in turn.

Axis correspondence

This representational component specifies which object axes will be represented in relation to which external axes. In the case of a two-dimensional representation two object-to-external axis mappings are possible. First, as illustrated in Figure 4A, the object's principal axis may be placed in correspondence with (i.e., represented in relation to) the external vertical axis, with the object's secondary axis mapped onto the external horizontal axis. We abbreviate this axis-to-axis mapping as PVSH (principal–vertical/secondary–horizontal). The other possible axis mapping is, of course, principal–horizontal/secondary-vertical (PHSV).

[2] Note that an orientation-invariant representation is not necessarily viewpoint independent. A representation of a three-dimensional object that described only the aspects of an object visible from the observer's viewpoint would be viewpoint dependent, but could still be invariant with respect to orientation in the picture plane. Hence, in positing orientation-invariant representations we do not intend to take a stance on the issue of viewpoint-dependent versus viewpoint-independent representations of three-dimensional objects.

We assume, then, that orientation representations include an axis correspondence component with two possible values (PVSH and PHSV).[3]

Establishing an object-to-external axis correspondence is necessary because the remaining components of the representation depend upon this correspondence. For example, given the stimulus in Figure 4A, the representation of the object's tilt depends on whether the object's principal axis is represented in relation to the external vertical axis (in which case the tilt is 30° counterclockwise), or instead in relation to the external horizontal axis (in which case the tilt is 60° clockwise).

For the moment we assume that orientation representations may adopt either of the two possible axis mappings (PVSH or PHSV) for any stimulus object. We speculate, however, that an object axis is more likely to be placed in correspondence with an external axis the smaller the angular difference between the axes. For the stimulus in Figure 4A, the PVSH mapping might therefore be more likely than the reverse mapping. Hence, for this stimulus the axis correspondence component may take a form something like the following:

AXIS CORRESPONDENCE: PVSH

Other possibilities can be envisioned. For example, an object axis may always be placed in correspondence with the external axis at the smallest angular distance. Alternatively, the axis correspondence could conceivably be constant (e.g., PVSH) in all orientation representations. As we shall see, patterns of orientation errors might provide a basis for distinguishing these possibilities.

Polarity correspondence

We assume that orientation representations specify not only which object axes correspond to which external axes, but also how the polarity of each object axis is related to the polarity of the corresponding external axis. In the present example, the principal object axis is aligned with its negative pole toward the positive pole of the corresponding external axis (i.e., the vertical axis, assuming a PVSH axis correspondence), as illustrated in Figure 4B. We refer to this negative-to-positive polarity correspondence as a negative polarity mapping. In contrast the secondary axis has a positive polarity relation to its corresponding (horizontal) external axis: The positive pole of the secondary object axis maps onto the positive pole of the external horizontal axis. For this stimulus the polarity correspondence component of the orientation representation might look something like the following:

POLARITY CORRESPONDENCE
PRINCIPAL: −
SECONDARY: +

The polarity correspondence component is critical for representing how the features of an object are positioned relative to the external reference frame. For example, the difference between Figure 8A and Figure 8B is one of polarity correspondence between the object's secondary axis and the external horizontal axis. We develop this point more fully in discussing forms of orientation error.

Tilt

Finally, we assume that orientation representations specify the tilt of the object axes relative to their corresponding external axes. For a two-dimensional representation, once the tilt is specified for one object–external axis pair, a representation of tilt for the other axis pair would be entirely redundant—for example, if the

[3] In a two-dimensional representation, once a mapping has been established between an object axis and an external axis, the other mapping is fixed; there are no other degrees of freedom. For this reason we posit a single axis correspondence component with two values, rather than assuming two separate representations, one for each object–external axis pair (e.g., P–V and S–H). For three-dimensional representations the situation is more complex: Establishing a mapping between one object axis and one external axis does not fully determine the other mappings. Therefore, positing a separate representation for each of the three object–external axis pairings may be most plausible. Given this point, one might want to assume individual object–external axis representations even in the two-dimensional case, to maintain consistency with the three-dimensional representations. However, as far as we can see the choice between a single representation (e.g., PVSH) and separate representations (PV, SH) in the two-dimensional case has no implications for any of the issues we discuss. Hence, for convenience we adopt the single-representation alternative.

object's principal axis is tilted 70° clockwise from the external vertical axis, the secondary axis must be tilted 70° clockwise from the horizontal axis. For the sake of simplicity we therefore assume that tilt is represented only for the object's principal axis.[4]

We assume that tilt is represented by specifying the direction and magnitude of the angular displacement between the object's principal axis and the corresponding external axis. For example, in Figures 3 and 4 the principal object axis is tilted 30° counterclockwise from the external vertical axis. Arbitrarily designating clockwise as the positive direction and counterclockwise as negative, tilt could therefore be represented as follows:

TILT
DIRECTION: –
MAGNITUDE: 30°

An important feature of the posited tilt representations is that direction and magnitude of tilt are represented separately, just as displacement direction and distance are represented separately in the location representations proposed by McCloskey and colleagues (McCloskey, 2004; McCloskey & Rapp, 2000a, 2000b; McCloskey et al., 1995). We assume that the direction and magnitude representations are based upon the smaller of the two angles between the object's principal axis and the corresponding external axis. For example, we assume that for the stimulus in Figure 3 the tilt would be represented as −30° and not as +330°.

Several alternative forms of tilt representation could be considered. For example, one might assume that, as in a typical polar coordinate system, angles are always defined in a standard direction (e.g., clockwise) and so can be specified solely in terms of magnitude, with no separate representation of direction. In such a scheme the angle in Figure 3 might be represented not as −30°, but rather as 330°. We argue, however, that positing separate direction and magnitude components provides a basis for interpreting certain forms of orientation error.

Substantive assumptions

Bringing together the various representational components that we have discussed, the orientation of the stimulus in Figure 3 might be represented as follows:

AXIS CORRESPONDENCE: PVSH

POLARITY CORRESPONDENCE
PRINCIPAL: –
SECONDARY: +

TILT
DIRECTION: –
MAGNITUDE: 30°

The details of the notation are largely irrelevant and should not be taken too literally. The substantive assumptions are as follows:

1. Mental representations of object orientation specify the relationship between an object-centred (orientation-invariant) frame of reference and a frame of reference external to the object.
2. Orientation representations are compositional, consisting of several independent components.
3. One component specifies which object axes map onto which external axes.
4. A second component specifies, for each object axis, how the poles of that axis map onto the poles of the corresponding external axis.
5. A third component specifies the tilt of the object reference frame relative to the external frame.
6. The tilt component separately represents direction and magnitude of tilt.

In relating an object-centred frame to an external reference frame the location of the object could also be represented, by specifying the location of the object frame's origin relative to the origin of

[4] Once again the situation is more complex for three-dimensional representations, and considerations of consistency with these representations might lead one to posit separate tilt representations for each object–external axis pair even in the two-dimensional case.

the external frame. However, in this article we focus on representation of orientation.

Relating external reference frames to one another

Once a representation relating an object-centred frame of reference to an external frame has been generated from a stimulus, this orientation representation may be used for a variety of purposes—for example, reaching for an object, describing the object's orientation verbally, or drawing the object. Using an orientation representation to perform a task will often (perhaps even always) involve relating the original external reference frame to a different external frame appropriate for the task. Consider, for example, an individual who views a stimulus object presented on a sheet of paper and then draws the object on another sheet, either by copying or from memory (see Figure 5). Assume that the orientation representation generated from the stimulus encodes the relationship between an object-centred frame of reference and an external frame defined by the stimulus sheet—that is, a frame centred on the sheet, with vertical and horizontal axes aligned with the sheet's edges. To produce a correctly oriented drawing, the individual must relate the external frame defined by the stimulus sheet to an external frame defined by the response sheet. In other words, the individual must represent the orientation of the stimulus external frame relative to the response external frame. Because the orientation of the stimulus object was initially represented relative to the stimulus external frame, relating this frame to the response external frame provides the link needed to orient the stimulus object relative to the response frame.

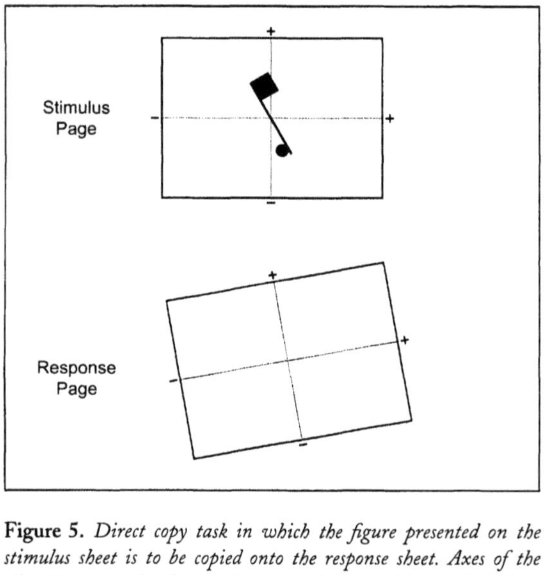

Figure 5. *Direct copy task in which the figure presented on the stimulus sheet is to be copied onto the response sheet. Axes of the stimulus external reference frame are shown on the stimulus sheet, and axes of the response external frame are shown on the response sheet. In performing the copying task the stimulus external frame must be mapped onto the response external frame.*

Representing the orientation of one external frame relative to another is, we assume, no different from representing the orientation of an object-centred frame relative to an external frame: Axis correspondences, axis polarity correspondences, and tilt must be specified. In the present example the vertical and horizontal stimulus frame axes correspond to vertical and horizontal response frame axes, respectively, and both axis polarity correspondences are positive (i.e., the positive pole of each stimulus axis maps onto the positive pole of the corresponding response axis). The response axes are, however, slightly tilted relative to the stimulus axes.

Processing of spatial information (including orientation) may often involve a progression through many different frames of reference; hence, several reference frames may conceivably intervene between an object-centred frame and the frame most directly involved in producing a response. We offer no specific assumptions about the processing that occurs in such circumstances. For instance, the representations linking each pair of reference frames may be used to generate a representation that directly relates the object-centred representation to the response frame of reference. Alternatively, the response may be generated from the chain of linked reference frames, without constructing a representation that directly places the object-centred frame in relation to the response frame.

Orientation errors

The assumptions of the COR hypothesis lead to clear predictions about potential types of orientation error and the underlying causes of the various error types. The hypothesis suggests that in any task that requires the processing of object orientation, orientation errors could arise from failures in the construction, retention or use of either (a) orientation representations that relate an object-centred representation to an external reference frame, or (b) orientation representations that relate one external frame to another. Consider once again a (normal or impaired) individual who copies, or draws from memory, the stimulus in Figure 3. The processes that construct an orientation representation from the stimulus might fail to represent, or misrepresent, one or more components—for instance, the magnitude of the tilt between object and external axes might remain unspecified, or might be misrepresented as 45°. Even if the orientation representation were initially complete and accurate, information could also be lost (or perhaps even altered) as the representation was held in memory, or misprocessed in some way when the representation was used to perform a task. The same points apply to representations that link one external reference frame to another.

In discussing types of orientation error we do not attempt to distinguish among errors arising in the construction, retention, and use of a representation; as far as we are able to see, failures at each of these points generally produce the same types of error. Rather, we focus our discussion on how error types should vary according to the particular representational component that is affected (e.g., tilt magnitude) and according to whether the orientation representation relates an object-centred frame to an external frame, or two external frames to one another. For convenience, we discuss errors largely in the context of constructing representations, with the understanding that the same forms or error are expected from failures at other points in processing.

We further limit our discussion by focusing on the tilt and polarity-correspondence components of orientation representations, because these are the components potentially relevant for understanding the orientation errors observed in the three developmental cases that we discuss. Certain forms of orientation error could conceivably arise from impairments affecting axis correspondence representations, but discussion of these error types is beyond the scope of the present article.

Tilt errors

We begin with tilt errors, because these are perhaps the most straightforward. The posited tilt representations have two elements: a direction element and a magnitude element. Failures affecting either element should produce orientation errors. We discuss tilt errors in the context of representing the relationship between an object-centred reference frame and an external frame. Analogous errors could arise for representations relating one external frame to another.

Tilt direction errors. In relating an object-centred frame to an external frame, misrepresenting the direction of tilt should lead to errors in which the object is tilted the correct amount but in the wrong direction relative to the external axes. For example, given the stimulus in Figure 6A, representing the tilt direction as + rather than − would yield the error shown in Figure 6B. Note that this error is not a mirror reflection of the object across the external vertical axis—the object is tilted in the wrong direction, but not mirror reflected. (See Figure 8D for the mirror reflection.)

Note also, however, that a tilt direction error cannot be distinguished from a mirror reflection across an external axis for stimuli that are bilaterally symmetric. Consider, for example, the arrow in Figure 7A. The error in Figure 7B could

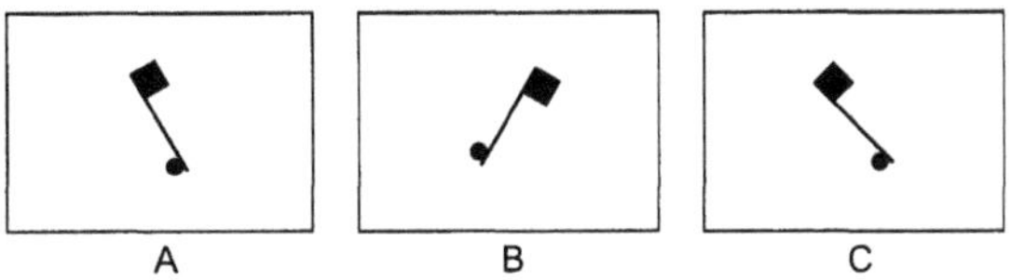

Figure 6. *A. Stimulus object. B. Tilt direction error. C. Tilt magnitude error.*

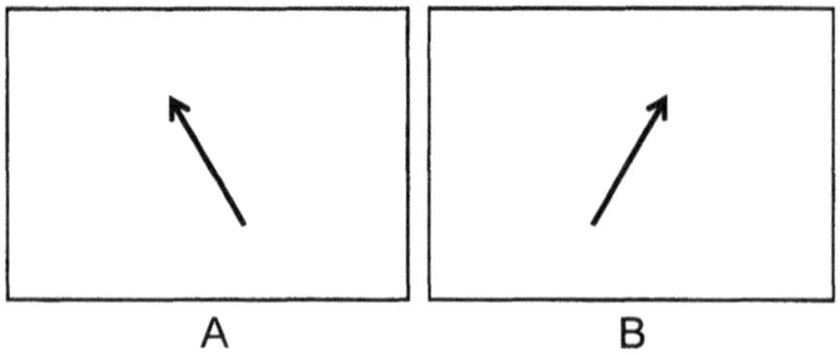

Figure 7. *A. Stimulus arrow. B. Reflection error.*

result either from misrepresentation of tilt direction, or instead from representation or processing failure that led to a reflection of the entire figure across an external vertical axis. (Below we discuss how such reflections might occur.) This observation is one instance of a general point that arises repeatedly: The stimuli used in most orientation tasks (including most of our tasks) are inadequate to distinguish among at least some forms of orientation error.

Tilt magnitude errors. Errors in representing tilt magnitude could take at least two forms. First, random error may be introduced into the representation or processing of tilt magnitude, due to noise or other limitations in perceptual, memory, motoric, or other processes. For example, a 30° tilt magnitude might be misrepresented or misproduced as 20° or 45° (see Figure 6C).

In tasks requiring participants to reproduce the orientation of stimuli (e.g., by copying or drawing from memory) this form of representational or processing imprecision should lead to a response pattern in which response orientations are clustered around the corresponding correct orientations, with a degree of scatter determined by the extent of random error. In normal adults the imprecision may be rather small, whereas in young children or individuals with tilt magnitude deficits the imprecision may be much larger (see, e.g., Dilks, Reiss, Landau, & Hoffman, 2004; Goodale, Milner, Jakobson, & Carey, 1991).

Tilt magnitude errors could also perhaps result from crude encoding of, memory for, or use of tilt magnitude information. For example, an orientation representation might specify tilt magnitude only with the precision afforded by a small number of crude tilt categories based on "standard" tilts, such as *roughly 0°*, *roughly 45°*, *roughly 90°*, and so forth. The 30° tilt magnitude in our example might thus be represented as *roughly 45°*, or perhaps *slightly less than 45°*. Crude representation of tilt magnitude should lead to errors in which response orientations are systematically displaced from the correct orientations toward or to the nearest standard orientation. This type of error pattern has been observed in tasks requiring normal participants to reproduce orientations from memory. For example, Barbara Tversky (1981) asked participants to place a cutout map of South America in the appropriate orientation on a page on which the compass directions were indicated. The long axis of the continent is tilted about 15° relative to the north–south axis, but three fourths of the participants positioned the cutout with the axis closer to a north–south orientation. Similar effects were obtained in tasks with artificial maps: Orientations of geographical features were recalled as being closer to north–south or east–west than they actually were.

Polarity correspondence errors

Polarity correspondence misrepresentations should lead to mirror reflection of the stimulus figure. According to the COR hypothesis, two major forms of reflection could occur—reflections across an object axis, and reflections across an external axis—with the form of error depending upon what frames of reference are implicated in the error.

Polarity correspondence errors in representations relating an object-centred reference frame to an external frame should result in reflection across an object axis. Consider once again our illustrative object (reproduced in Figure 8A). If the polarity correspondence between the object's secondary axis and the external horizontal axis were misrepresented as negative (negative secondary axis pole corresponding to positive horizontal axis pole) the result would be a reflection across the object's principal axis, as shown in Figure 8B. Similarly, misrepresenting the polarity relation between the object's principal axis and the external vertical axis would lead to a reflection across the object's secondary axis, as illustrated in Figure 8C.

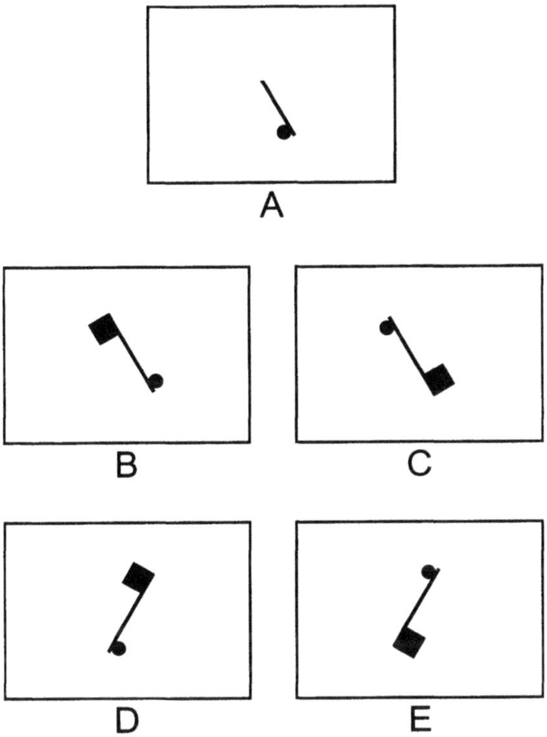

Figure 8. *A. Stimulus object. B. Reflection across the object's principal axis, resulting from misrepresentation of the polarity correspondence between the secondary axis and an external horizontal axis. C. Reflection across the object's secondary axis, resulting from misrepresentation of the polarity correspondence between the principal axis and an external vertical axis. D. Reflection across an external vertical axis, resulting from misrepresentation of the polarity correspondence between the horizontal axes of two external reference frames. E. Reflection across an external vertical axis, resulting from misrepresentation of the polarity correspondence between the vertical axes of two external reference frames.*

In contrast polarity correspondence errors in representations relating the stimulus external frame of reference to another external frame should produce a subtly different form of error: reflection across an axis of the stimulus external frame. For example, given the stimulus in Figure 8A, misrepresenting the polarity correspondence between stimulus and response frame horizontal axes (e.g., in a copying task) would lead to a (left–right) reflection across the vertical axis of the external stimulus frame (see Figure 8D). If the polarity correspondence were misrepresented for the external vertical axes, a reflection across the external stimulus frame's horizontal axis would occur (Figure 8E).

Note that polarity correspondence errors take a different form from tilt direction errors. In a tilt direction error the stimulus is tilted in the wrong direction but is not reflected across any axis (e.g., Figure 6B). In polarity correspondence errors, however, the stimulus is reflected across either an object axis or an external axis. Compare, for example, Figures 6B (tilt direction error), 8B (polarity correspondence error in relating an object-centred frame to an external frame), and 8D (polarity correspondence error in relating the stimulus external frame to another external frame).

Here again, however, we encounter the point that many stimulus types are inadequate for distinguishing among certain forms of orientation error. We have already noted that for bilaterally symmetric stimuli (e.g., the arrow in Figure 7) tilt direction errors cannot be distinguished from reflections across an external stimulus axis (which we have now attributed to polarity correspondence errors in relating the external stimulus frame to another external frame). Bilaterally symmetric stimuli also have the shortcoming that some difficulties in processing polarity correspondence information simply cannot be detected. For an arrow, which is symmetric about its principal axis, polarity correspondence errors in relating the secondary axis to an external axis are undetectable—reflecting the arrow across its principal axis (the result of a polarity correspondence error for the secondary axis) would not produce a detectable change. (For objects that are symmetric across both object axes, such as a simple line, neither principal- nor secondary-axis polarity correspondence errors can be detected.)

A different ambiguity arises for stimuli in which the object axes are aligned with the axes of the external reference frame, as in Figure 9A. Specifically, polarity correspondence errors in the mapping between object-centred and external stimulus frames (which lead to reflections across object axes) cannot be distinguished from polarity correspondence errors in relating the external stimulus frame to another external frame (which lead to reflections across external stimulus axes).

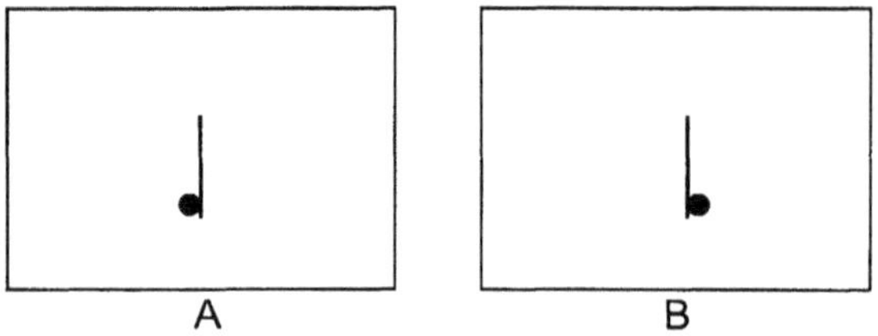

Figure 9. *A. Vertically oriented stimulus object.* ***B.*** *Reflection error. This error could have been caused by misrepresentation of polarity correspondence either in relating an object-centred representation to a stimulus external frame, or in relating one external frame to another.*

Thus, the reflection in Figure 9B could be caused by either form of polarity correspondence error.

An alternative formulation

The orientation representations that we have posited may seem unnecessarily complex. We assume that an object's shape is represented within an object-centred frame of reference and that orientation is represented in terms of a complex relationship between the object-centred frame and an external reference frame (which in turn may be mapped onto other external frames). Perhaps, then, we should consider simplifying the proposal. Perhaps in particular we could dispense with the object-centred representations, by assuming that an object's parts are represented directly within the external stimulus frame, without an object-centred reference frame as an intermediary.

Adopting this direct-representation approach, the object in our example might be represented by specifying the location and tilt of each part (line, square, circle) in the external reference frame. The representation might look something like the following:

BAR
  LOCATION (+20, +20)
  TILT (−30°)

CIRCLE
  LOCATION (+25, +15)

SQUARE
  LOCATION (+15, +30)
  TILT(−30°)

This representation, which is no more complex than the object-centred representations that we have posited, carries all the information necessary to determine not only the object's shape, but also its orientation relative to the external stimulus frame. Hence, if we were to assume this sort of direct representation of object parts in the external frame, we could dispense with the added complexity of orientation representations that relate object-centred frames to external stimulus frames. Why, then, have we opted for the more complex hypothesis?

Three points may be made in response to this question. First, many researchers have argued on theoretical and empirical grounds that the visual system constructs some form(s) of object-centred representation for the purposes of object recognition (e.g., Marr, 1982). If object recognition processes generate representations that describe an object's shape independent of external reference frames, it seems plausible to suppose that these representations could provide a basis for representing the object's orientation. Second, even if we were to dispense with representations that relate object-centred to external stimulus frames, we would still need to posit the same type of representation for purposes of relating other reference frames to one another (in the processing of orientation information and in many other forms of spatial processing). The direct-representation hypothesis does not therefore eliminate a type of representation, but serves only to deny that one particular frame-to-frame relationship is implicated in processing orientation information. Given that many reference frames may well intervene between stimulus and response in most orientation tasks, the direct-representation hypothesis seems neither strongly motivated nor particularly effective in reducing complexity.

However, the strongest reason for preferring the object-centred representation version to the direct-representation alternative is that the latter has difficulty accounting for certain forms of orientation error. Specifically, the direct-representation position has no way to account for reflections across an object axis, such as those shown in Figures 8B and 8C. (Note that stimuli in which the object axes are tilted with respect to the external axes are required to distinguish these errors from reflections across external axes.) According to our proposal, reflections across object axes result from polarity correspondence errors in relating object axes to external stimulus axes. Representations in which individual object parts are represented directly with respect to the external stimulus frame predict that such errors should not occur. As we shall see, however, A.H. clearly makes such errors.

THREE CASES OF ORIENTATION IMPAIRMENT

In the following discussion we present results from three individuals with deficits in representing or processing orientation, and we attempt to interpret the major features of their performance patterns by reference to the COR hypothesis.

B.C.

B.C. is a left-handed girl with severe visual-spatial impairment resulting from a presumed herpes encephalitis infection at age 3. Magnetic resonance imaging (MRI) at age 5 years revealed cortical damage in both right and left occipital regions, intruding into the secondary and tertiary areas of the occipital and parietal regions of the left hemisphere. Both grey and white matter were affected.[5] Ophthalmologic evaluations at ages 7 and 15 years found right hemianopia and partial left hemianopia, with about 10° of spared visual field. Visual acuity was 20/30 to 20/40.

In a neuropsychological evaluation at age 10 years, B.C.'s WISC-III (Wechsler Intelligence Scale for Children, 3rd Edition; Wechsler, 1991) Verbal IQ was 85, reflecting average performance on most subtests, above-average performance on digit span, and below-average scores on arithmetic and comprehension. Performance IQ was considered untestable due to her severe visuo-spatial impairment.

B.C. was tested at Johns Hopkins University over a period of 9 months, during which time she was 15–16 years old. She presented as a young woman of normal intelligence, engaging in conversation fluently and with a sense of humor, picking up quickly on social cues and expressing herself in an age-appropriate manner. Unlike A.H., B.C. was able to reach accurately for objects on a table in front of her. In other visual-spatial tasks, however, B.C. was profoundly impaired. She was able to name simple geometric shapes (e.g., square, circle, triangle) accurately, but was impaired in recognizing line drawings of objects. On the Boston Naming Test (Goodglass & Kaplan, 1983) she scored in the 5–6-year-old range (24/60), with erroneous responses (e.g., "bicycle" for wheelchair) apparently based on object parts.

B.C. also showed severe and broad-ranging impairment on the Developmental Test of Visual Perception (DTVP-2), a standardized test assessing a variety of visuo-spatial abilities (Hammill, Pearson, & Voress, 1993). On the four administered subtests her age equivalents ranged from below 4 years to 6 years. In the Block Construction Test from the Differential Ability Scales (Elliott, 1990), B.C. scored at the first percentile, for an age equivalent of 4;1. Her visuo-spatial short-term memory performance on the Corsi Block Span Task (Milner, 1971) was extremely limited: She consistently erred on sequences of two or more blocks. (In contrast she obtained a digit span of 7.)

Tasks involving copying or drawing from memory also revealed severe impairment. B.C.'s drawing of a person appeared similar to that of a very young child, and when asked to draw a house

[5] If developmental deficits are contrasted with acquired deficits, B.C.'s impairment clearly falls into the acquired category because it resulted from obvious neural insult. However, her deficit is developmental in the sense of arising before brain development was complete. It is this sense of developmental that we consider most relevant to questions concerning the validity of inferences about normal cognition drawn from developmental deficits. See the General Discussion.

she gave up after failing to produce a rectangle (see Figure 10). She was able to copy individual lines and right angles (although often at incorrect orientations), but she was almost entirely unable to reproduce a stimulus of any greater complexity. Copying a square, for example, was consistently impossible. On the Beery–Buktenica Developmental Test of Visual-Motor Integration (VMI; Beery & Buktenica, 1997), which involves direct copying of visual stimulus figures, her age equivalent was less than 5 years (see Figure 11 for two examples).

Profound visuo-spatial impairment was evident not only in neuropsychological testing, but also in other aspects of B.C.'s behaviour. She was often not fully able to avoid bumping into objects while walking, despite being always guided, and she was unwilling to walk alone down a straight corridor with no obstacles. B.C. and her parents reported that she could find her way around their house, but had to be guided from class to class at school.

B.C.'s difficulties cannot be entirely explained by her restricted visual field. Although limited, her visual field is sufficient to support adequate performance in navigating the environment, drawing, recognizing objects, constructing spatial patterns and memorizing visuo-spatial sequences. Her difficulties in these tasks suggest instead a more central visual-spatial deficit, perhaps involving a severe reduction in the resources available for spatial representation and processing, leading often to a complete breakdown with stimuli of any significant complexity.

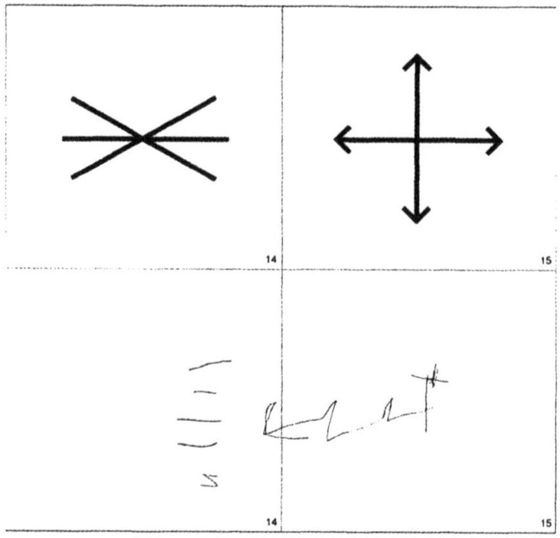

Figure 11. *B.C.'s direct copies of two stimulus figures from the Beery–Buktenica Developmental Test of Visual-Motor Integration (VMI; Beery & Buktenica, 1997).*

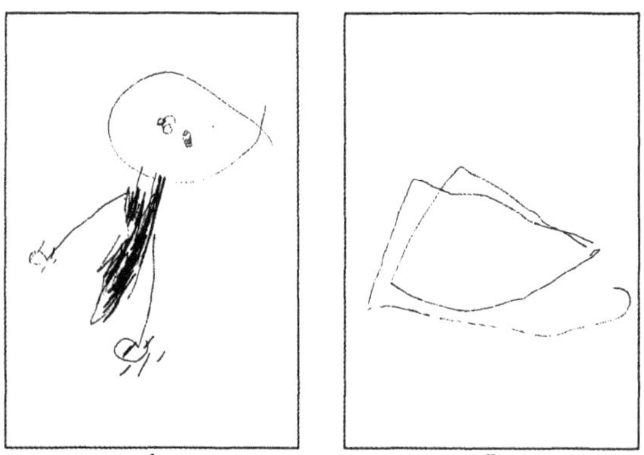

A B

Figure 10. *A. B.C.'s drawing of a person. B. B.C.'s attempt to draw a house. She gave up after being unable to draw a rectangle to represent the lower part of the structure (i.e., the part below the roof).*

Experimental tasks

Because of B.C.'s profound problems with complex visual stimuli, experimental testing was limited to tasks with very simple line stimuli.

Reproducing line orientation: Visual stimuli

In this task a target line was displayed on the upper half of a computer screen, and a response line was presented on the lower half of the screen (see Figure 12A). B.C.'s task was to adjust the orientation of the response line until it matched that of the target line, by turning a dial that caused the response line to rotate about its centre. The 12 target orientations ranged from 0° (horizontal) to 165° in 15° increments. Six trials per orientation were presented in random order, for a total of 72 trials.

B.C.'s performance was highly inaccurate: Her absolute orientation errors ranged from 1° to 88°, with a mean of 29°. Considering that the

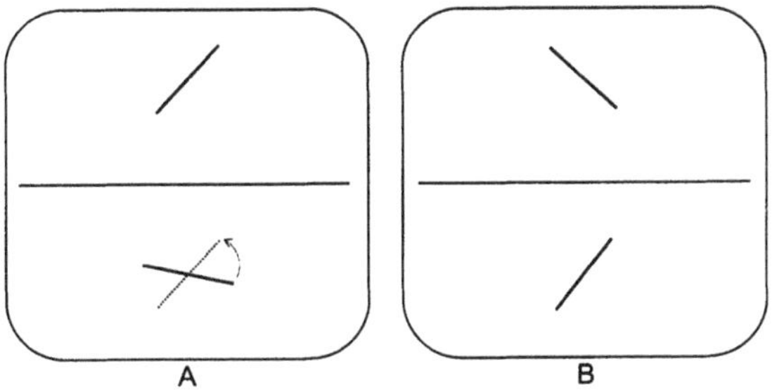

Figure 12. *A. The line orientation reproduction task presented to B.C. A target line was presented on the upper half of a computer monitor, and B.C. turned a knob to adjust the orientation of a response line displayed on the lower half of the monitor.* ***B.*** *One of B.C.'s reflection errors.*

largest possible error in the task was 90°, B.C.'s errors were remarkably large. Examination of B.C.'s responses suggested that many of her errors took the form of mirror reflections; an example is presented in Figure 12B. The scatterplot in Figure 13 confirms this impression. For each trial the response orientation (y axis) is plotted against the target orientation (x axis). The diagonal with positive slope indicates correct responses (e.g., target 135°, response 135°), whereas the negative diagonal corresponds to mirror reflection responses (e.g., target 135°, response 45°). B.C.'s responses are distributed along the two diagonals, with a substantial proportion (27/72) falling closer to the mirror-reflected orientation than to the correct orientation. This pattern indicates a systematic tendency to mirror-reflect the target orientation.

Also apparent from the scatterplot is that most of the points do not lie exactly on the diagonals. This finding indicates that B.C.'s responses—both reflections and nonreflections—show substantial imprecision. Nonreflection responses differed from the target orientation by an average of 13.4°, and reflection responses differed from the reflection orientation by an average of 15.7°.

B.C.'s performance pattern suggests that two distinct forms of error play a role in her responses: imprecision, and a tendency to mirror-reflect the target orientation. Some responses show imprecision alone, whereas others show mirror-reflection plus imprecision. Results from control participants reveal, not surprisingly, that B.C.'s performance is strikingly impaired. Dilks et al. (2004) tested 12 normal adults in the task, and found highly accurate performance (mean absolute error = 1.6°). Results from 10 normal 3–4-year-olds showed greater imprecision (mean absolute error = 13.9°) and only occasional reflection errors. Hence, B.C.'s imprecision was comparable to that of 3–4-year-olds, and her rate of reflection errors was higher.

Reproducing line orientation: Visual stimuli with differentiated ends

This task was identical to the preceding task, except that each target and response line had a red tip at one end (see Figure 14A). B.C. was instructed to adjust the response line so that it matched the target line in orientation and in placement of the tip. Our aim in introducing the red tip was to learn more about the nature of B.C.'s reflection errors. The simpler stimuli in the first task were insufficient to distinguish reflections across a vertical axis (left–right reflections) from reflections across a horizontal axis (up–down reflections). For example, the error shown in Figure 12B could have resulted from either a left–right or an up–down reflection of the stimulus line. Given lines with differentiated ends, however, left–right and up–down reflections can be distinguished (see Figure 14B).

To control for possible effects of the placement of target and response lines on the computer monitor, two conditions were presented. In the first condition the target line was positioned above the response line (as in the preceding task); in the second condition the target line was to the left of the response line. B.C.'s performance was virtually identical in the two conditions. Accordingly, the scatterplot shown in Figure 15 presents the results collapsed across conditions.

This scatterplot is more complex than that from the preceding task. Because the ends of the lines were differentiated, target and response orientations range from 0° to 345°, rather than 0° to 165°. For example, whereas the first task included

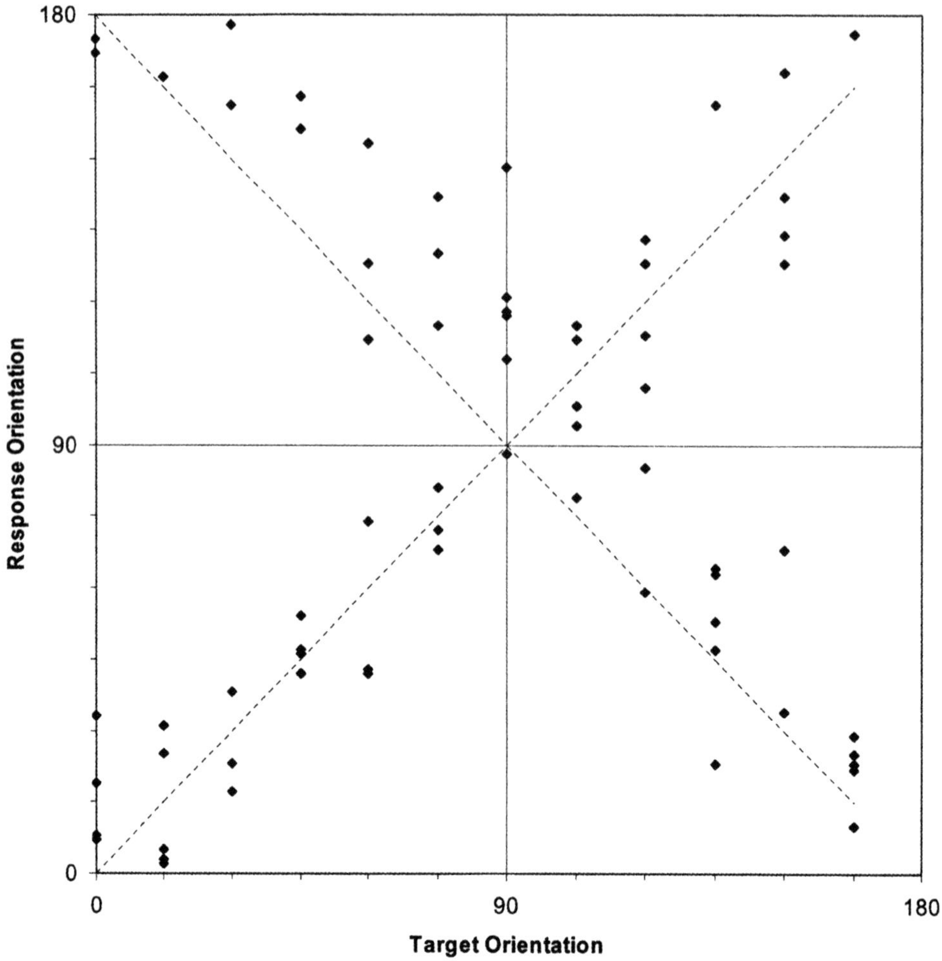

Figure 13. *Scatterplot of results from the line orientation reproduction task. The response orientation (y axis) is plotted against the stimulus orientation (x axis) for each trial. The diagonal with positive slope (from lower left to upper right) corresponds to correct responses, and the negative diagonal corresponds to mirror reflections.*

only a single horizontal target orientation (0°), the modified task included two: 0° (horizontal with red tip on the right) and 180° (horizontal with red tip on the left). In the present scatterplot correct responses once again fall along the positive diagonal. Up–down reflections (e.g., target 45°, response 315°) lie along the negative diagonal, and left–right reflections (e.g., target 45°, response 135°) lie along the negative diagonals through the lower left and upper-right quadrants of the plot.

Several points are apparent from the scatterplot. First, B.C.'s responses again show considerable imprecision. For nonreflection responses (i.e., those falling closer to the target orientation than to either the left–right or the up–down reflection orientation) B.C.'s mean absolute error was 12.7°.

Second, B.C. made many left–right reflection errors: Approximately one fourth of her responses (43/192) were closer to the left–right reflection orientation than to the correct orientation (mean distance from reflected orientation = 11.1°).

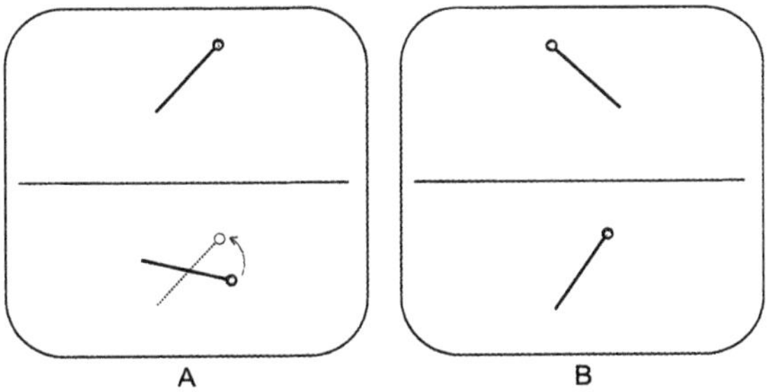

Figure 14. *The line orientation reproduction task in which stimulus lines had a red tip at one end (indicated by the grey dots in the figure). A. Target and response lines displayed on a computer monitor. B. Example of a left–right reflection error made by B.C.*

Interestingly, left–right reflection errors were observed primarily for target orientations at least 30° from horizontal; only 3 of the 43 left–right reflections occurred for targets that were horizontal or within 15° of horizontal.

The third point apparent from the scatterplot is that B.C. made far fewer up–down than left–right reflection errors. In fact it is unclear whether any of her responses were true up–down reflections. Only 13 of the responses (7%) were closer to the up–down reflection orientation than to the correct orientation. Further, 10 of these 13 responses involved target orientations only 15°

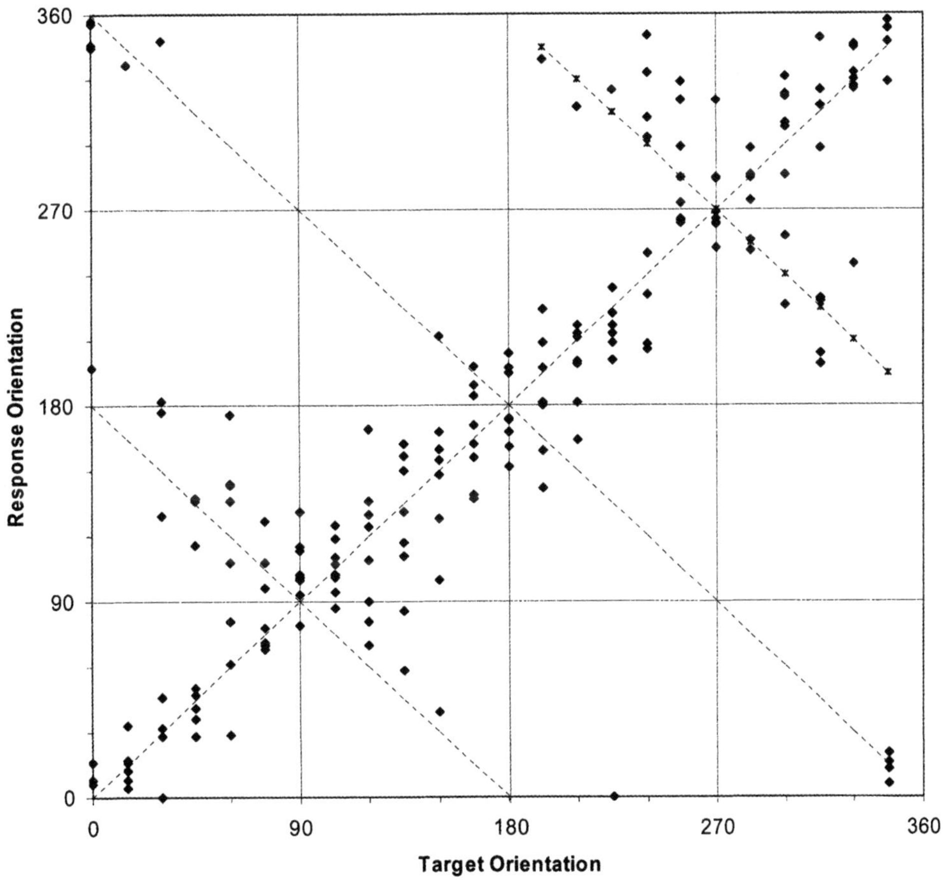

Figure 15. *Scatterplot of results from the orientation reproduction task involving lines with differentiated ends. The response orientation (y axis) is plotted against the stimulus orientation (x axis) for each trial. The diagonal with positive slope (from lower left to upper right) corresponds to correct responses. The major negative diagonal (upper left to lower right) corresponds to up–down mirror reflections. The minor diagonals in the lower left and upper right quadrants correspond to left–right mirror reflections.*

away from horizontal (e.g., 195°, 345°), and the remaining 3 involved targets 30° from horizontal. For nearly horizontal targets, random imprecision alone could conceivably produce responses closer to the up–down reflection orientation than to the correct orientation. For example, given a target orientation of 165° a random error of more than 15° in the counterclockwise direction would yield a response orientation closer to the up–down reflection orientation of 195° than to the correct orientation. Given that B.C.'s non-reflection errors averaged nearly 13° (and some were as large as 50°), it seems likely that at least some of the apparent up–down reflections resulted simply from random imprecision.[6] However, it is also possible that some of these errors were true up–down reflections.

Note that in contrast to the apparent up–down reflections, the left–right reflections clearly cannot be attributed to random imprecision. Many of the left–right reflection responses—in particular, those occurring for target orientations that are not close to vertical—are very distant from the corresponding correct responses and are clearly separated in the scatterplot from the responses clustering around the correct orientation.

Reproducing line orientation: Tactile stimuli

A third task was carried out to determine whether B.C.'s deficit affected only visual stimuli or extended to other modalities. The task was similar to the visual line orientation tasks, except that the stimuli were tactile. B.C. was blindfolded and felt the orientation of a wooden target bar placed on the table in front of her. As in the first visual orientation task, the two ends of the stimulus were not differentiated. B.C.'s task was to rotate a response bar to match the orientation of the target.

The results, presented in Figure 16, were very similar to those obtained with visual stimuli: Responses were distributed along the correct and mirror-reflection diagonals and showed imprecision comparable to that observed in the visual tasks. These findings suggest that B.C.'s orientation errors may arise not in the visual system, but rather at a more central supramodal level of representation. Another possibility, however, is that B.C. drew upon impaired visual-system mechanisms in performing the tactile orientation task (e.g., by generating visual orientation representations from the tactile input).

Interpreting B.C.'s performance

Within the COR framework, B.C.'s performance can be interpreted in terms of impairment in representing tilt magnitude and tilt direction when relating object-centred and external reference frames. The imprecision in her responses may be explained by assuming that her representations of tilt magnitude are much cruder or noisier than those of normal individuals. The left–right reflection errors may be interpreted by assuming that B.C. usually represented the tilt of the principal object axis relative to a vertical external axis (axis correspondence = PVSH), and that she often misrepresented the direction of tilt. For example, Figure 14B illustrates one of B.C.'s errors, in which she set the response line to an orientation of 58° in response to a target orientation of 135°. For this target orientation, the tilt direction should have been represented as negative (assuming that clockwise is the positive direction), and the tilt magnitude should have been represented as 45°. B.C.'s response may be explained by assuming that she represented the tilt direction as positive and also represented

[6] The points in the upper left and lower right corners of the scatterplot might seem to represent responses that were far from the correct orientation and very close to the up–down reflection orientation. For such responses, an interpretation in terms of random imprecision might be implausible. In fact, however, the responses in these corners are not very distant from the correct orientations. For example, one of the points in the upper left corner represents a target orientation of 30° and a response orientation of 348°. This response is not in fact 318° away from the target orientation (as it may appear in the scatterplot), but only 42° from the target. The points in the upper left corner of the scatterplot may be thought of as lying just below those in the lower left corner, and the points in the lower right corner may be thought of as lying just above the upper right corner.

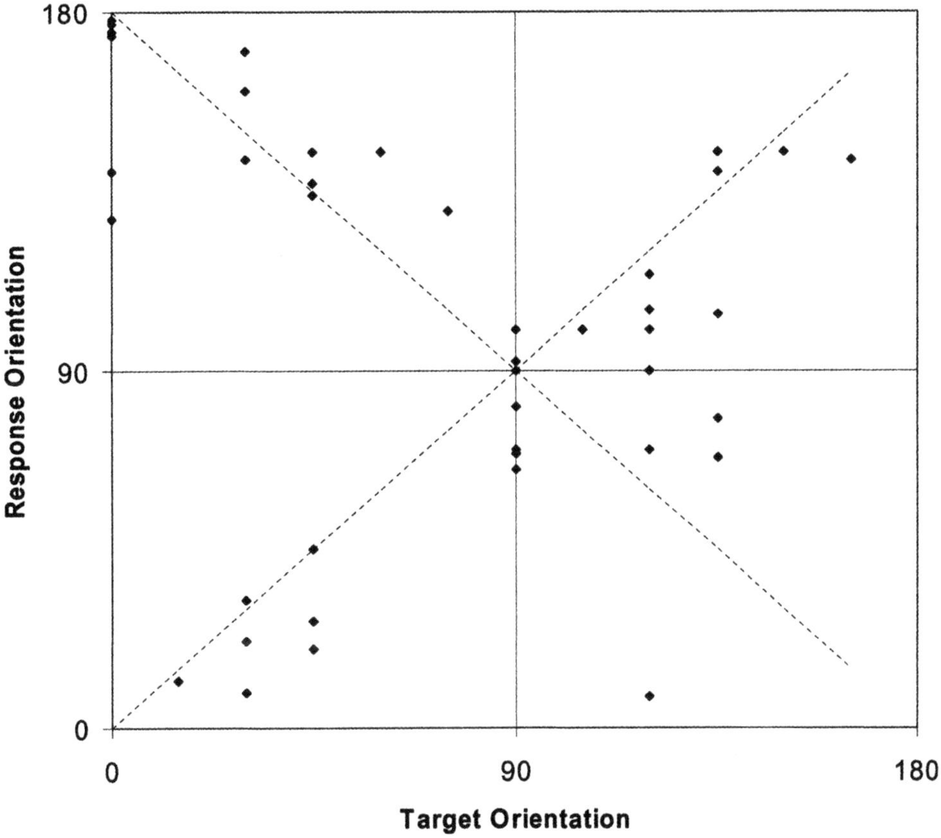

Figure 16. *Scatterplot of results from the tactile line orientation reproduction task. The response orientation (y axis) is plotted against the stimulus orientation (x axis) for each trial. The diagonal with positive slope (from lower left to upper right) corresponds to correct responses, and the negative diagonal corresponds to mirror reflections.*

the magnitude imprecisely (perhaps as something like *roughly 60°*).[7]

The finding that B.C. made few left–right reflections for near-horizontal target orientations may be interpreted by assuming that these orientations were usually represented relative not to the vertical but rather to the horizontal external axis (i.e., axis correspondence = PHSV). When tilt is specified relative to a horizontal axis, left–right reflections should not be observed; if tilt direction is misrepresented, the result should be an up–down reflection. As we have noted, it is not entirely clear whether B.C. made up–down reflections. Her responses to near-horizontal targets occasionally fell closer to the up–down reflection orientation than to the correct orientation, but these responses could have resulted from imprecision in representing tilt magnitude. Accordingly, one possibility is that whereas B.C. is impaired in representing the direction of tilt relative to vertical external axes, she is intact in representing tilt direction with respect to horizontal axes. However, it is also possible that B.C. sometimes misrepresented tilt direction relative

[7] For convenience we have stated the interpretation in terms of representing the target line. However, errors could also have originated in B.C.'s representations of response lines.

to a horizontal external axis, leading to true up–down reflections for some near-horizontal target stimuli.

Although we have attributed B.C.'s reflection errors to misrepresentation of tilt direction in relating object and external reference frames, another interpretation is also possible. Even in the task involving lines with red tips, the stimuli were symmetric about the principal axis of elongation. As a consequence, tilt direction errors cannot be distinguished from polarity correspondence errors in relating one external reference frame to another external frame. For example, if B.C. frequently established a negative polarity correspondence in mapping the horizontal axis of the stimulus external frame onto a response external frame (mapping the positive pole of the stimulus frame's horizontal axis to the negative pole of the response-frame horizontal axis) then left–right reflections would be the result. We could have distinguished these two interpretations only by testing B.C. with stimuli asymmetric about the principal object axis. The tilt direction misrepresentation interpretation would predict errors of the sort shown in Figure 6B, whereas the polarity correspondence account would predict the type of error illustrated in Figure 8D. However, tasks with such stimuli proved too complex for B.C.

T.M.

T.M. is a right-handed girl with a family history of reading problems and other language-based learning disabilities. During testing for the present study she was 13–15 years old. Neurological examination at age 14 years revealed no sensory deficits or other disturbance of neurological function.

In elementary school T.M. experienced some difficulty with reading, spelling, and mathematics. Evaluated in her school at ages 9 and 12 years, she obtained average-range Verbal, Performance, and Full Scale IQ scores on the Wechsler Intelligence Scale for Children–3rd Edition (WISC-III; Wechsler, 1991). In both evaluations, however, her Performance IQ (90 and 95 at ages 9 and 12 years, respectively) was lower than her Verbal IQ (106 and 101), and the difference was significant at age 9 years. At age 12 years T.M.'s performance was especially poor on the Block Design subtest (2nd percentile), a measure of visuo-spatial construction. Difficulty with visual orientation was also noted in an occupational therapy evaluation report from age 9 years. T.M. scored at the 13th percentile on the Visual Motor Integration Test (Beery & Buktenica, 1997), which involves direct copying of simple and complex stimulus figures, and she was described as having "significant difficulty with visually determining direction of forms".

At age 13 years T.M. was evaluated at the Massachusetts General Hospital Psychology Assessment Center. On the Differential Ability Scales (DAS; Elliott, 1990) she demonstrated average verbal abilities (Verbal Cluster Score = 101; 53rd percentile), but her scores on both the Spatial (7th percentile) and the Nonverbal Reasoning clusters (9th percentile) were below average. She achieved her lowest scores on the Pattern Construction (8th percentile) and Sequential and Quantitative Reasoning (8th percentile) subtests, with errors on these measures suggesting difficulty with visual orientation. T.M. also showed mild impairment on reading and spelling tasks.

The most remarkable aspect of T.M.'s performance was her direct copy of the Rey–Osterrieth Complex figure (Rey, 1941; Osterrieth, 1944), shown in Figure 17. Although the stimulus remained in view while she drew it, her copy was largely left–right reflected, and it also contained errors in placement of elements within the figure. T.M.'s difficulties with orientation were investigated in eight additional sessions over a period of three years.

Complex figures

Direct copying

Over the course of the study complex visual stimuli were presented for direct copy on 15 occasions. The stimuli included the Rey–Osterrieth figure, the Taylor figure (Taylor, 1969), and several

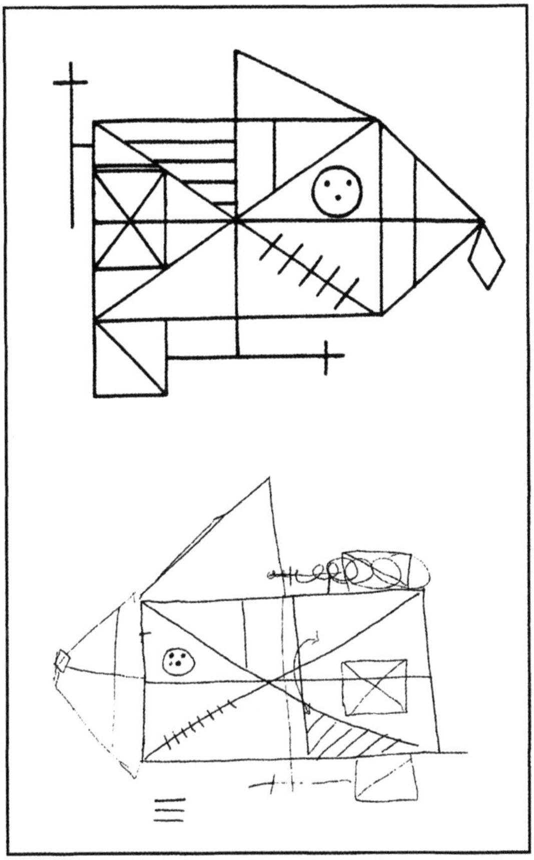

Figure 17. *T.M.'s direct copy of the Rey–Osterrieth complex figure.*

other figures of comparable complexity (Savage et al., 2001). On two of the trials T.M. copied the figure accurately, and on five trials she oriented the figure correctly but made relatively minor errors in locating or orienting internal features within the overall stimulus shape. However, on the remaining eight trials she left–right and/or up–down reflected the entire stimulus (and in some of these cases also made errors on internal features). Three examples are presented in Figure 18.

Detection of errors

One striking feature of T.M.'s copying performance suggested that her errors arose in constructing perceptual representations of the visual stimuli, rather than in producing the response drawing: She was entirely unaware of her copying errors, even when asked to make a careful comparison between the stimulus figure and her drawing. For example, asked to compare the stimulus and copy shown in Figure 18B, T.M. made a lengthy examination and then pointed to the spiral in her copy, stating that "the circle things are a little bit different". When asked what she meant, she said that the shapes were different. She failed to notice any further differences when asked to examine the figures again. T.M. also failed to detect orientation errors when asked to inspect copies made by the examiner.

Direct description task

T.M. also made reflection errors when asked to describe visual stimuli that remained in view on a computer monitor while she gave her descriptions. For example, presented with the stimulus in Figure 19, T.M. responded as follows:

> T.M.: There are two triangles, one with a banana in it, one with a house and then there's a wave on the side.
>
> E: Tell me about each triangle.
>
> T.M.: The triangle that is pointing to the *left* has a banana in it on the *right* side and it has a line down the middle. The arrow that is pointing up has a house pointing down.
>
> E: Where is the house?
>
> T.M.: On the *left* side.
>
> E: Where is the wave?
>
> T.M.: On the *left* side too.
>
> E: Tell me about what's in the first triangle.
>
> T.M.: The banana is on the *right* side.

This description is consistent with a left–right reflection of the entire stimulus figure. The errors are unlikely to stem from difficulty in using the words *left* and *right* because T.M.

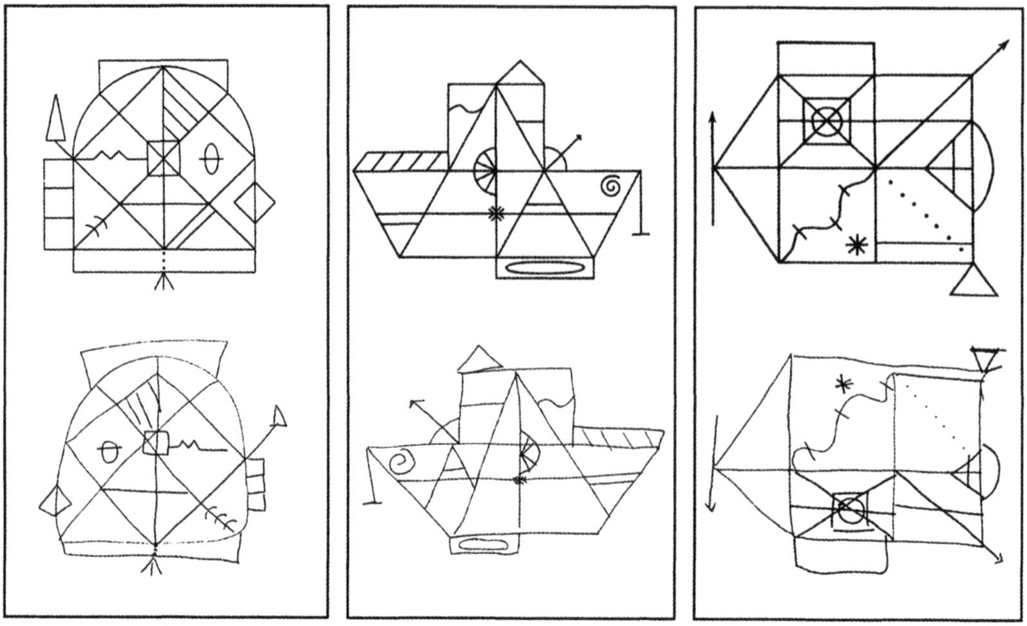

Figure 18. *T.M.'s direct copies of three additional complex figures (Savage et al., 2001).*

consistently used these terms correctly in a pretest in which she named the locations of individual shapes presented at left, right, up, or down locations on the computer screen.[8]

Simple stimuli

Whereas T.M. frequently made major orientation errors in tasks with complex visual stimuli, her performance was somewhat better with simpler stimuli. For example, she performed well in a task requiring her to indicate whether an arrowhead (<or >) was pointing to the left or right. She was also more accurate in copying simple than complex figures, although some reflection errors were observed even with simple stimuli (see Figure 20). These results suggest that T.M. may have less difficulty representing and processing orientation information under low- than high-load conditions (although we have no specific interpretation for why reduced load should be helpful).

T.M. also performed reasonably well on a task involving 21 line drawings of real objects with

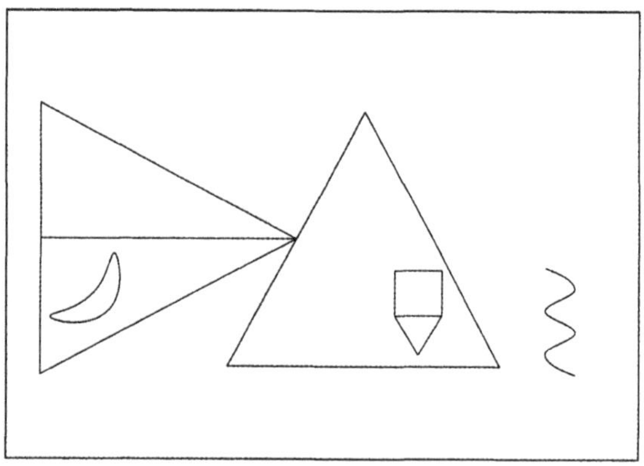

Figure 19. *Stimulus figure described by T.M.*

[8] Unlike A.H. (but like B.C.) T.M. was accurate in localizing visual stimuli relative to herself. She made no errors in reaching for a wooden block on a table in front of her, and she also reached accurately for a specified object within a complex array of objects.

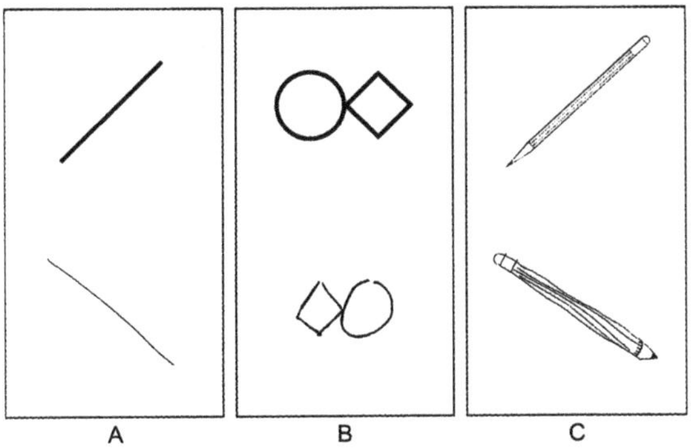

Figure 20. *T.M.'s direct copies of three simple stimuli. **A** and **B**. Stimuli from the Visual-Motor Integration test (Beery & Buktenica, 1997). **C**. Stimulus from the Boston Naming Test (Goodglass & Kaplan, 1983).*

canonical upright orientations (e.g., camel, house). On each of 21 trials she was asked to indicate whether the object was displayed right side up or upside down, and also whether a particular feature (e.g., the chimney on the house) was on the left or right side of the stimulus display. She made only two errors in the task, both involving left–right judgements. Conceivably, the line drawings imposed a lighter representational or processing load than stimuli such as the Rey–Osterrieth complex figure, because the arrangement of elements is much less arbitrary for real objects than for the abstract figures.

Interpreting T.M.'s performance

As Figure 20 illustrates, T.M. occasionally made reflection errors in copying tilted stimuli. These errors are similar to those observed for B.C. and have the same two potential interpretations: (a) misrepresentation of tilt direction in relating an object-centred reference frame to an external frame, or (b) polarity correspondence errors in mapping one external frame onto another. As in the case of B.C., the errors are ambiguous because the stimuli were bilaterally symmetric.

Most of the stimuli presented to T.M. (e.g., the Rey–Osterrieth complex figure) were not tilted—that is, the major axes of the stimulus were aligned with external horizontal and vertical axes. In copying or describing these stimuli T.M. frequently made left–right and/or up–down reflections of the entire stimulus figure (at least for complex stimuli). The whole-figure reflections may be interpreted as polarity correspondence errors in relating the axes of one reference frame to those of another. Consider, for example, the left–right reflection shown in Figure 18B. Assume for convenience that the principal axis of the object-centred reference frame coincides with the long axis of the stimulus figure, and that the end of the principal axis near the small spiral is defined as the positive pole. In relating the object-centred frame to an external frame (e.g., a frame defined by the page upon which the figure was printed) a correspondence might be established between the object frame's principal axis and the external horizontal axis (axis correspondence = PHSV). For this axis pair a positive polarity correspondence should be established—in other words, the positive pole of the object's principal axis should be placed in correspondence with the positive pole of the external horizontal axis. If the axis polarity were misrepresented as negative (i.e. positive pole of principal axis mapped onto negative pole of horizontal axis) the result would be a left–right reflection of the entire stimulus figure. On this interpretation the error is a reflection across the secondary object axis.

The whole-figure reflections could also have resulted from polarity correspondence errors in relating one external reference frame to another; whenever object axes are aligned with external horizontal and vertical axes, polarity correspondence errors in relating object to external reference frames cannot be distinguished from polarity correspondence errors in relating one external frame to another. For example, the left–right reflection in Figure 18B could have occurred in the process of relating a reference frame defined by the stimulus page to a frame defined by the page on which the copy was to be made. If the horizontal-axis polarity correspondence were represented as negative rather than positive, a left–right reflection would be the result. On this interpretation the error is a reflection across an external reference axis. The reflection errors for nontilted stimuli point clearly to misrepresentation of polarity correspondence. However, we cannot determine whether the errors arose in relating object frames to external frames, in relating external frames to one another, or both.[9]

In addition to whole-figure reflections T.M. made some errors in which she misplaced internal details within the larger stimulus figure. These errors may also have arisen from impairment in relating reference frames to one another. However, we postpone discussion of this point until considering results from A.H., at which time we can develop the point in the context of simpler examples.

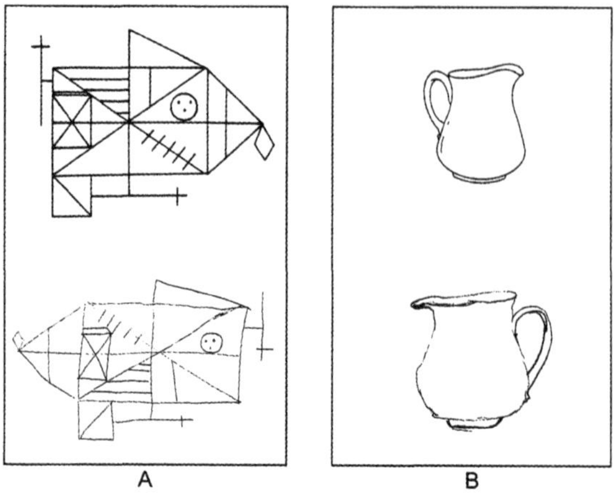

Figure 21. *A. A.H.'s direct copy of the Rey–Osterrieth complex figure. B. A.H.'s direct copy of a line drawing (Snodgrass & Vanderwart, 1980).*

A.H.

As we discussed at the beginning of this article, A.H. is severely impaired in localizing visual stimuli, making frequent left–right and up–down reflection errors. However, she also makes left–right and up–down orientation errors in tasks with visual stimuli.

Direct copying

Left–right and up–down reflections of orientation were observed in several direct copying tasks. Figure 21A presents A.H.'s copy of the Rey–Osterrieth figure (Rey, 1941; Osterrieth, 1944). Note the multiple left–right and up–down reflections. Note also how similar A.H.'s copy appears to that produced by T.M. Figure 21B shows a left–right reflection in A.H.'s direct copy of a picture from the Snodgrass and Vanderwart (1980) set.

Arrows experiment

In this task A.H. viewed a line drawing of an arrow that extended from the centre to the edge of a circle. The arrow pointed in one of eight directions: up, down, left, right, up left, up right, down left, or down right. Three response conditions were tested: drawing, pointer, and verbal. In the drawing response condition A.H. copied the stimulus arrow: She was given a response sheet showing a circle with a dot at the centre, and she drew in the arrow. The pointer response condition involved a wooden pointer that was out of sight inside a box. The pointer was mounted at the centre of a cardboard square by a bolt that allowed it to be rotated. A.H. reached into the box through a small hole and adjusted the pointer to indicate the direction of the stimulus arrow. Finally, in the verbal response condition A.H. reported the direction in words (e.g., "down right"). In the drawing and pointer response conditions a response was counted as correct if the arrow's orientation was within 10° of the correct orientation.

A.H. was severely impaired for all three forms of response. In the drawing condition she copied only 50% of the stimuli (12/24) correctly. Her

[9] Although T.M.'s errors for both tilted and nontilted stimuli are each subject to two potential interpretations, one of the interpretations is shared by the two types of error: Both error types could have resulted from misrepresentation of polarity correspondence in relating one external reference frame to another. However, we do not consider this point a sufficient basis for ruling out the other possible interpretation for each error type.

performance was equally poor in the pointer and verbal conditions: 42% (10/24) and 54% (13/24) correct, respectively. In all three conditions her errors were left–right and up–down reflections; some examples are shown in Figure 22.

Letter recognition

McCloskey and Rapp (2000a) found that A.H. made high rates of orientation errors in recognizing letters, whether the letters were presented in isolation or in the context of words. Of the 26 lower-case letters, 8 may be described as *orientation-critical*, meaning that reflecting the letter across a horizontal or vertical axis will yield a visual form corresponding to a different letter. For *b*, *d*, *p*, and *q* a left–right reflection, an up–down reflection, or both will transform one of the letters into another. For example, *b* becomes *d* by left–right reflection, *p* by up–down reflection, and *q* by left–right plus up–down reflection. Also, *n* and *u* are potentially confusable through up–down reflection, as are *m* and *w*. In a letter-naming task A.H. made orientation errors on about one fourth of the trials with orientation-critical letters. For example, across 21 presentations of *d*, she responded "b" six times, "p" three times, and "q" twice. Similarly, A.H. named *w* as "m" on 5 trials, and *m* as "w" twice. Results from control tasks demonstrated that the errors resulted

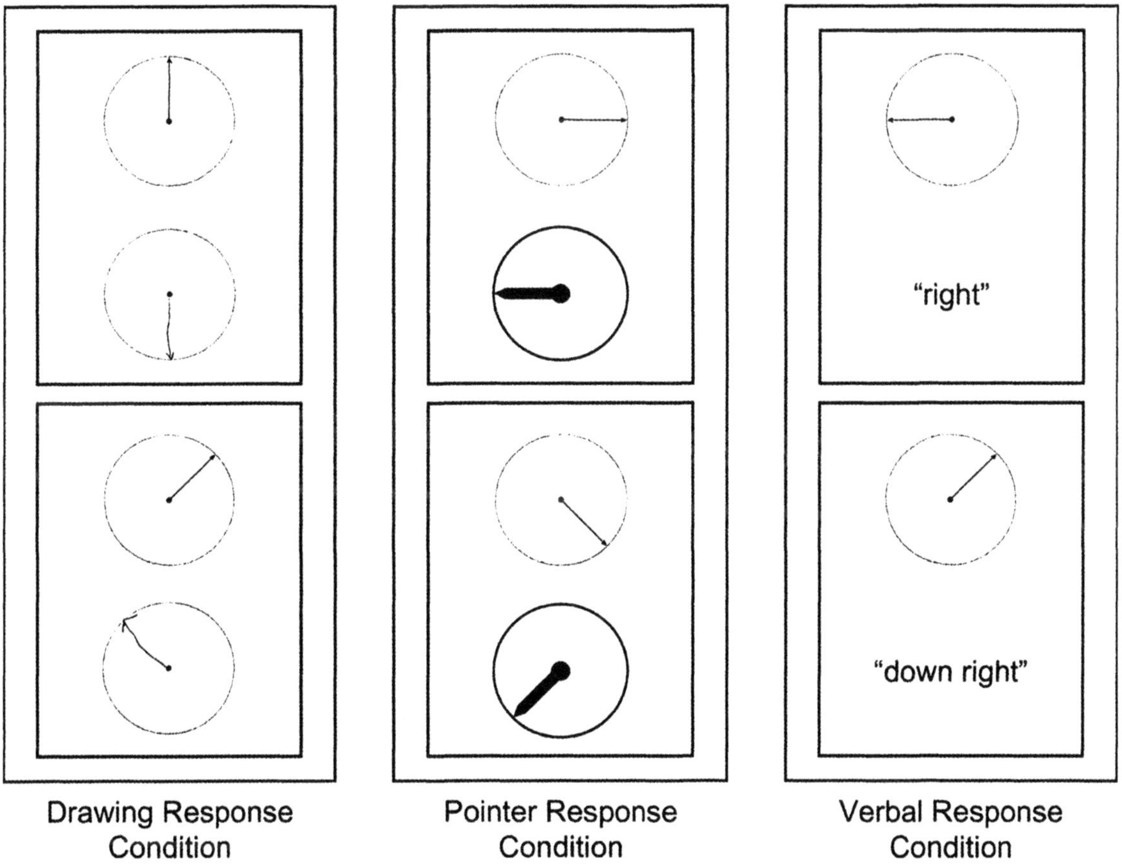

Figure 22. *Examples of A.H.'s reflection errors in the arrows experiment. Each panel shows a visual stimulus at the top and A.H.'s drawing, pointer-setting, or verbal response at the bottom.*

from misrepresentation of stimulus orientation and not from errors in associating names with letter shapes.

In another task A.H. read aloud words. For some of the stimulus words a letter orientation error could lead to confusion with a different word (e.g., *dark*, for which an orientation error for the *p* could lead to confusion with *bark* or *park*). A.H. made orientation confusions for nearly one third of these words (e.g., *bill* → "pill"; *dean* → "bean"; *wink* → "mink").

Possible interpretations

The errors in which A.H. left–right or up–down reflected a stimulus object—for example, in copying the drawing of a pitcher, or naming *w* as *m*—may be interpreted as polarity correspondence errors. For most stimuli, such as the pitcher, the object-centred axes were aligned with external vertical and horizontal axes. For these stimuli the reflections could have resulted from misrepresentation of polarity correspondence either in mapping between the object-centred and stimulus external reference frames, or in relating one external frame to another.

In the arrows task some of the arrows were tilted 45°. A.H.'s errors for the tilted arrows (see Figure 22) are also ambiguous, but for a different reason. Like the red-tipped line stimuli presented to B.C., the arrows were bilaterally symmetric. For such stimuli, tilt direction errors cannot be distinguished from polarity correspondence errors in relating external reference frames to one another. As a consequence, A.H.'s left–right and up–down reflections for tilted arrow stimuli could have resulted from misrepresentation of tilt direction in relating the object-centred frame to the external stimulus frame, or from polarity correspondence errors in relating one external frame to another.

Direct copying of tilted asymmetric figures

A.H. was also tested in a direct copying task not subject to these problems of ambiguity. In this task A.H. copied simple stimulus figures that were asymmetric across both primary and secondary axes and tilted relative to external reference axes. As illustrated in Figures 23 and 24, each stimulus consisted of a straight line with an additional feature at one or both ends. Three blocks of 24 stimuli were presented. On 16 of the 24 trials in each block the principal object axis was tilted 45° from vertical (8 clockwise, 8 counterclockwise). Each block also included four horizontally-oriented and four vertically-oriented stimuli.

Most of A.H.'s errors involved left–right or up–down reflection of the entire stimulus figure. However, she also made some errors in which she misoriented a feature within a stimulus object. We first discuss the whole-figure reflections and then consider the within-object errors.

Whole-figure reflections

A.H.'s errors for vertical and horizontal stimuli were similar to those observed in previous tasks. Collapsing across the vertical and horizontal orientations, A.H. made seven left–right and two up–down reflections of the entire stimulus figure.

Results for the tilted stimuli were more interesting. A.H. made seven errors in which she reflected the stimulus object across its principal axis; an example is presented in Figure 23A. She

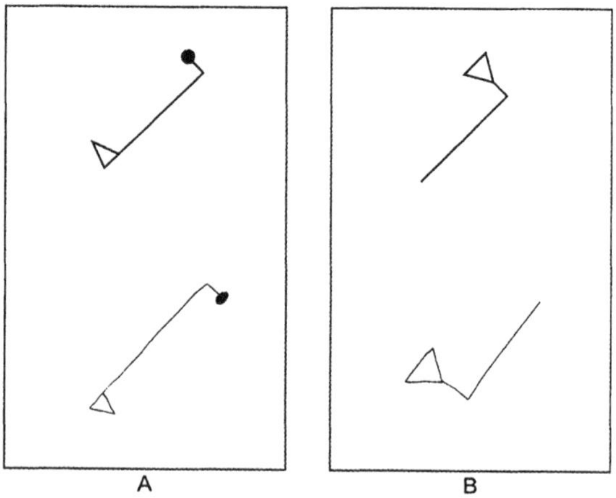

Figure 23. *A.H.'s direct copies of two asymmetric figures. A. Reflection across the principal object axis. B. Reflection across the secondary object axis.*

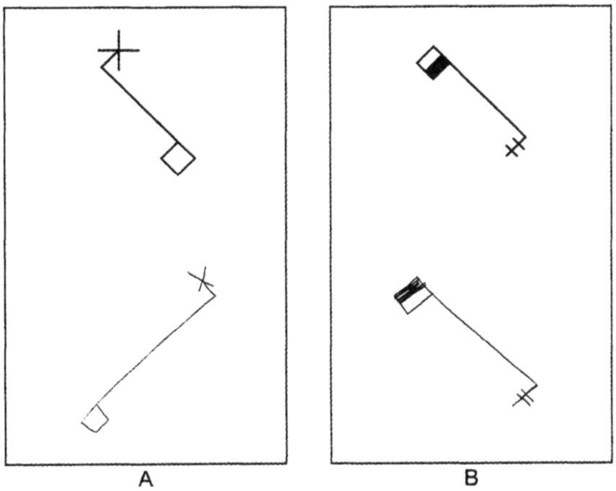

Figure 24. *A.H.'s direct copies of two additional asymmetric figures. A. Reflection across a vertical external axis. B. Within-object orientation error.*

also made one error in which the stimulus was reflected across its secondary axis (see Figure 23B). These errors indicate impairment in representing polarity correspondence between object-centred and external reference frames. The reflections across the principal axis may be attributed to misrepresentation of polarity correspondence between the secondary object axis and an external axis. Assume, for example, that for the stimulus in Figure 23A the principal object axis was placed in correspondence with the vertical external axis (i.e., axis correspondence = PVSH). Misrepresenting the polarity correspondence between the secondary object axis and the external horizontal axis would produce the error made by A.H. For instance, if the feature-laden side of the secondary axis were designated positive, the secondary-to-horizontal polarity correspondence should be negative, indicating that the feature-rich side of the secondary axis should be related to the left side of the horizontal axis. Misrepresenting the correspondence as positive would yield the observed error. By the same logic, the error in which A.H. reflected the stimulus object about its secondary axis may be attributed to misrepresentation of the polarity correspondence between the principal object axis and the relevant external axis.

In addition to the reflections across object axes A.H. made one error in which she left–right reflected the stimulus across a vertical external axis. This response, shown in Figure 24A, is interpretable as a polarity correspondence error in relating the horizontal axes of two external reference frames. For example, A.H. may have misrepresented the polarity correspondence between the horizontal axes of stimulus and response external frames as negative rather than positive. Unlike reflection errors for bilaterally symmetric stimuli, the error cannot be interpreted as a tilt direction error; misrepresenting tilt direction would have produced a response in which the × feature extended diagonally down and to the right from the upper end of the central line, and the square feature extended diagonally up and to the left.

A.H. also made four errors in which her response was 180° rotated relative to the stimulus. Even in the context of tilted asymmetric stimuli, such responses are ambiguous. We do not develop this point at length, but simply assert that 180° rotations could result from misrepresentation of polarity correspondence for both axis pairs either in relating an object frame to an external frame, or in relating one external frame to another.

To summarize, the results for the tilted asymmetric stimuli clearly demonstrate that A.H. is impaired in representing polarity correspondences between object and external axes, especially in relating a secondary object axis to an external axis. The single left–right reflection across a vertical external axis may also suggest some difficulty in representing polarity correspondences when relating one external frame to another. This suggestion is buttressed by the results from the previously discussed arrows task. The left–right and up–down reflections observed for tilted arrows cannot be attributed to polarity correspondence errors in relating object to external reference frames. However, these errors could have resulted from misrepresentation of polarity correspondences when relating external frames to one another.

Within-object misorientations

In addition to errors involving reflection of the entire stimulus object, A.H. also made a number of errors in which she reflected individual object parts within the object as a whole. Figure 24B presents an example, in which A.H. reflected the half-filled square relative to the object's principal axis. A detailed discussion of the within-object errors is beyond the scope of this article. However, we note briefly that these errors are consistent with the assumption made by some theorists (e.g., Marr, 1982) that object-centred representations are hierarchically structured. In the present example, representing the stimulus figure may involve (among other things) generating an object-centred representation of the half-filled square and then specifying the position of the square within the object by relating the square's reference frame to a frame for the object as a whole. Errors in specifying relationships among reference frames within an object-centred representation could lead to mis-placement or misorientation of object parts relative to one another. For example, the error shown in the figure might have occurred when A.H. misrepresented the polarity correspondence between an axis of the square's reference frame (more specifically, an axis perpendicular to the division between light and dark halves), and the principal axis of the whole-object frame. The within-object errors made by A.H. and T.M. when copying complex figures may admit of similar explanation.

Location versus orientation errors

One important question about A.H.'s performance concerns the relationship between her location and orientation errors. McCloskey and colleagues (McCloskey, 2004; McCloskey et al., 1995) have attributed A.H.'s reflection errors in localizing visual stimuli to an impairment in representing direction of displacement along reference axes, whereas we have argued that her reflection errors in orientation tasks probably stem from polarity correspondence errors in relating one reference frame to another. The co-occurrence of reflection errors in location and orientation tasks is unlikely to be a coincidence, especially given that the same variables affect A.H.'s accuracy in both task types (see McCloskey, 2004). One possibility is that A.H.'s developmental deficit affects a neural mechanism implicated in representing both displacement direction along reference axes and polarity mappings between axes. A more intriguing possibility is that A.H.'s location errors as well as her orientation errors arise from misrepresentations of polarity correspondence: Given a representation of an object's location within an external reference frame (as illustrated in Figure 2B), a polarity correspondence error in mapping the external frame onto another external frame could lead to a reflection error.[10]

GENERAL DISCUSSION

In this article we proposed a coordinate-system hypothesis of orientation representation (COR) and showed that the hypothesis allows us to interpret the orientation errors observed in three studies of developmental deficits. In the following

[10] We might also consider the possibility that A.H.'s location and orientation errors both result not from misrepresentation of polarity correspondence but from misspecification of displacement direction along reference axes. For the orientation errors we might posit that A.H. frequently misspecifies the direction of displacement along object axes when representing the locations of object parts within an object-centred frame (e.g., specifying the location of an object part as 20 units in the negative rather than the positive direction on the secondary object axis). This interpretation could conceivably be applied to the errors involving reflection across object axes; however, for whole-object reflections involving objects with multiple features (as in Figure 23A), we would have to posit multiple errors in which the displacement direction for each feature was misspecified for the same object axis. In contrast the polarity-correspondence interpretation needs to posit only a single representational error to account for the whole-object reflections. Also, mislocation of object parts in object-centred representations cannot account for the orientation errors involving reflection across external axes (see Figure 24A, and the reflections observed with diagonal arrow stimuli, illustrated in Figure 22). The association between location and orientation errors in A.H. clearly deserves careful consideration, especially in the light of the fact that location errors do not always co-occur with orientation errors. (For example, T.M. and B.C. did not make visual localization errors in tasks for which A.H. showed gross impairment, such as visually guided reaching.) More generally, the relationship between location and orientation representations is in need of careful exploration. However, this is a topic for subsequent theoretical and empirical work.

discussion we briefly consider three sets of issues arising from our results and interpretations.

Interpretation of results

In discussing the results from B.C., T.M., and A.H. we have focused almost exclusively on how the observed errors could have arisen within coordinate-system orientation representations. As a consequence, we have left several significant issues largely unexplored. One such issue concerns where in the stream of processing each participant's errors arose. Results reported more fully elsewhere (McCloskey, 2004; McCloskey et al., 1995) demonstrate that A.H.'s errors originate within the visual system—for example, she showed normal performance in location and orientation tasks with nonvisual stimuli. However, B.C. made reflection errors with tactile as well as visual stimuli, raising the possibility that her deficit implicates a more central amodal level of representation (although as we noted in discussing B.C.'s results, a visual-system locus of impairment is also possible). T.M. made reflection errors in describing as well as copying visual stimuli, suggesting that her deficit affects a level of representation not tied to a specific response modality. However, we cannot determine from the evidence we collected whether the affected representations lie within the visual system or instead at some more central level.

Identifying the level at which errors arise is crucial for tying conclusions about the form of a representation to a particular perceptual-, cognitive-, or motor-system locus. We have argued that reflection errors are a signature of coordinate-system orientation representations. Hence, the systematic patterns of reflection errors observed for B.C., T.M., and A.H. constitute evidence for coordinate-system representations of orientation. However, we can draw only limited conclusions about the functional loci at which orientation is represented in coordinate-system form. A.H.'s results imply that some level(s) of the visual system implement coordinate-system orientation representations. T.M.'s results are consistent with this conclusion, although a more central locus for her errors is possible. B.C.'s performance pattern is perhaps most plausibly interpreted as evidence for coordinate-system orientation representations at some central amodal level, although her errors could conceivably have arisen within the visual system. Most other studies of orientation errors are subject to similar uncertainties. Hence, an important goal in future research should be to pin down more precisely the functional locus at which the observed orientation errors arise, so that conclusions can be drawn about the form of orientation representations at particular levels of representation.

A related issue concerns the reference frames implicated in orientation errors. We have suggested that some of A.H.'s errors, and perhaps also some of B.C.'s and T.M.'s errors, involved representations that relate one external (i.e., nonobject-centred) reference frame to another. However, we have no firm evidence about what specific reference frames were implicated in the errors. Consider, for example, A.H.'s errors involving reflection across an external horizontal or vertical axis (e.g., Figure 24A). These errors might have originated in representations relating an external frame defined by the stimulus page to a frame based on head or body axes, or in representations relating a head- or body-based frame to a frame defined by the response page. Alternatively, the errors might have occurred in relating the stimulus external frame directly to the response frame, without the intervention of frames defined by body axes.[11] Hence, another goal in future research should be to identify the reference frames within which orientation errors arise.

The importance of these goals is underlined by the observation that orientation information is

[11] McCloskey and Rapp (2000b) have reported evidence that at least some of A.H.'s localization errors arise within an attention-centred frame of reference, in which the origin of the coordinate system is defined by the focus of attention. However, A.H.'s orientation errors were not addressed in their study. Further, the conclusion about attention-centred representations has to do only with how the origin of the coordinate system is defined, and not with the basis for defining reference axes.

almost certainly processed at multiple loci within the brain. For example, Milner and Goodale (1995) have proposed that the visual system includes two largely independent subsystems: a vision-for-action subsystem that mediates natural visually guided actions such as reaching for an object, and a vision-for-perception subsystem that underlies other visual functions, including conscious awareness of visual stimuli. Both subsystems must represent orientation: The vision-for-action subsystem requires orientation information for such purposes as positioning a reaching hand to grasp an object, and the vision-for-perception subsystem needs orientation information for such functions as processing visual symbols (e.g., *b* vs. *d*, ← vs. →), interpreting visual scenes, and giving rise to conscious awareness of object orientations. Orientation may also be processed within the somatosensory system, within systems that manipulate multimodal or amodal spatial representations, and so forth. Furthermore, within each of these brain systems, orientation information may be represented in multiple frames of reference. A central issue for subsequent research is whether orientation representations take the same basic form at all of these representational levels, or whether instead the form of orientation representations varies across brain systems and/or across frames of reference within systems.

Developmental deficits

In most cognitive neuropsychological research inferences about normal cognition are drawn from adult acquired deficits, in which an initially normal and fully developed system suffers damage. Inferences from an adult acquired deficit to normal cognitive representations and processes are founded on the assumption that the damaged brain has not substantially reorganized and hence that the observed performance reflects a largely normal brain with one or more specific malfunctions (e.g., Caramazza, 1986).

In this article we have presented evidence from developmental deficits, in which abnormalities arise before brain development is complete, due to genetic defects, neural insult (as in B.C.), or unknown causes (as for A.H. and T.M.). However, the use of developmental deficits as a basis for inferences about normal cognition has been controversial (see, e.g., the target article and commentaries in Thomas & Karmiloff-Smith, 2002). The principal concern is as follows: In a developmental deficit neural development could conceivably have followed a far-from-normal course, producing not a basically normal brain with specific malfunctions, but instead a brain that differs in its fundamental structure and functioning from the normal brain. Conclusions about normal cognition drawn on the basis of a brain with fundamentally abnormal organization would probably be erroneous, especially if the possibility of abnormal organization were not recognized. Given that one usually has no way of knowing whether brain organization is fundamentally normal or abnormal in cases of developmental impairment, developmental deficits do not provide a sound basis for inferences about normal cognition.

In our view this argument is too strong. We agree that inferences from developmental deficits to normal cognition must be drawn with some caution and are subject to some uncertainty. However, a blanket rejection of all such inferences does not appear to be warranted. We suggest that the issue should be considered on an inference-by-inference basis: Given a potential inference about normal cognition from a pattern of performance observed in a case of developmental impairment, one should ask whether the performance could be explained in terms of abnormal brain organization without making claims about normal cognition. To the extent that plausible abnormal-organization accounts can be formulated, the inference about normal cognition is weakened. However, to the extent that abnormal-organization interpretations appear implausible, the inference can be drawn (albeit with caution).

For example, we have inferred from the reflection errors observed for B.C., T.M., and A.H. that normal brains implement coordinate-system representations of orientation. The implicit chain of reasoning was as follows: (a) The reflection errors imply that B.C.'s, T.M.'s, and A.H.'s brains implement coordinate-system representations of orientation; (b) the brains of these developmentally impaired individuals have the same forms of orientation representation as normal brains (although malfunctions occur in the generation or use of these representations); and (c) therefore, normal brains implement coordinate-system representations of orientation.

An alternative interpretation positing abnormal brain organization would not question Step (a) of the argument: What is at issue is not whether one can draw valid conclusions about the representations and processes of the developmentally impaired individuals themselves, but whether the conclusions can be generalized to normal individuals. The point of attack for an abnormal-organization account would be Step (b). The interpretation would assert that our participants' brains do not have the same forms of representation as normal brains and therefore that conclusions about orientation representations cannot be generalized from these participants to normal individuals.

This interpretation is committed to a very strong and implausible claim—namely, that abnormal brain development in B.C., T.M., and A.H. somehow produced a new form of orientation representation not used by the normal brain. Our participants clearly made use of orientation information—they often gave correctly oriented responses, and their orientation errors were definitely not random. Therefore, one presumably must assume that B.C., T.M., and A.H. represented orientation in some form or another, even if one does not agree with our suggestion that the representations were in coordinate-system form. Hence, an abnormal-organization account must assume that the brains of these developmentally impaired individuals implement some specific form of orientation representation that is not used in the normal brain. This claim cannot be dismissed entirely, but strikes us as quite implausible. Hence, we suggest, inferences from our participants' performance to normal orientation representations are reasonable. More generally, formulaic rejection of inferences from developmental deficits to normal cognition is unjustified.

Ultimately, the value of developmental deficits as a basis for conclusions about normal cognition can be determined only by accumulating experience with the approach. If we find, over time, that inferences from developmental deficits tend to converge with those from other methods (e.g., studies of normal children and adults, studies of adult acquired deficits) then we will have more confidence that developmental deficits can inform us about normal cognition. If, however, we find that conclusions from developmental deficits do not fit well with those emerging from other types of research, we will have to consider the possibility that developmental deficits are not a sound basis for conclusions about normal cognition (or at least that inferences need to be more complex, taking into account abnormal development more explicitly).

The coordinate-system orientation representation hypothesis

The COR hypothesis is at an early stage of development, in several respects. As we noted when introducing the hypothesis, many of the assumptions are tentative, and plausible variants can be envisioned. Also, in formulating the hypothesis we have focused largely on reflection errors. Hence, an important goal for subsequent theoretical work is to evaluate and refine the hypothesis by considering other types of error observed in studies of orientation. For example, in copying visual stimuli young children often have difficulty with diagonal lines, tending to align them with external vertical and horizontal axes (e.g., copying an × shape as a +; see, e.g., Tada & Stiles, 1996). Perhaps this phenomenon can be understood in terms of difficulty in relating an object-centred frame of reference (with axes aligned with the diagonal lines in the stimulus) to external reference frame with vertical and horizontal axes.

Even in its current preliminary state, however, the COR hypothesis has significant value. The hypothesis provides something that has been lacking in cognitive research on orientation: a conceptual framework for thinking about how the orientation of objects might be represented. Also, the hypothesis calls attention to nonobvious differences among forms of orientation error (e.g., tilt direction errors, reflections across object axes, reflections across external axes) and suggests underlying causes for each error type. Most notably, the hypothesis provides specific interpretations for the various forms of mirror reflection error. These striking errors have been observed in many previous studies, but distinctions among types of reflection error have not been defined, nor have specific interpretations been offered. The COR hypothesis also allows us to recognize the characteristics a stimulus must have for distinguishing among potential underlying causes of orientation error. To tease apart the various potential error types we have described, a stimulus object must be asymmetric across both primary and secondary axes and must be presented with object axes tilted relative to external axes.

Finally, the hypothesis suggests directions for subsequent research. Patterns of orientation errors should be explored systematically with tilted, asymmetric stimuli, in studies that aim to identify the functional loci at which errors arise and the reference frames affected. Pursuing this agenda in studies of normal and impaired children and adults should add significantly to our understanding of how orientation is represented in the human brain.

PrEview proof published online 30 March 2006

REFERENCES

Appelle, S. (1972). Perception and discrimination as a function of stimulus orientation: The "oblique effect" in man and animals. *Psychological Bulletin, 78*, 266–278.

Beery, K. E., & Buktenica, N. A. (1997). *VMI: The Beery–Buktenica Developmental Test of Visual-Motor Integration* (4th rev. ed.). Parsippany, NJ: Modern Curriculum Press.

Bornstein, M. H. (1982). Perceptual anisotropies in infancy: Ontogenetic origins and implications for inequalities in spatial vision. *Advances in Child Development, 16*, 77–123.

Caramazza, A. (1986). On drawing inferences about the structure of normal cognitive systems from the analysis of patterns of impaired performance: The case for single-patient studies. *Brain and Cognition, 5*, 41–66.

Corballis, M. C., & Beale, I. L. (1976). *The psychology of left and right.* Hillsdale, NJ: Lawrence Erlbaum Associates, Inc.

Davidoff, J., & Warrington, E. K. (2001). A particular difficulty in discriminating between mirror images. *Neuropsychologia, 39*, 1022–1036.

Deregowski, J. B., McGeorge, P., & Wynn, V. (2000). The role of left–right symmetry in the encodement of spatial orientations. *British Journal of Psychology, 91*, 241–257.

Dilks, D. D., Reiss, J. E., Landau, B., & Hoffman, J. E. (2004). *Representation of orientation in Williams syndrome.* Unpublished manuscript.

Elliott, D. E. (1990). *Differential ability scales.* New York: Psychological Corporation.

Goodale, M. A., Milner, A. D., Jakobson, L. S., & Carey, D. P. (1991). A neurological dissociation between perceiving objects and grasping them. *Nature, 349*, 154–156.

Goodglass, H., & Kaplan, E. (1983). *Boston Naming Test.* Philadelphia: Lea & Febiger.

Hammill, D. D., Pearson, N. A., & Voress, J. K. (1993). *Developmental Test of Visual Perception (DTVP-2)* (2nd ed.). Austin, TX: Pro-Ed.

Harris, I. M., Harris, J. A., & Caine, D. (2001). Object orientation agnosia: A failure to find the axis? *Journal of Cognitive Neuroscience, 13*, 800–812.

Howard, I. P. (1982). *Human visual orientation.* Chichester, UK: Wiley.

Howard, I. P., & Templeton, W. B. (1966). *Human spatial orientation.* London: Wiley.

Hubel, D. H., & Wiesel, T. (1968). Receptive fields and functional architecture of monkey striate cortex. *Journal of Physiology, 160*, 106–154.

Ittelson, W. H., Mowafy, L., & Magid, D. (1991). The perception of mirror-reflected objects. *Perception, 20*, 567–584.

Lacquaniti, F., Guigon, E., Bianchi, L., Ferraina, S., & Caminiti, R. (1995). Representing spatial information for limb movement: Role of area 5 in the monkey. *Cerebral Cortex, 5*, 391–409.

Marr, D. (1982). *Vision.* New York: W. H. Freeman.

McCloskey, M. (2000). Spatial representation in mind and brain. In B. Rapp (Ed.), *The handbook of cognitive neuropsychology: What deficits reveal about the human mind* (pp. 101–132). Philadelphia: Psychology Press.

McCloskey, M. (2004). Spatial representations and multiple visual systems hypotheses: Evidence from a developmental deficit in visual location and orientation processing. *Cortex, 40*, 677–694.

McCloskey, M., & Palmer, E. (1996). Visual representation of object location: Insights from localization impairments. *Current Directions in Psychological Science, 5*, 25–28.

McCloskey, M., & Rapp, B. (2000a). A visually based developmental reading deficit. *Journal of Memory and Language, 43*, 157–181.

McCloskey, M., & Rapp, B. (2000b). Attention-referenced visual representations: Evidence from impaired visual localization. *Journal of Experimental Psychology: Human Perception and Performance, 26*, 917–933.

McCloskey, M., Rapp, B., Yantis, S., Rubin, G., Bacon, W. F., Dagnelie, G. et al. (1995). A developmental deficit in localizing objects from vision. *Psychological Science, 6*, 112–117.

Milner, B. (1971). Interhemispheric differences in the localization of psychological processes in man. *British Medical Bulletin, 27*, 272–277.

Milner, A. D., & Goodale, M. A. (1995). *The visual brain in action*. Oxford: Oxford University Press.

Noble, J. (1968). Paradoxical interocular transfer of mirror-image discriminations in the optic chiasm sectioned monkey. *Brain Research, 10*, 127–151.

O'Keefe, J. (1993). Kant and the sea-horse: An essay in the neurophilosophy of space. In N. Eilan, R. McCarthy, & B. Brewer (Eds.), *Spatial representation: Problems in philosophy and psychology* (pp. 43–64). Oxford, UK: Blackwell.

O'Keefe, J., & Nadel, L. (1978). *The hippocampus as a cognitive map*. Oxford, UK: Oxford University Press.

Osterrieth, P. A. (1944). Le test de copie d'une figure complex: Contribution a l'étude de la perception et de la mémoire. *Archives de Psychologie, 30*, 286–356.

Priftis, K., Rusconi, E., Umiltà, C., & Zorzi, M. (2003). Pure agnosia for mirror stimuli after right inferior parietal lesion. *Brain, 126*, 908–919.

Rey, A. (1941). *L'examen clinique en psychologie*. Paris: Press Universaire de France.

Riddoch, M. J., & Humphreys, G. W. (1988). Description of a left/right coding deficit in a case of constructional apraxia. *Cognitive Neuropsychology, 5*, 289–315.

Rudel, R. G. (1982). The oblique mystique: A slant on the development of spatial coordinates. In M. Potegal (Ed.), *Spatial abilities: Development and physiological foundations* (pp. 129–146). New York: Academic Press.

Savage, C. R., Bohne, A., Deckersback, T., Bitran, S., Chugani, H., & Rauch, S. L. (2001). Validation of 3 alternate figures for the Rey–Osterrieth Complex Figure Test. *Journal of the International Neuropsychological Society, 7*, 134.

Snodgrass, J. G., & Vanderwart, M. (1980). A standardized set of 260 pictures: Norms for name agreement, image agreement, familiarity, and visual complexity. *Journal of Experimental Psychology: Human Learning and Memory, 6*, 174–215.

Soechting, J. F., & Flanders, M. (1989). Errors in pointing are due to approximations in sensorimotor transformations. *Journal of Neurophysiology, 62*, 595–608.

Soechting, J. F., & Flanders, M. (1992). Moving in three-dimensional space: Frames of reference, vectors, and coordinate systems. *Annual Review of Neuroscience, 15*, 167–191.

Tada, W. L., & Stiles, J. (1996). Developmental change in children's analysis of spatial patterns. *Developmental Psychology, 32*, 951–970.

Taylor, L. B. (1969). Localization of cerebral lesions by psychological testing. *Clinical Neurosurgery, 16*, 269–287.

Thomas, M., & Karmiloff-Smith, A. (2002). Are developmental disorders like cases of adult brain damage? Implications from connectionist modeling. *Behavioral and Brain Sciences, 25*, 727–788.

Turnbull, O. H. (1997). A double dissociation between knowledge of object identity and object orientation. *Neuropsychologia, 35*, 567–570.

Turnbull, O. H., Beschin, N., & Della Salla, S. (1997). Agnosia for object orientation: Implications for theories of object recognition. *Neuropsychologia, 35*, 153–163.

Turnbull, O. H., Della Salla, S., & Beschin, N. (2002). Agnosia for object orientation: Naming and mental rotation evidence. *Neurocase, 8*, 296–305.

Turnbull, O. H., Laws, K. R., & McCarthy, R. (1995). Object recognition without knowledge of object orientation. *Cortex, 31*, 387–395.

Turnbull, O. H., & McCarthy, R. (1996). Failure to discriminate between mirror-image objects: A case of viewpoint-independent object recognition? *Neurocase, 2*, 63–72.

Tversky, B. (1981). Distortions in memory for maps. *Cognitive Psychology, 13*, 407–433.

Wechsler, D. (1991). *Wechsler intelligence scale for children* (3rd ed.). New York: Psychological Corporation.

COGNITIVE NEUROPSYCHOLOGY, 2006, 23 (5), 714–747

Psychology Press
Taylor & Francis Group

Prosopagnosia as an impairment to face-specific mechanisms: Elimination of the alternative hypotheses in a developmental case

Bradley C. Duchaine
Institute of Cognitive Neuroscience, University College London, London, UK

Galit Yovel
Tel Aviv University, Tel Aviv, Israel

Edward J. Butterworth
Institute of Imaging Science, Vanderbilt University, Nashville, TN, USA

Ken Nakayama
Harvard Vision Sciences Laboratory, Cambridge, MA, USA

For more than 35 years, researchers have debated whether face recognition is carried out by face-specific mechanisms or whether it involves more general mechanisms that are also used for objects. Prosopagnosic patients have furnished powerful evidence for face-specific mechanisms. Yet for each case that has been tested there have always been several untested alternative explanations that could account for the case. As such, each of these individuals has not been sufficiently tested to provide conclusive evidence for face-specific processes. Here we make a stronger argument with a single case of severe developmental prosopagnosia by exhaustively addressing all extant alternatives. We reject each in turn and thus eliminate all alternative accounts. Because this case is developmental in etiology the results also indicate that face recognition involves developmental mechanisms different from those producing other visual recognition mechanisms.

Face perception has played a central role in social interaction for millions of years in a wide range of species. Information from faces is used to infer emotional state (nonhuman primates: Darwin, 1872; human infants: Klinnert, Campos, Sorce, Emde, & Svejda, 1983), gender (human infants: Quinn, Yahr, Kuhn, Slater, & Pascalis, 2002), attractiveness (macaques: Waitt et al., 2003; human infants: Rubenstein, Langlois, & Kalakanis, 1999), attentional focus (snakes: Burghardt, 1990; plovers: Ristau, 1991; macaques: Perrett & Mistlin, 1990; human

Correspondence should be addressed to Bradley C. Duchaine, Institute of Cognitive Neuroscience, University College London, 17 Queen Square, London WC1 N 3AR, UK (Email: b.duchaine@ucl.ac.uk).

This work was supported by grants from NIH (F 32 MH64246–03 and R01 EY13602). Some of the images were provided courtesy of Mike Tarr (Brown University, Providence, RI). Special thanks to Anne Grossetete, Gayle Speck, Kerry Dingle, and Nancy Kanwisher for their contribution to this project.

http://www.psypress.com/cogneuropsychology

DOI:10.1080/02643290500441296

infants: Papousek & Papousek, 1979), age, and physical prowess (adult humans: Fox, 1997). Possibly because of the richness of these social signals (Bruce & Young, 1998), faces have also become a primary means for individual identification in many species, and the primacy of the face for human identification is demonstrated by our use of faces for photographs, portraits, identification cards, and police sketches. Face recognition is also an important issue within cognitive neuroscience that has been approached with a wide variety of methods over the past forty years. Herein we investigate the nature of the mechanisms that humans use for the identification of individual faces by assessing the recognition abilities of an individual with lifelong face recognition impairments.

Our findings will bear on fundamental issues in cognitive neuroscience. Despite years of discussion, it remains a matter of debate whether the brain contains mechanisms that are specialized for processing information about domains described by natural kind terms (e.g., faces, animate beings, plants, language, children)—mechanisms often called domain specific (Caramazza & Mahon, 2003; Caramazza & Shelton, 1998; Hirschfeld & Gelman, 1994). Such mechanisms are typically contrasted with domain-general mechanisms or horizontal faculties that operate over a wide range of domains (Fodor, 1983; Tooby & Cosmides, 1992). The two abilities most often pointed to as products of domain-specific mechanisms are language and face recognition (Bruce & Young, 1986; Chomsky, 1980; Cowie, 1998; Fodor, 1983; Jackendoff, 1992; Pinker, 1994). Language, however, is a more difficult test case, because language appears to involve a number of mechanisms, and it is difficult to isolate one of these and determine if it is language specific. In contrast, the relative simplicity of face recognition makes it a more tractable ability to explore. A second, related, issue is whether the brain contains mechanisms specialized for social cognition. While research on social cognition has begun to flourish, it remains an open question whether any social computations are handled by mechanisms dedicated to social interaction.

In addition, because this case is developmental in nature, it provides a means to investigate the developmental processes that produce the mechanisms used for visual recognition. Unlike acquired dissociations, dissociations found in developmental cases are not only functional dissociations but also developmental dissociations. Thus, if this case is best accounted for by an impairment to face-specific mechanisms, it will indicate that these mechanisms are produced, at least in part, by developmental processes that are uninvolved in the development of other visual-recognition mechanisms. Our results also bear on a current theoretical debate about developmental disorders. Some have argued that developmental impairments in one mechanism will necessarily impact the functioning of other developing mechanisms (Thomas & Karmiloff-Smith, 2002) and so predict that residual normality, as it has been called, for other mechanisms should not exist. However, investigations of specific developmental disorders in other domains (e.g., dyslexia, dyscalculia, semantic amnesia, episodic amnesia) suggest that functionally unrelated mechanisms can develop normally (Landerl, Bevan, & Butterworth, 2004; Ramus et al., 2003; Temple & Richardson, 2004; Vargha-Khadem, Gadian, & Mishkin, 2001; Vargha-Khadem et al., 1997). Whether this is the case for visual recognition mechanisms remains to be determined. Apparently face-selective cases of developmental prosopagnosia indicate that other recognition mechanisms can develop normally (Duchaine & Nakayama, 2005; Nunn, Postma, & Pearson, 2001), but further evidence is necessary to draw firm conclusions.

Dissociations within visual recognition

Evidence from a number of sources indicates that some of the mechanisms used for face recognition are different from the mechanisms used for other types of visual recognition. Studies of prosopagnosics have shown that face and object recognition can dissociate even when task demands are equivalent and speed/accuracy trade-offs are ruled out (Duchaine & Nakayama, 2005; Farah, 1996).

Conversely, a number of patients have been reported who show normal (Moscovitch, Winocur, & Behrmann, 1997) or relatively spared (McMullen, Fisk, & Phillips, 2000) face recognition despite severe impairments with objects. Evidence from lesion studies, neurophysiology, and neuroimaging indicate that the inferior right temporal lobe is involved in face recognition (Barton, Press, Keenan, & O'Connor, 2002; Kanwisher, McDermott, & Chun, 1997; Kreiman, Koch, & Fried, 2000; Landis, Cummings, Christen, Bogen, & Imhof, 1986; McCarthy, Puce, Belger, & Allison, 1999; McCarthy, Puce, Gore, & Allison, 1997; Yin, 1970). Behavioural experiments using different methods have demonstrated that faces are processed in a more configural or holistic manner than many object classes including inverted faces (Freire, Lee, & Symons, 2000; McKone, Martini, & Nakayama, 2001; Tanaka & Farah, 1993; Tanaka & Sengco, 1997; Yin, 1969; Young, Hellawell, & Hay, 1987). Although these studies demonstrate that face recognition relies on different mechanisms from those for many other types of recognition, they do not demonstrate that the mechanisms are face specific.

To make this point more clearly, we display some of the potential architectures that might be used to process faces in Figure 1. For example, selective deficits could result from an architecture that contains a battery of mechanisms that are each specialized for a particular processing task such as parts-based processing, configural processing, individual item recognition, or expert processing. These mechanisms could be applied to any class depending on the properties of that class and/or an individual's experience with the class. Recognition of items from a particular stimulus class could activate one, some, or all of the mechanisms, and selective impairments could result from problems with a subset of these mechanisms. Visual recognition could also be performed by an array of domain-specific mechanisms that only operate on the class for which they are specialized. Of course, impairment to some of these mechanisms would produce selective dissociations. Finally, there could be a mixed architecture with a battery of more general-purpose mechanisms as well as domain-specific

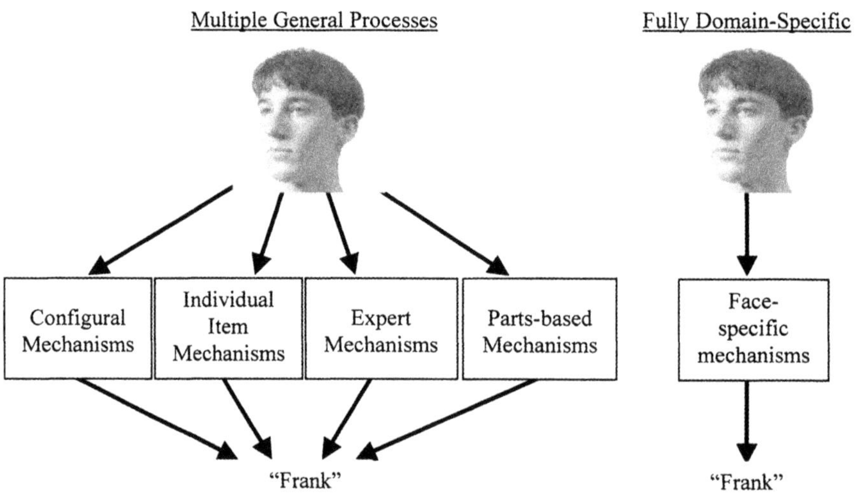

Figure 1. *Possible organizations for mechanisms involved with face recognition. For the multiple general process model, faces are recognized by a number of mechanisms that are also used with other object classes. Note that the battery of mechanisms included in the model that we present is only one of many possibilities. In a fully domain-specific model, upright face recognition depends almost exclusively on face-specific mechanisms. A hybrid organization is also a possibility; faces would be processed by both face-specific mechanisms and more general-purpose mechanisms. Impairments to any of these mechanisms could cause prosopagnosia.*

mechanisms. The more general mechanisms may contribute to the recognition of the classes for which domain-specific mechanisms exist, or they may be uninvolved in recognizing such items. Each of these architectures would lead to different patterns of dissociations, but current evidence does not clearly support a particular organization.

To draw firm conclusions, all alternative explanations must be addressed in a single case

Over the years, many explanations for prosopagnosia have been proposed, and we discuss each explanation below. All agree that some mechanisms in the visual system are not working properly, but they differ in how to characterize the domain of the impaired mechanisms and thus on what classes the mechanisms operate. Because the proposed classes differ, the hypotheses make different predictions about which nonface classes prosopagnosics will be impaired with. In many past studies of prosopagnosia, researchers have tested some of these predictions and have demonstrated that a single explanation for prosopagnosia cannot account for the observed pattern of normal object recognition and impaired face recognition. They have then often concluded that defective mechanisms proposed by one of the explanations are the best account of the case and the best account of prosopagnosia in general. However, there are many alternative explanations, and all of the alternatives have not been addressed in a single case. Until this is done, no one hypothesis is implicated as the best explanation, and so past cases do not provide strong evidence about the nature of the mechanisms performing face recognition in normal subjects.

To illustrate this issue, consider the following case: An individual with severe face recognition impairments shows normal or relatively spared recognition for individual televisions and individual lamps. This pattern would demonstrate that the individuation explanation could not account for this subject's prosopagnosia, because this explanation proposes that prosopagnosia is caused by impairment to mechanisms used for individual item recognition within any class. Comparable results have often been considered supportive of the face-specific explanation. However, though the results are consistent with the face-specific explanation, they are also consistent with a number of the remaining alternative explanations as well. For instance, there is little reason to believe that either object class (televisions or lamps) requires configural processing so the configural processing explanation remains a possibility. Similarly, subjects are unlikely to have significant visual expertise with either class so the expertise explanation may account for the face impairment. In fact, normal performance with televisions and chairs only eliminates the individuation explanation so the results are only a first step in ascertaining which explanation is the best account. To draw firmer conclusions, the predictions of the other alternatives must be tested as well.

Furthermore, each alternative must be tested in a single case. Above, we discussed that many possible architectures could give rise to the dissociations seen in previous cases of prosopagnosia, and for some of these architectures, face recognition relies on a number of different mechanisms. If multiple mechanisms contribute to face recognition, then impairment to any of these mechanisms could result in prosopagnosia, and there would be different varieties of prosopagnosia (Davidoff, 1986; Schweich & Bruyer, 1993). Therefore, past demonstrations that an explanation cannot account for a prosopagnosic's deficits does not rule it out as an explanation in another prosopagnosic. To provide support for a particular explanation, all explanations need to be addressed in a single case study. Before proceeding, we provide a list of the extant explanations of prosopagnosia to be addressed in the present study.

Here are the proposed explanations and their predictions:

Face-specific explanation. This account proposes that prosopagnosia results from an impairment to mechanisms specialized for faces—in particular, upright faces (Moscovitch et al., 1997). Because it suggests face-specific mechanisms, it makes no predictions about other impairments that should accompany impairments to face recognition. Although single subjects cannot provide evidence against it, the face-specific hypothesis predicts that some cases with face-specific impairments should exist, and it would be weakened if the field failed to find any selective cases (Gauthier, Behrmann, & Tarr, 1999).

Individuation explanation. The individuation explanation proposes that face recognition deficits result from impairment to mechanisms used for the recognition of individual items from within a class (Damasio, Damasio, & Van Hoesen, 1982; Rosch, Mervis, Gray, Johnson, & Boyes-Braem, 1976). It is often called the within-class hypothesis or the subordinate-level hypothesis, but following Moscovitch et al. (1997) we refer to it as the individuation hypothesis. Intuitions about "within class" and "subordinate level" usually lead researchers to consider them to refer to individual items, but neither term is clear about the specificity involved. Note, however, that individual item is not well suited to describe recognition of mass-produced artifacts that are identical in appearance (Henke, Schweinberger, Grigo, Klos, & Sommer, 1998), and most researchers have treated these as individual items for experiments addressing the hypothesis (Gauthier, Skudlarski, Gore, & Anderson, 2000; Henke et al., 1998; Sergent & Signoret, 1992). The individuation explanation predicts that impairment to the mechanisms used for individual-item object recognition will impair performance whenever recognition of individual items from a particular class is required.

Holistic explanation. Another alternative explanation for prosopagnosia is that it represents the malfunction of one of two hypothetical shape representation systems proposed to generate structural descriptions of objects (Farah, 1990). Farah's two-process theory was based upon her review of 99 cases of agnosia not attributable to lower level perceptual deficits. She found that there were cases with pure prosopagnosia, pure alexia (an inability to read words), alexia with object agnosia, prosopagnosia with object agnosia, and cases with all three deficits. However, she did not find any cases of pure object agnosia or any cases of alexia with prosopagnosia. This led Farah to postulate that there are two shape representation systems: One constructs structural descriptions for objects that are decomposable into numerous parts, and one constructs structural descriptions for objects that allow little shape decomposition and so must be represented as a complex whole. In her account, words are handled by the part-based system, faces are handled by the holistic system, and objects are handled by a combination of the two systems. Alexia results from a deficit in the part-based system whereas prosopagnosia is produced by damage to the holistic system. Different varieties of object agnosia are produced when one or both systems are malfunctioning. This proposal predicts that prosopagnosia will always be accompanied by deficits with object classes that allow little shape decomposition.

Configural processing explanation. Many results indicate that a key difference between face recognition and object recognition is that configural information in faces is represented in a more precise manner than it is in objects (Freire et al., 2000; Le Grand, Mondloch, Maurer, & Brent, 2001; Leder & Bruce, 1998). While configural processing has been defined in a number of ways, here we refer to it as representation of the spacing between features (Freire et al., 2000; Leder & Bruce, 2001; Le Grand et al., 2001). However, what produces this type of representation is unclear. It could result from the operation of face-specific mechanisms or domain-general configural mechanisms. Levine and Calvanio (1989) proposed that faces are processed by domain-general configural processing mechanisms, and they suggested that prosopagnosia results from impairment to these mechanisms. In many ways this proposal is similar to Farah's holistic hypothesis (Farah, 1990), but it places more emphasis on the configural nature of face representation. It of course predicts that prosopagnosics will fail with object tasks requiring configural processing.

Curvature explanation. The curvature hypothesis is the most recently proposed explanation for prosopagnosia. Two versions of this hypothesis have been discussed, and both suggest that impairments that leave individuals unable to represent items with curvature may result in prosopagnosia. One version proposes that the perception of any curved stimulus is impaired (Kosslyn, Hamilton, & Bernstein, 1995) whereas the more specific version proposes that it is the perception of geometric volumes made of curved surfaces that is impaired (Laeng & Caviness, 2001). Faces, of course, have many curved surfaces, and the hypothesis predicts that prosopagnosia caused by curvature deficits will also have impairments with object classes with substantial curvature.

Expertise explanation. The final explanation for prosopagnosia is one of the most commonly discussed possibilities, and it has been investigated with many different approaches. It contains elements of all of the other domain-general hypotheses except the curvature hypothesis, and so it attempts to account for many of the results discussed above. This explanation proposes that face recognition is performed by mechanisms that operate on classes for which subjects have developed expertise (Diamond & Carey, 1986; Gauthier & Tarr, 1997). It claims that expertise with a class is acquired when viewers must repeatedly recognize individual items from a visually homogeneous class that share a first-order configuration. This expertise allows subjects to represent items from expert classes in a configural or holistic manner. Because all expert classes are handled by the same expert mechanisms, this view predicts that when these mechanisms are defective subjects will have difficulty acquiring and/or using expertise for faces or any other object class. The amount of exposure needed for expertise development is a matter of debate. The rapid expertise view proposes that it can be acquired in hours (Gauthier & Tarr, 1997) whereas the extended view suggests that years of experience are required (Diamond & Carey, 1986).

Developmental prosopagnosia

Our prosopagnosic subject reports lifelong face recognition problems, and so he is classified as a developmental prosopagnosic. Because he knows of no events that may have caused brain damage, he may also be a congenital prosopagnosic, but because we do not know the developmental course that led to his face recognition problems, we prefer to classify him more conservatively as a developmental prosopagnosic. Until the last few years, there were few documented cases of developmental prosopagnosia, and so it appeared to be an extremely rare condition. However, there has been a sharp increase in the number of cases of developmental prosopagnosia coming to the attention of researchers recently. This seems to be primarily because the Internet and media have raised awareness of the condition, and the Internet has allowed prosopagnosic individuals to contact researchers easily. Our laboratory created a Web site four years ago to recruit prosopagnosic subjects, and we have been contacted by more than 450. Few of these individuals acquired their prosopagnosia as adults so developmental prosopagnosia seems to be more common than acquired prosopagnosia.

There appear to be a number of possible routes to developmental prosopagnosia. These include genetic conditions (de Haan, 1999; Duchaine & Nakayama, 2005), early brain damage (Barton, Cherkasova, Press, Intrilligator, & O'Connor, 2003; Michelon & Biederman, 2003), and possibly early visual problems such as infantile cataracts (Le Grand et al., 2001; Le Grand, Mondloch, Maurer, & Brent, 2003) or severe myopia. A number of problems are commonly associated with developmental prosopagnosia, and, not surprisingly, many of the associated deficits are handled by brain areas in the vicinity of areas involved with face recognition. However, for each ability that is sometimes impaired, some developmental prosopagnosics have been shown to perform normally. Some show deficits with other types of face processing such as emotion recognition (Ariel & Sadeh, 1996; de Haan & Campbell, 1991; Duchaine, 2000; Kracke, 1994) and gender discrimination (Ariel & Sadeh, 1996; de Haan & Campbell, 1991; Jones & Tranel, 2001). Many, though not all (Bentin, Deouell, & Soroker, 1999; Duchaine & Nakayama, 2005; Nunn et al., 2001) developmental prosopagnosics have trouble with nonface object recognition (Ariel & Sadeh, 1996; Duchaine & Nakayama, 2005; Laeng & Caviness, 2001; McConachie, 1976), but usually this affects only exemplar recognition (a particular car, a particular horse), not basic-level recognition (cars or horses, in general). About one third of those who have contacted us have difficulties with everyday large-scale navigation (Duchaine, Parker, & Nakayama, 2003b), and approximately one fifth report that they have trouble understanding speech in noisy settings. In addition, many individuals with autism-spectrum disorder have problems with face perception (Barton, Cherkasova, Hefter, Cox, O'Connor, & Manoach, 2004; Cipolotti, Robinson, Blair, & Frith, 1999; Duchaine, Nieminen-von Wendt, New, & Kulomaki, 2003a).

EDWARD

Edward is a 53-year-old married right-handed man who has PhDs in theology and physics. He currently works as a physicist in a magnetic resonance research laboratory, and his interests in magnetic resonance imaging and prosopagnosia led to our collaboration. He recalls face recognition difficulties during childhood, such as problems recognizing his father. Edward is unaware of any head trauma that may have caused his prosopagnosia. While discussing his prosopagnosia recently with his sister, she reported that she had difficulties with facial identity and emotion as a teen especially in stressful situations but she reports no problems as an adult.

Despite his difficulties, Edward is able to manage in most social situations, and we believe that his object recognition provides him with an alternative means that many other prosopagnosics with agnosia cannot use as proficiently. For individual recognition, he reports using context, hair, body types, facial hair, gait, voices, and distinctive facial features. Edward's problems with faces extend to aspects of face perception other than identification. Below we present data showing that he has problems recognizing expressions and gender from the face. His wife has told him that he sometimes fails to notice subtle facial expressions (though we note that such complaints are commonly heard by nonprosopagnosic spouses as well!). Recordings done with magnetoencephalography show that Edward, unlike normal subjects, fails to show a face-selective M170 signal (Harris, Duchaine, & Nakayama, 2005), and he also does not show any face-selective voxels when face activation is compared to object activation (Yovel, Duchaine, Nakayama, & Kanwisher, 2005).

Edward has scored normally on all tests dependent on early visual processes. He performed normally on the Pelli–Robson test of contrast sensitivity (Pelli, Robson, & Wilkins, 1988), and he also was in the normal range on the low-level visual tests (Tests 1–5) from the Birmingham Object Recognition Battery (Riddoch & Humphreys, 1993). On a demanding visual spatial attention test involving tracking of multiple objects (Pylyshyn & Storm, 1988), Edward scored normally. He also had no difficulty naming 100 common objects from Snodgrass and Vanderwart's (1980) set of line drawings.

Edward's face perception

Face recognition

First we demonstrate that Edward is impaired with different aspects of face perception including, most importantly, face recognition. Edward was tested individually. Our first testing session was in May 2002, and the most recent was in January 2005. Controls were also tested individually, and because the composition of the control groups varied we present information about each control group prior to discussing test results. In some cases, we used age- and education-matched controls. However, we often used undergraduate and graduate student controls because Edward scored in the normal range even when compared to these younger subjects.

Famous face identification. Edward and the control subjects were presented with 23 famous faces (Duchaine, 2000). Most of these images were in colour, and they had been cropped so that little of the hair was visible (see Figure 2 Panel A for examples). Each image was presented for 10 s, and subjects were asked to provide the name or other uniquely identifying information (e.g., movie role, political office).

Results and comment. Edward's performance was compared to that of a group of 17 male and female subjects between the ages of 55 and 64 years. Edward was able to identify only three faces whereas the control average was 18.0 (*SD* = 3.3). Figure 2 Panel B shows the scores sorted from worst to best for Edward (black column) and each control subject. This figure makes it clear that Edward's correct identification of only three of the faces was far worse than any of the control subjects. Among the approximately 40 developmental prosopagnosics who have been assessed with this test, Edward's score is one of the worst. It was particularly striking that Edward failed to identify Bill Clinton, because nearly all of the developmental prosopagnosics we have tested are able to identify him. After completing the test, we asked Edward about his exposure to the individuals that he was unable to name. He was confident that he had significant exposure to 18 of the 23 individuals.

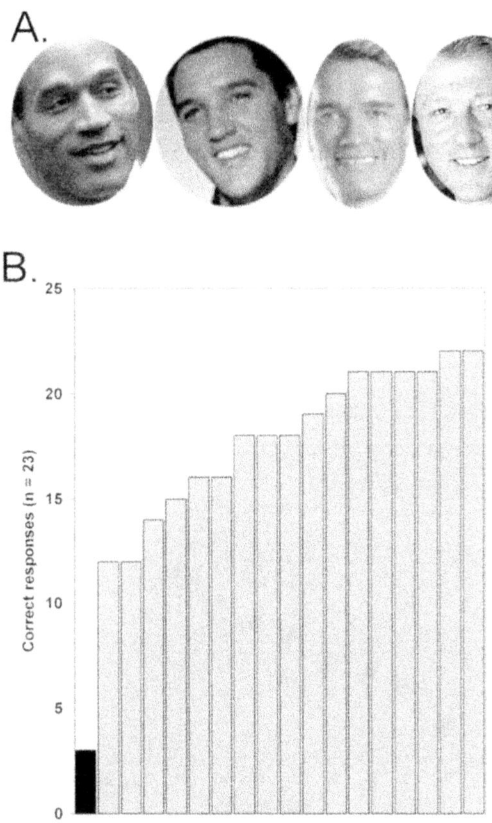

Figure 2. *Famous-face test. Panel A shows examples from the famous-face test. Panel B shows scores on the famous-face test for Edward (black) and each age-matched control subject (grey). The scores have been sorted from worst to best.*

The three faces that Edward correctly identified were Michael Jackson, Ronald Reagan, and Martin Luther King Jr. His comments suggested that he might not have identified these faces through normal means. He uncertainly identified Michael Jackson by his formerly telltale strands of hair on his forehead. Edward correctly identified Reagan and King, but afterward reported that we used well-known images that he had seen before in situations in which he was aware of their identity. Thus he may have recognized the image rather than the face.

Edward's famous face results suggest that he has a severe face recognition deficit. However, all subjects have different amounts of exposure to famous faces so we tested him with a test of unfamiliar-face recognition in which exposure was equivalent for all subjects.

Cambridge Face Memory Test. The Cambridge Face Memory Test is a recently designed test from our laboratory. We are distributing it free of charge if used for research, and it is fully described in Duchaine and Nakayama (2006).

The test has three stages. In the introduction, subjects are introduced to the six target individuals that they will attempt to recognize throughout the test (see Figure 3A). Target individuals are

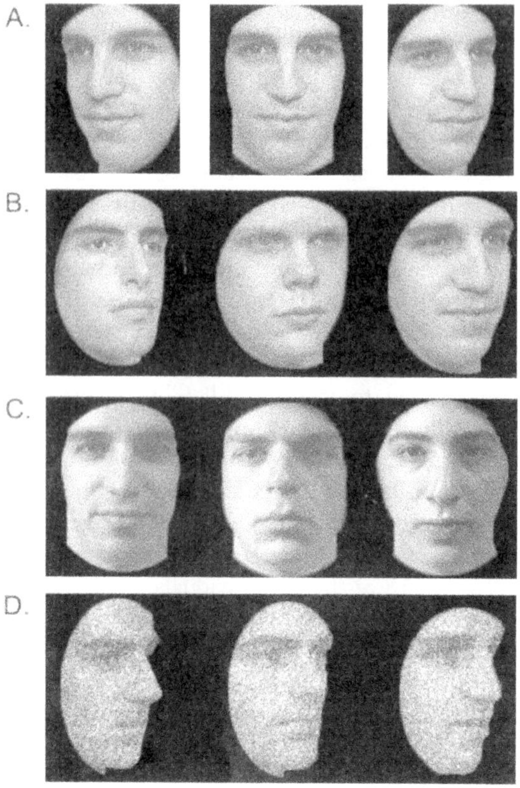

Figure 3. *Sample stimuli from the Cambridge Face Memory Test. None of these items was used in the test. In the test, test faces are numbered 1, 2, and 3 from left to right, but we omitted this to save space. Panel A shows study views of a target face. Study views are presented for 3 s each. Panel B displays a test item from the introduction. Face 3 is the same image as the rightmost study view in Panel A. Panel C shows an item from the novel images section (Face 1 is the target). Panel D displays a test item from the novel images with noise section (Face 3 is target).*

introduced one at a time by presenting a three-quarter left profile, a frontal view, and a three-quarter right profile for 3 seconds each. All of the faces throughout the test have been cropped so that no hair is visible. Following the three study faces, subjects are simultaneously presented with three faces photographed in identical poses and under identical lighting. Two are distractors, and the other is one of the study views presented seconds before (Figure 3B). Subjects are to choose the target face. Two more items are then presented consisting of the two other study views along with two distractors. This procedure is repeated for the five other target faces so there are 18 test items in the introduction.

Following this, there are two sections: novel images and novel images with noise. During the novel images section, subjects are tested with 30 trials, each of which consists of the presentation of a target with two distractors (Figure 3C). In this section and in the novel images with noise section, any of the six target faces can be presented so these items are much more difficult than the introduction items. In addition, all of the images are novel views in which the pose and/or lighting differ from the study views. In the novel images with noise sections, Gaussian noise was added to the 24 test items (Figure 3D). There are a total of 72 possible points on the test (18 + 30 + 24).

Results and comment. Figure 4 shows the cumulative scores for Edward and 9 age-matched and education-matched control subjects (average age 46.5, SD = 7.7). The plot is divided into the three sections of the test (introduction, novel images, novel images with noise). As is apparent

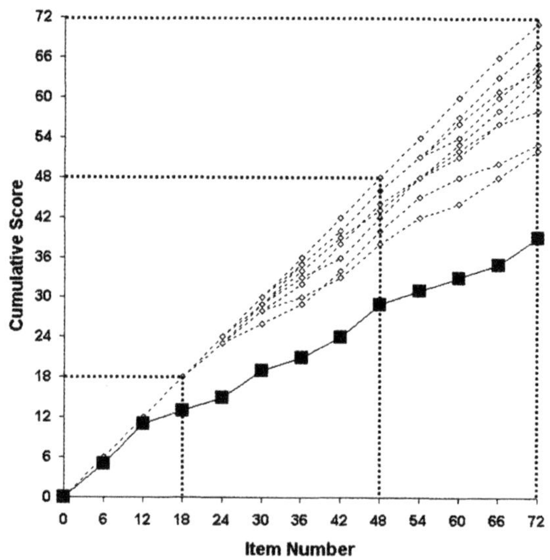

Figure 4. *Cumulative scores for Edward (black square) and 9 age- and education-matched control subjects (open diamonds). The plot is divided into the tests three sections: introduction, novel images, and novel images with noise.*

from the figure, Edward had more difficulty with all parts of the test than the control subjects did. In the introduction the correct test choice was identical to study images that subjects had just viewed, yet Edward was able to respond correctly on only 13 of the 18 items. In contrast, our control subjects made no errors in this section. On the 30 novel images, Edward scored 13 while controls averaged 26, and on the 24 novel images with noise, Edward scored 10 compared to the controls' average of 18. His total score of 39 was 3.5 standard deviations below the control average of 62.8 ($SD = 6.8$). Edward's errors were distributed fairly evenly between all of the faces. There were 12 test items for each of the six target faces, and the number of errors that Edward made per face ranged between 3 and 7.

These results make it clear that Edward is worse than control subjects even when all subjects are provided with identical exposure to the faces. In later sections, we present face recognition results that further demonstrate Edward's face recognition impairment. A number of these experiments demonstrate that Edward is impaired with facial identity even in tasks with minimal memory demands (Duchaine, Dingle, Butterworth, & Nakayama, 2004).

Face detection

Most prosopagnosics (de Gelder & Rouw, 2000; Duchaine, 2000; Duchaine et al., 2003a) score normally when asked to detect the presence of faces or discriminate between faces and nonfaces. We investigated Edward's ability to detect faces with two tests.

Face detection. Two-tone faces were created for this experiment by adjusting the threshold controls in Adobe Photoshop. This left a face in which the darker areas were black, and the lighter areas were white (see Figure 5). Faces were composed of black areas for the major features (irises, eyebrows, lips, bottom of nose) while the rest was white. Each test image contained one of these faces surrounded by a large field of individual features drawn from other faces that served to make the facial configuration more difficult to perceive.

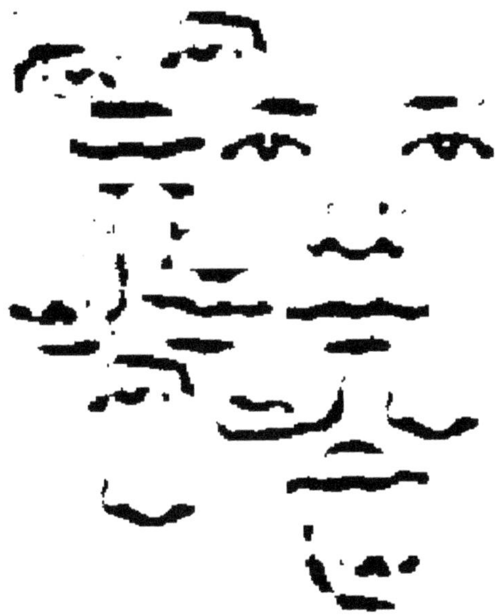

Figure 5. *Example of a stimulus from the face detection task. The stimulus was presented for 150 ms, and subjects indicated whether the face was on the left or on the right.*

The face was placed on either the left or the right side of the test image. A total of 90 of these images were presented to subjects for 150 ms each, and subjects indicated with a key press whether the face was on the right or the left. Subjects were run on two blocks of upright trials and two blocks of inverted trials.

Results and comment. A total of 16 controls between the ages of 35 and 45 years averaged 87.2% ($SD = 6.0$). Edward's score of 91.2% was slightly above the control mean. This indicates that he can detect upright faces normally. In addition, it demonstrates that he can perceive briefly presented displays. He was also in the normal range with inverted faces. His average was 78.9% while the controls averaged 69.4%. Thus, both Edward and the controls showed large inversion effects with face detection. Next we test his face detection with a different method.

Face decision. In this test (Duchaine et al., 2003a), subjects decided whether an image showed a normally configured face or a scrambled face. Both types of faces were created by pasting features from hand-drawn faces into face outlines. Features were placed in the typical locations for the normally configured faces whereas they were misplaced in scrambled faces. There were 30 of each type, and the faces were presented for 100 ms. A total of 23 controls between 35 and 45 years of age averaged 93.2% (*SD* = 7.1). Edward's score of 88.3% placed him within one standard deviation of the control mean.

Results and comment. Edward's normal scores on both of these tests demonstrate that he has no difficulty categorizing a face as a face. His difficulties only become obvious when he is asked to do finer processing of faces.

Emotion perception tests

In addition to his problems with facial identity, Edward reports difficulties with emotion recognition so we assessed his abilities with three tests of emotion recognition. His scores for the tests were compared to those for a group of 14 subjects who ranged in age from 55–64 years.

Emotion hexagon. In this test (Duchaine et al., 2003b), we presented faces created by morphing between four individuals from Ekman and Friesen's emotion face set (Ekman & Friesen, 1976). After Calder, Young, Perrett, Etcoff, and Rowland (1996), our morph sequence was happy–surprise–fear–sadness–disgust–anger–happy, and we presented five morph proportions: 90–10, 70–30, 50–50, 30–70, and 10–90. This created 120 images (4 individuals × 6 morph series × 5 morphs per series). Subjects were presented with each image twice in a random order, and they were asked to label the predominant emotion with one of the six emotion labels.

Results and comment. We did not analyse the 50–50 morph trials, because they did not have a predominant emotion. The black square in Figure 6 shows the average percent correct for the control subjects, and the error bars display two standard deviations above and below the control mean. Performance at chance would be

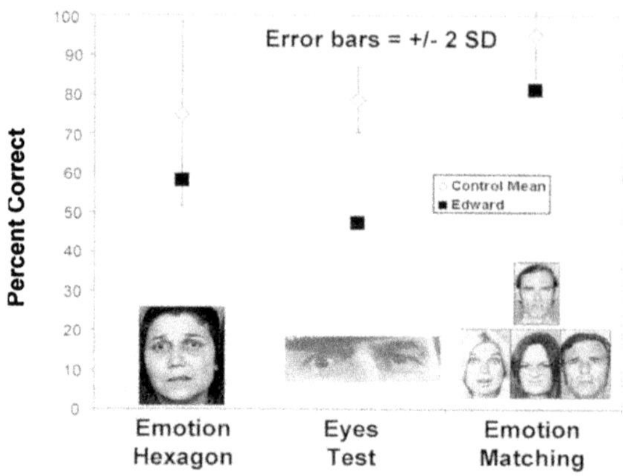

Figure 6. *Performance on three tests of emotion recognition. The open diamond displays the control mean for each test, and the error bars represent 2 standard deviations above and below the control mean. The black squares are Edward's percent correct for each test. Images below the scores show examples from each test.*

16.7%. Edward's score of 58.4% correct was 1.4 standard deviations below the control mean of 75% (*SD* = 11.7).

Eyes Test. Baron-Cohen and his colleagues designed the Eyes Test to assess advanced theory of mind (Baron-Cohen, Wheelwright, Hill, Raste, & Plumb, 2001). Subjects were presented with the eye region of a face along with four emotion state words on a computer. They were asked to pick the word that best described the eye region. There were 36 items.

Results and comment. Figure 6 shows that Edward's percent correct was far out of the normal range. In fact, his score was more than seven standard deviations below the mean. Whereas the controls chose correctly on 78.6% of the items (*SD* = 4.1), Edward was correct on only 47.2% items. This test clearly revealed the emotion recognition deficits that Edward reported.

Emotion matching. This test assesses the ability to categorize emotional expressions as the same despite changes in the models portraying the emotions. Subjects were briefly presented with a target face from the Ekman and Friesen set (Ekman & Friesen, 1976) portraying surprise, disgust, happiness, or neutrality. Following this, they were presented with three faces simultaneously. Each face portrayed a different emotional expression, and the individual used in the preceding target photo was not presented. One of the individuals portrayed the same emotion as that of the target model, and subjects were to choose which of the three faces depicted the same emotion as that of the target image. There were 8 trials for each of the four emotions for a total of 32 trials.

Results and comment. The control subjects correctly matched 95% (SD = 5.3) of the items so this test suffers from ceiling effects. Despite these ceiling effects, Edward's percent correct of 81% placed him 2.6 standard deviations below the control mean, and his score was lower than that of any of the controls (see Figure 6). On five of his six errors, the target face portrayed disgust. Taken together, these three tests indicate that Edward does, in fact, have difficulties with the recognition of facial expressions of emotion. Next we examine Edward's gender discrimination ability.

Gender discrimination

College-age male and female faces were cropped so that little or no hair was visible. The 35 images were briefly presented, and subjects categorized them as male or female.

Results and comment. Edward's performance was compared to 22 college-age control subjects. Controls found this task easy. Scores ranged between 33 and 35, and the control mean was 34.5 (SD = 0.7). Edward's score was 29. Although Edward was able to categorize most of the faces successfully, it is clear that he has gender discrimination problems.

Summary of face perception experiments

These experiments show that Edward has problems not only with face recognition but also with face processing more generally. However, he had no difficulties with face detection tasks. We have also recently collected data showing that Edward makes atypical attractiveness judgments when asked to sort faces in order of attractiveness (Sadr, Duchaine, & Nakayama, 2004).

TESTING PREDICTIONS OF THE ALTERNATIVE EXPLANATIONS

Next we present six experiments that test the predictions of the explanations for prosopagnosia.

Old–new discriminations

The first set of experiments compare Edward's individual item recognition for faces to seven nonface classes. Old–new recognition memory tests with 10 target items and 30 nontargets are used for all of the classes. The nonface classes include horses, cars, guns, sunglasses, tools, houses, and natural scenes. A wide range of object classes was used, because a number of experiments have suggested that nonface classes may be recognized by dissociable mechanisms (Cipolotti et al., 1999; Duchaine et al., 2003a; Farah, McMullen, & Meyer, 1991; Sartori & Job, 1988). These dissociations have often been segregated roughly as animate objects, inanimate objects, and places. By including classes from each of these categories, we increase the chances of discovering impairments with classes other than faces.

His performance with the nonface recognition tests tests three explanations. The individuation hypothesis predicts that prosopagnosics will show impairments with tests of individual item recognition. Consequently, normal performance by Edward with some or all of the nonface classes would be inconsistent with this hypothesis. The holistic explanation claims that prosopagnosia is caused by impairment to mechanisms used to represent complex parts that must be represented holistically (Farah, 1990). Although the hypothesis is not explicit about what classes other than faces consist of complex parts, Farah does mention animals as a likely candidate. Consideration of our nonface classes shows that the cars and horses are at least as nondecomposable as the faces. Therefore, Edward's performance with cars and horses appears to be a test of the holistic hypothesis. Lastly, the curvature hypothesis predicts that Edward will have impairments with any class for which curved surface representation is important. The horses, cars, guns, and sunglasses all have curved surfaces so normal performance with these classes would be inconsistent with the curvature hypothesis.

Method

Control participants

A total of 17 graduate students (9 women and 8 men) served as controls for the old/new recognition memory tests, and their mean age was 27.8 years with a range from 24 to 34. Each control participant produced a score for each old/new test except for 4 instances out of a possible 136 (17 controls × 8 tests). The control results showed no significant sex differences for any of the tests, and in fact the means for each sex were quite similar.

Stimuli

In each test, 40 items from within a category were used. Of these, 10 items were target items, and they were shown during the study phase of the experiment; 30 items were nontargets that were presented along with the target items during the test phase. See Figure 7 for examples.

Faces. Greyscale yearbook photographs of women's faces were cropped so that very little or no hair was visible. In order to achieve a fairly standard pose, some of the images were flipped or rotated. All of the images were the same size.

Cars. The cars used in these greyscale photographs had all conspicuous ornaments removed, and they were placed on a white background facing the same direction. Each car was categorized into one of three styles (compact, sedan, truck), and they were divided proportionally into target cars and nontarget cars. The sizes of the cars were adjusted so that they were the proper size relative to the other cars.

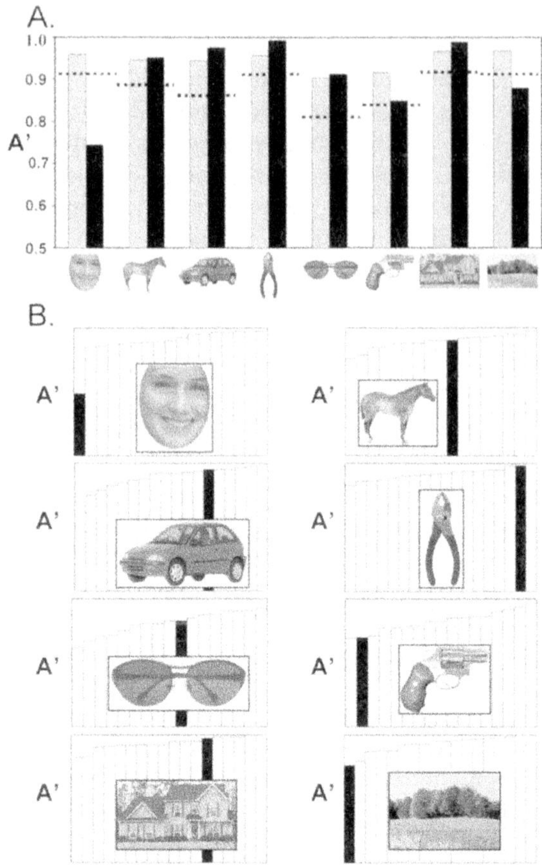

Figure 7. *Performance on the old–new discriminations. Panel A displays the average A′ scores for the controls (grey bars) and Edward's A′ score (black bars). Dashed lines indicate the point 2 standard deviations below the control mean. Panel B shows individual A′ scores for each test. Edward's score is in black, and the control scores are in white. Each set of scores has been sorted from worst to best. The images labelling the class for each test are items drawn from the test.*

Tools. Eight tool images were drawn from five categories (saws, hammers, pliers, wrenches, and screwdrivers), and these greyscale items were presented on a white background. Two items from each category were chosen as targets, and all items from particular categories were presented with a similar orientation and size.

Guns. Colour images of handguns were used. All conspicuous decorations were erased, and the guns were presented in the same orientation and were scaled similarly.

Horses. The images for this test consisted of colour photographs of model horses made by Breyer Animal Creations placed on a white background. The photographs presented a side view of the horses, and their poses and sizes were similar.

Sunglasses. Each colour image consisted of a pair of sunglasses in a standard pose on a white background.

Natural landscapes. Greyscale photographs of natural landscapes that did not have any man-made structures were used. Eight landscapes were chosen from each of the following five categories: beaches, lakes, meadows, mountains, and deserts. Two images were chosen from each category to serve as targets, and six served as nontargets. All images were the same size.

Houses. The colour photographs used in this test contained typical-looking houses photographed from the front with some of the yard surrounding the house visible. The sizes of the images were similar.

Procedure

Participants were tested individually in a normally lit room and were seated approximately 40 cm from the monitor. Prior to each test, instructions were given both verbally and on the monitor to ensure that participants understood the procedure. For the study portion, participants were presented with the 10 target items for 3 s per item. The 10 items were cycled through twice so that control performance would be high enough that we would be better able to identify impaired performance. The target images were identical throughout each task. During the test phase, participants were presented with items one at a time and were asked to respond whether an item was a target item (old) or a nontarget item (new) as quickly as possible with a mouse click. A total of 50 test items were presented consisting of 20 target items (10 targets $\times$ 2 presentations) and 30 nontargets (30 nontargets $\times$ 1 presentation). The order of the stimuli remained the same for all participants.

Results

A' was used as the measure of discrimination in the following comparisons. It is a bias-free measure that varies between 0.5 and 1.0 with higher scores indicating better discrimination (Macmillan & Creelman, 1991). Unlike d', A' values can be computed when zero values are present.

Figure 7 Panel A shows Edward's A' score along with the mean A' for the control subjects. Dashed lines were placed two standard deviations below the control mean. As is evident, Edward's A' score for faces was far below the control mean. In contrast, all of his A' scores for nonface objects were within two standard deviations of the control mean except for his natural scenes score, which was just out of the normal range. Note that the mean A' for the controls for faces was as high as or higher than the mean A' for the other classes. This demonstrates that the nonface tests were at least as difficult as the face test, and a number were more difficult than the face test. As a result, Edward's normal performance cannot be due to the nonface tests being less demanding than the face test.

In Figure 7 Panel B we present individual A' scores for Edward and the controls for each class. Individual scores have been sorted from least to best, and Edward's score is in black whereas the controls' scores are white. Consideration of the face test scores shows that Edward's score was far below that of even the lowest scoring control subject. However, when we consider the other tests, we see that Edward is scoring much better. For example, for the horse test, Edward's A' score is right in the middle of the scores of the control subjects. For the other tests, Edward's score was well within the normal range with the exception of his natural scenes score, and this presentation of the results demonstrates that his natural scenes score is not an outlier from the control group.

Earlier we discussed that measurement of response times is critical to demonstrate that a dissociation is not the result of speed/accuracy

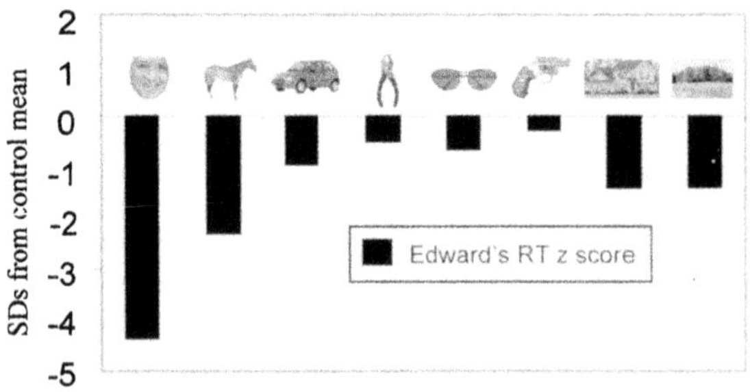

Figure 8. *The z scores for Edward's average response time on each old–new discrimination. Scores below zero are longer than the mean control response time.*

trade-offs. Thus, it could be that apparently selective deficits in prosopagnosia are due to their propensity to take more time with nonface tasks, thus elevating their performance (Gauthier et al., 1999). To address this issue, we present z values computed from the response times for Edward on each test in Figure 8. These were computed by subtracting Edward's score from the control average so that any of Edward's response times longer than the control mean would be negative z values. For speed/accuracy trade-offs to account for dissociation seen in Edward's A' scores, his object response times need to be longer than those of the control group. His z score for the face test was more than four standard deviations longer than the mean response time. Inspection of his z scores for the nonface tests shows that none of his nonface z scores were as low as his face z score. In fact, nearly all of them were just slightly below the control mean. In addition, the actual length of his face response times was also longer than any of the nonface response times. Hence differentiated speed/accuracy trade-offs between face and nonface tasks cannot explain Edward's pattern of A' results.

Comment

Edward's performance with faces for both A' and response time was far worse than that of the controls. In contrast, his performance with the nonface classes was quite good. His results are the clearest demonstration in the literature that a prosopagnosic can perform normally on comparable nonface tests. Not only were his accuracy scores in the normal range but his response times were as well. This is especially impressive considering that Edward is a 53-year-old while the controls were in their twenties and thirties.

His results are clearly inconsistent with the individuation explanation. All of the tasks involved individual item recognition yet he only had substantial difficulties with the face test. His normal performance with horses and cars suggests that the holistic explanation also cannot account for his prosopagnosia. Finally, many of the nonface classes had curved surfaces (horses, cars, guns, sunglasses) yet Edward was normal with these classes. As a result, the curvature account does not appear to be an appropriate explanation for his face recognition difficulties. In the other experiments discussed below, we present more results that reinforce our conclusions about these three explanations.

The meaning of Edward's low score with the natural scenes is unclear to us, and we plan to conduct more tests with similar stimuli. He reports neither navigational difficulties nor difficulties recognizing places, and he performed normally on a famous-places test. Neuropsychological (Carlesimo, Fadda, Turriziani, Tomaiuolo, & Caltragirone, 2001; Incisa de la Rocchetta, Cipolotti, & Warrington, 1996; Whiteley & Warrington, 1978) and neuroimaging (Aguirre, Zarahn, & D'Esposito, 1998; Epstein, De Yoe, Press, Rosen, & Kanwisher, 2001; Epstein & Kanwisher, 1998) studies indicate that place recognition involves specialized mechanisms that differ from those used for face and object recognition. Thus, if further experiments show that Edward's scene recognition is impaired, this may be due to problems with mechanisms unrelated to his prosopagnosia.

Face matching: Upright and inverted

Inverted- and upright-face recognition has been contrasted in many experiments, because inverted faces are an almost ideal control class for upright faces. They are identical to upright faces except for orientation so they are matched on many dimensions that have been considered critical for face recognition. They have equivalent curvature, second-order configural information, complexity, and within-class similarity. As a result, comparing upright and inverted face performance allows researchers to look into the importance of these dimensions as factors underlying our impressive abilities with faces.

In the next experiment, we use upright faces and inverted faces to examine whether the explanations involving curvature, holistic representation, configural processing, and individuation can account for Edward's face recognition impairments. If Edward is impaired with upright faces in this paradigm all of these hypotheses predict that he will also be impaired with inverted faces. However, if he is out of the normal range with upright faces and in the normal range with inverted faces, this will indicate that these hypotheses cannot account for his prosopagnosia.

The previous face recognition experiment demonstrated that Edward has impairments with face memory tests, but these difficulties could result from perceptual problems, memory problems, or a combination of perceptual and memory problems. To compare upright and inverted face recognition, we use a sequential face matching test. Subjects must match faces presented only a few hundred milliseconds apart, and so the memory demands are minimal. If Edward has difficulties with the upright faces in this paradigm it will demonstrate that his impairments with faces do not only involve long-term memory for faces.

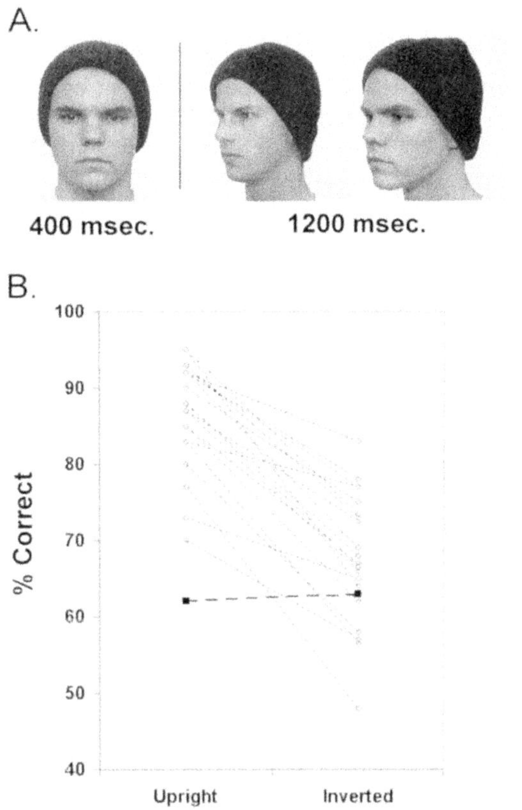

Figure 9. *Sequential face matching. Panel A shows a target face and two test faces. The test face on the right is the correct answer. The difference between upright presentation and inverted presentation can be experienced by rotating the page. Panel B shows the percent correct for upright and inverted trials. Controls are represented by open diamonds, and a dashed line connects each subject's upright and inverted scores. The black squares show Edward's scores.*

Method

Control participants

The controls consisted of 10 men and 10 women between 35 and 45 years of age.

Stimuli

Images consisted of full-frontal and three-quarter-profile shots of Caucasian college-age men wearing black ski hats so that their hair was not visible (see Figure 9 Panel A).

Procedure

On each trial, a frontal shot was presented for 400 ms, after which 2 three-quarter views were presented side by side for 1,200 ms. Subjects indicated which of the 2 three-quarter views matched the frontal shot with a key press. There were 120 trials; half consisted of upright faces, and half consisted of inverted faces. The upright and inverted trials were interleaved.

Results

Figure 9 Panel B displays the percent correct for Edward (filled black square) and the controls. It is immediately apparent that Edward shows a different pattern from that of the controls. There are three significant things to note in these results. First, Edward's upright percent correct is well out of the normal range. The controls averaged 86.4% (*SD* = 7.0) ranging from 70.0% to 95.0% while Edward responded correctly to only 61.7%. Second, Edward's inverted score is well within the normal range. The controls inverted average was 69.6% (*SD* = 7.1) with a range from 56.7% to 83.3%, and Edward's percent correct was 63.3%. Lastly, the figure makes it clear that unlike every control subject, Edward showed no advantage for the upright faces. The average difference for the controls between upright and inverted was 16.8% (*SD* = 8.3). The differences ranged from 6.6% to 31.6% so Edward's −1.6% difference is very atypical. Edward's response times for upright and inverted trials were in the normal range and were similar in length (upright = 973 ms, inverted = 1,017 ms).

Follow-up experiment

Because chance performance was 50% correct in the face matching experiment, we wanted to be sure that Edward's normal performance with inverted faces was not due to floor effects. To test this possibility, we created another face matching task involving only inverted faces. Again a frontal shot was presented for 400 ms, but three test faces rather than two were presented for 3,000 ms. With three test faces, chance performance was 33%. There were a total of 120 trials. Six college-age controls averaged 51.3% (*SD* = 13.1), and their range was 29 to 64. Edward's score of 53% placed him in the midst of the controls and 20% above chance.

Comment

Edward manifested a severe deficit with upright faces in this matching paradigm. In contrast, he was well within the normal range with inverted-face matching. Because the inverted faces are identical as a stimulus class to upright faces, his poor performance with upright faces cannot be attributed to any aspect of upright faces shared by the inverted faces. These include curvature, the complexity of the face, or the type of second-order configural information present in the face, and so these results are inconsistent with the curvature hypothesis, the holistic hypothesis, and the configural processing hypothesis. Later experiments investigate whether Edward manifests difficulties after he and controls have had extensive experience with classes with these characteristics. In addition, the inverted trials required individual item recognition so the results are also consistent with the individual item hypothesis.

For years, it has been recognized that normal subjects apply a qualitatively different type of processing to upright faces than that used with inverted faces or other objects (Moscovitch et al., 1997; Yin, 1969; Young et al., 1987). However, Edward's nearly identical performance with upright and inverted faces indicates that he processes upright and inverted faces in the same manner. Similar results were reported for EP, another developmental prosopagnosic (Nunn et al., 2001). Because Edward's upright score and inverted scores were comparable to the inverted scores for the control participants, he may apply to all faces processes that normal subjects apply to inverted faces. He does not treat upright faces as a special class.

This test also placed few memory demands on Edward yet he was far out of the normal range. Consequently, the results demonstrate that Edward's problems with face recognition do not lie solely with long-term memory for faces, and they are consistent with the notion that Edward has perceptual problems with faces. An experiment discussed later reinforces this possibility.

Tests of visual closure

When the configural processing explanation was first proposed, tests of visual closure were used to assess configural processing in a prosopagnosic (Levine & Calvanio, 1989). These tests required subjects to identify basic-level objects and words from images in which portions of the objects had been deleted or occluded. Because individual parts are meaningless in these images, subjects had to rely on the general configuration of the object. As mentioned above, this type of configural processing is not comparable to second-order configural processing applied to faces. Nevertheless, because this has been a commonly discussed explanation of prosopagnosia, we test Edward with the tests of visual closure. The three tests were drawn from the Kit of Factor-Referenced Cognitive Tests (Ekstrom, French, & Harman, 1976), and these are the same tests as those that were used in the paper proposing the configural processing hypothesis (Levine & Calvanio, 1989).

Control subjects
Norms were drawn from the manual for the battery of tests in the Kit of Factor-Referenced Cognitive Tests (Ekstrom et al., 1976). Edward was compared with a sample of young adults.

Results

In the Gestalt Completion Test (which is very similar to the Street Test), subjects must identify a common object from a group of black blotches created by deleting parts of the object (see Figure 10 Panel A for examples from the three tests). Figure 10 Panel B presents Edward's scores and the control subjects' scores. Edward's score of 14 is close to the control mean of 15.2 (SD = 3.6). In the Concealed Words Test, in which subjects identify words based on fragments of a printed word, Edward scored 24 whereas

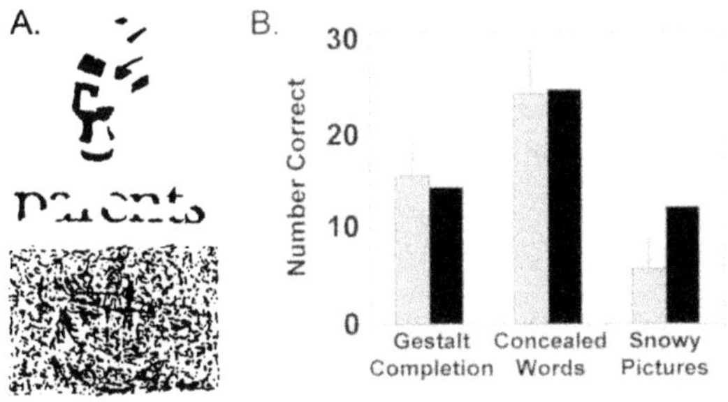

Figure 10. *Test of visual closure. Panel A displays practice items from the Gestalt Completion Test (hammer), Concealed Words Test (parents), and Snowy Pictures (anchor). Panel B shows the control mean in grey, and error bars represent 1 standard deviation. Edward's scores are in black.*

controls averaged 23.6 (SD = 6.4). Finally, on the Snowy Pictures Test, subjects must identify objects from an outline drawing that is partly obliterated by snow-like splatters. Edward's score of 12 places him above the control mean of 5.7 (SD = 3.0). In summary, Edward scored at or above the mean on the three tests of visual closure.

Comment
Edward performed very well on the tests of visual closure. However, these tests do not require the second-order configural processing that upright face recognition involves. Next we present results from a test that involved second-order configural processing in a nonface object class.

Discrimination of second-order spacing changes and part changes: Faces and houses

The configural processing explanation proposes that prosopagnosia results from impairment to domain-general configural processing mechanisms. To investigate whether Edward's abilities are consistent with these predictions, we compare his ability to process second-order configural information in faces and houses. The domain-general configural processing hypothesis predicts that he will have comparable deficits with faces and houses. We use a paradigm that has recently been used to look at sensitivity to two types of change in faces (Freire et al., 2000; Le Grand et al., 2001) and more recently faces and houses (Yovel & Kanwisher, 2004). Second-order configural processing is examined by presenting faces or houses that vary in the spacing of the parts, while part processing is assessed with faces or houses that vary only in the parts themselves.

If Edward has difficulty with the faces in this paradigm, the house results are also relevant to other explanations of prosopagnosia. Both tasks require individual item discrimination so normal performance with houses would be inconsistent with the individuation hypothesis. The faces and houses (see Figure 11) also appear to be similar in their decomposability (ease with which they

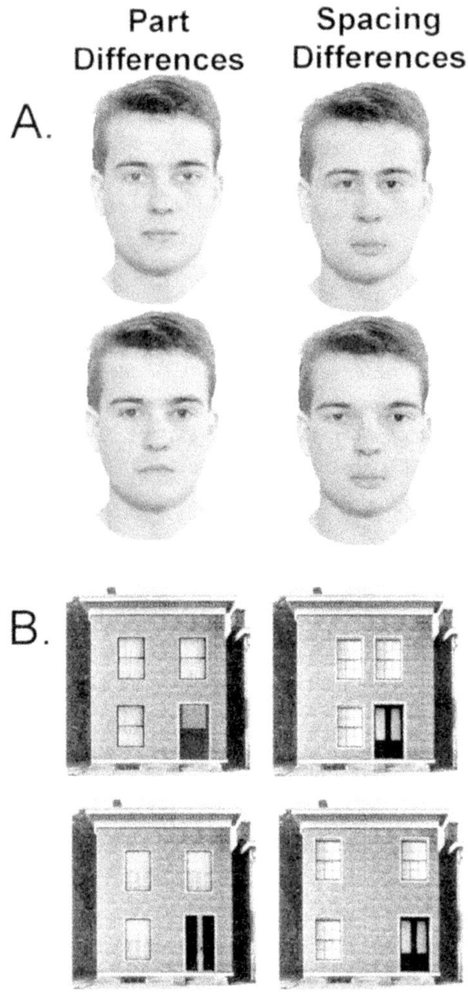

Figure 11. *Examples drawn from the face and house discrimination task with part difference versions on the left and spacing difference versions on the right. Panel A shows versions of Jeff. The changes were always made to the eyes and the mouth. Panel B displays versions of the house with changes made to the windows and the door.*

can be divided into parts) so should be similar in their need to be represented holistically (Farah, 1990). Hence the house results also provide a test of the holistic explanation.

Control participants
A total of 18 college-age students and young adults participated as controls.

Stimuli
The base stimuli consisted of a male face ("Jeff") and a house. The base stimuli were modified to create stimuli that differed in one of two ways. Spacing variants were created by changing the location of the features. For faces, the spacing of the eyes and the distance between the mouth and the nose were varied while house spacing changes involved the windows and the door. Part variants were created by substituting the features of the stimuli with features from other face/house images while keeping the spacing of the parts as similar as possible. The replaced parts were the eyes, the mouth, the windows, and the door. Four variants of each type were created for each stimulus so there were 16 stimuli (2 stimuli × 2 types × 4 variants). The original face and house stimuli were also included and were paired with modified stimuli.

Procedure
Participants took part first in the face experiment and then in the house experiment. Trials with spacing changes and part changes were presented in a random order. Participants were informed that some trials would involve changes while others would not, but they were not told what sort of changes would occur. There were a total of 80 trials for each experiment with an equal number that were same or different and an equal number of spacing and part trials. Subjects were introduced to each experiment with five practice trials.

Trials consisted of stimulus presentation for 250 ms followed by a 1,000-ms interstimulus interval with a fixation cross. The second stimulus was then presented for 250 ms. Subjects indicated whether or not a change occurred with a key press.

Results

Figure 12 displays scatter plots with the results for the controls and Edward. As expected, the scatter plot for the face experiment clearly shows that Edward performed much worse than the control subjects for both the spacing and the part trials. Controls averaged 84.2% (SD = 7.9) for the spacing items while Edward was correct on only

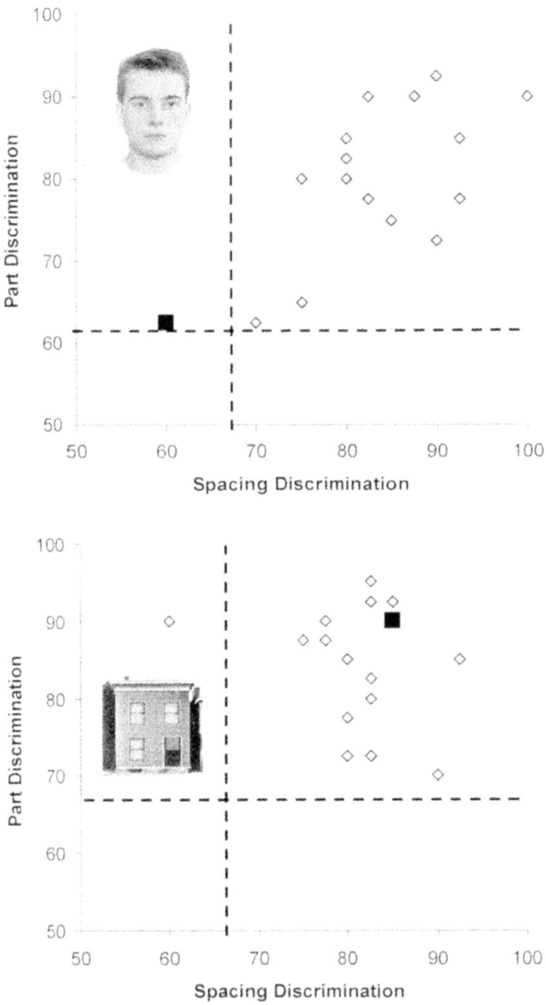

Figure 12. *Plots for Edward (black square) and control subjects (open diamonds) for the face and house tests. Percent correct for configural items is shown on the x axis and for feature items on the y axis. The tests were same–different tasks so chance was 50% correct. Dashed lines display 2 standard deviations below the mean.*

60% of the spacing items. Edward's score is 3.0 standard deviations below the mean. Similarly, the control mean for the part items was 80.3% (SD = 9.0), and Edward scored only 62.5%. Edward's score is two standard deviations below the mean.

Edward's response times with faces were normal. Controls averaged 501 ms (SD = 53) on the spacing trials, and Edward averaged 458 ms. On the face part trials, the control mean was 480 ms (SD = 93), and Edward's mean was 455 ms.

The house results quite clearly demonstrate that Edward has normal sensitivity to both types of house change. Contrary to the predictions of the configural processing explanation, his percent correct for the house spacing items of 85% was slightly higher than the control mean of 80.7% (SD = 7.3). Similarly, his score of 90% on the house part items was slightly higher than the control mean of 84.0% (SD = 8.0).

As with faces, Edward's house response times were normal. Controls averaged 436 ms (SD = 91) on spacing trials while Edward averaged 471 ms. On the part trials, the control mean was 483 ms (SD = 68), and Edward's mean was 514.

Comment

Edward's normal performance with the house configural items demonstrates that he does not have a problem representing second-order configural information for objects in general, and so these results are inconsistent with the configural-processing hypothesis. In a recent paper, Behrmann and colleagues used the Navon task (Navon, 1977) to investigate configural processing in five developmental prosopagnosics (Behrmann, Avidan, Marotta, & Kimchi, 2005). They found that some of these prosopagnosics did not process the global stimuli, which require spatial integration, normally whereas others showed normal configural effects. We believe that the house test used in our experiment provides a more direct comparison to configural processing in faces, but we plan to test Edward with a Navon task in the near future. The house results are also inconsistent with the individual item hypothesis and the holistic hypothesis.

An interesting aspect of Edward's face performance is his poor sensitivity with both spacing and part changes. Dissociations between spacing and part discrimination have led some to suggest that the special processing applied to upright faces may be limited to configural representation (see Maurer, Le Grand, & Mondloch, 2002, for a review). According to this view, the parts of a face are processed by domain-general mechanisms regardless of a face's orientation, but the configuration in upright faces is processed by a face-specific mechanism. This view predicts that individuals with face-specific deficits will have difficulty with configural processing but will perform normally with part changes. Edward's performance with objects indicates that his other recognition mechanisms are normal so his results are inconsistent with this prediction. His results are, however, consistent with models in which the entire face is represented holistically (Farah, Wilson, Drain, & Tanaka, 1995; Tanaka & Sengco, 1997; Yovel & Kanwisher, 2004), and parts and configuration are not processed separately (Yovel & Duchaine, in press; Yovel & Kanwisher, 2005).

Because this test is a matching task with minimal memory demands, these results support our previous conclusion that Edward's prosopagnosia involves a poor perceptual representation of the face. He may also have memory problems with faces that contribute to his difficulties, but his apparent perceptual difficulties make that difficult to determine.

Greeble training

The previous experiments demonstrate that Edward's face recognition problems are not elicited by stimulus properties considered important for face recognition (curvature hypothesis, holistic hypothesis, configural processing hypothesis) or the task demands of face recognition (individual item hypothesis). However, none of the experiments discussed so far have addressed the expertise hypothesis. The expertise hypothesis contends that some of the stimulus properties just mentioned are important as are task demands, but it also claims that substantial experience with an object class is necessary for special processing to occur (Diamond & Carey, 1986). After enough experience recognizing individual items from an object class with the same first-order configuration, observers begin to represent objects from the expert class in a configural or holistic manner.

The amount of experience necessary for this to occur is a matter of debate, and this has led us to refer to one view as the rapid expertise hypothesis and the other as the extended expertise hypothesis (Duchaine et al., 2004). Whereas the rapid-expertise hypothesis claims that expertise requires 10 hours or less to emerge, the extended view has suggested that it requires years. Regardless of the temporal issue, both hypotheses predict that an individual who cannot acquire expertise with faces will also be unable to acquire expertise with other object classes. Edward's performance with upright and inverted faces suggests that his years of experience with upright faces have not led to the development of any expertise with them. As a result, the expertise view predicts that Edward will also be unable to develop expertise with nonface classes.

The rapid expertise hypothesis claims that expertise can be activated in laboratory-based training in 10 hours or less when trained with an artificial stimulus class known as greebles (see Figure 13; Gauthier & Tarr, 1997; Gauthier, Williams, Tarr, & Tanaka, 1998). However, a close inspection of the results supporting these claims raises questions about this conclusion (McKone & Kanwisher, 2005). The

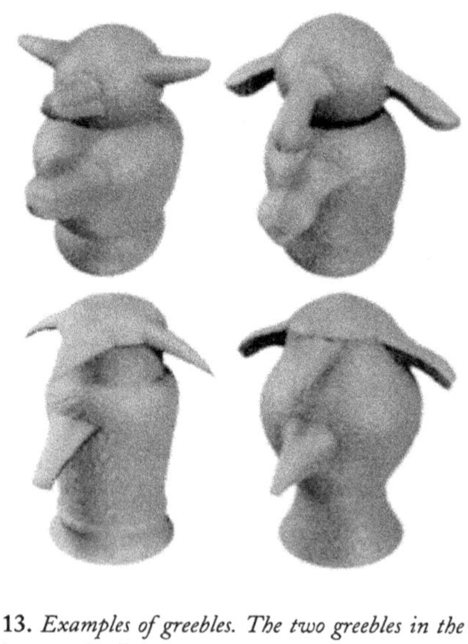

Figure 13. *Examples of greebles. The two greebles in the top row are in the same family, because they share a similar body shape.*

rapid expertise hypothesis predicts that Edward will perform similarly to the control subjects in the early training sessions, because in early sessions neither Edward nor the controls will process the greebles with expert mechanisms. However, in the later sessions, it predicts that Edward's performance will not improve like the controls, because they will be becoming greeble experts. To investigate Edward's performance in the greeble training, we designed a set of greeble training sessions nearly identical to those in a recent paper (Gauthier & Tarr, 2002), and we compared Edward and a group of age-matched control subjects in a recent paper (Duchaine et al., 2004) that we review next; we also present further relevant results.

As their criterion for expertise, Gauthier and colleagues have used response times for correct family and individual verification trials that presented consistent label–greeble pairs (trial types are discussed below). When family verification response times and individual verification response times are not significantly different, it has been claimed that subjects have become experts. This criterion was based on two previous findings. Tanaka and Taylor (1991) found that bird experts, but not bird novices, showed equivalent response times for basic-level verifications and subordinate-level verifications. Similarly, Tanaka (2001) found that subordinate verification (e.g., Bill Clinton) was as fast as basic verification (face). With greebles, it is claimed that individual recognition is a subordinate-level categorization while family recognition is a basic-level categorization. We have serious reservations with this as a measure of expertise, but because it is been used as a criterion we compare Edward's verification response times to determine whether he meets this criterion.

Control participants

Our six age- and education-matched control participants all had graduate degrees, and their average age was 48 (SD = 10.2). All showed a normal inversion effect on the sequential face-matching task described above and performed normally on the famous faces test (Duchaine et al., 2004). These results demonstrate that they have normal expertise with faces.

Stimuli

A total of 30 greyscale greebles were used in the experiment. Figure 13 shows examples of greebles used in the training, and all had the same first-order configuration. Thus, as with faces, subjects are forced to rely on second-order configural differences and feature differences. There are five greeble families, and greebles in the same family share the same general body shape.

Procedure

There were eight training sessions. In the first session, subjects were introduced to five greebles and the five greeble families. They were given practice and feedback with the greebles. In each of the first four sessions, five individual greebles were introduced so that after four sessions subjects were familiar with 20 different greebles. Subjects' knowledge of the greebles was assessed with two types of trial. In verification trials, a label is presented (either an individual name or a family name) for 600 ms after which a greeble is presented. The greeble remains visible until the subject indicates whether or not the label and the greeble are consistent. On naming trials, subjects are presented with a greeble and identify it by pressing the letter key corresponding to the first letter of its name. In the final four sessions, subjects were not introduced to any new greebles, but we continued to assess their knowledge with naming and verification trials. The first four sessions each took approximately one hour, and the last four sessions each took about 15 minutes.

Results

Figure 14 shows the percent correct for Edward and the control subjects. We have scaled the percent correct for the naming and individual verification panels to reflect the number of greebles known in each session (5, 10, 15, 20). For example, in Session 1, only 5 of the 20 (25%) individual greebles had been introduced so we scaled the maximum percent correct to 25%. Figure 14

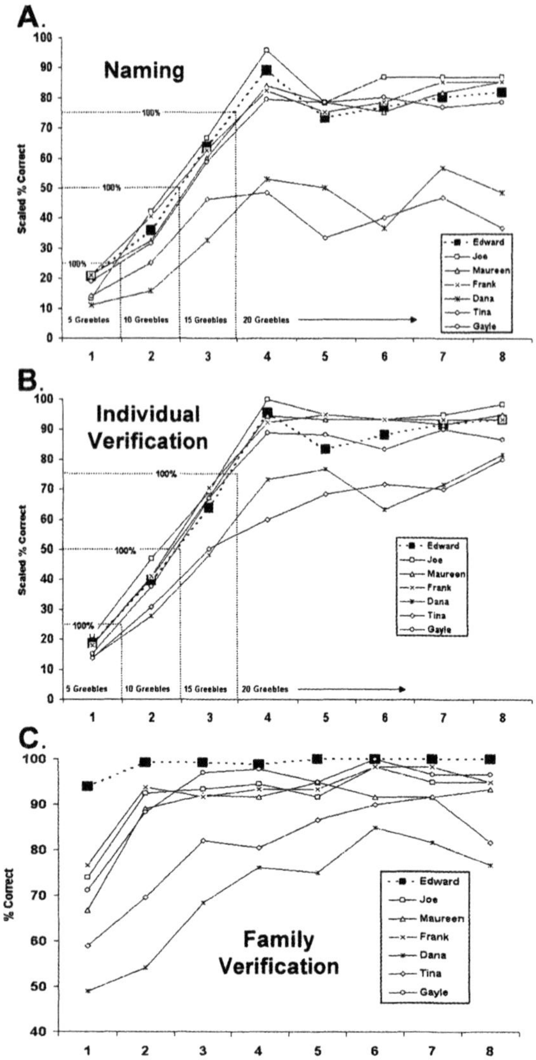

Figure 14. *Greeble training accuracy results. Percent correct for the three types of trial assessing greeble knowledge. For the naming trials (Panel A) and the individual verification trials (Panel B), we have scaled the scores to reflect the number of named greebles at each point in the training. For example, subjects had only been introduced to 5 of the 20 greebles in Session 1 so we divided their percent correct by 4 and placed the 100% level for Session 1 at 25% of the total percent correct. Panel C displays the family verification trials.*

Panel A displays the percent correct for the naming trials, and it is clear that, contrary to the predictions of the rapid expertise hypothesis, Edward's performance is normal. In fact, his score is comparable to that of our best performing subjects and considerably better than that of two of the control subjects. Figure 14 Panel B shows the results for the individual verification trials, and again it is clear that Edward is performing normally. Finally, Edward's family verification in Figure 14 Panel C was better than that of any of the control subjects. Edward's response times for all three trial types were in the normal range so speed/accuracy trade-offs cannot explain his normal accuracy (see Duchaine et al., 2004, for details).

Figure 15 displays Edward's response times, and arrows indicate the sessions in which the two types of response time were not significantly different from one another (Session 1, $p = .69$; Session 3, $p = .09$; Session 4, $p = .10$; Session 6, $p = .27$; Session 7, $p = .19$). Edward met this criterion for expertise in Sessions 1, 3, 4, 6, and 7. Thus, at least according to this criterion, Edward is a greeble expert.

Comments

Edward's results were clearly inconsistent with the rapid-expertise hypothesis (Duchaine et al., 2004). He was as good as our best control subjects with all

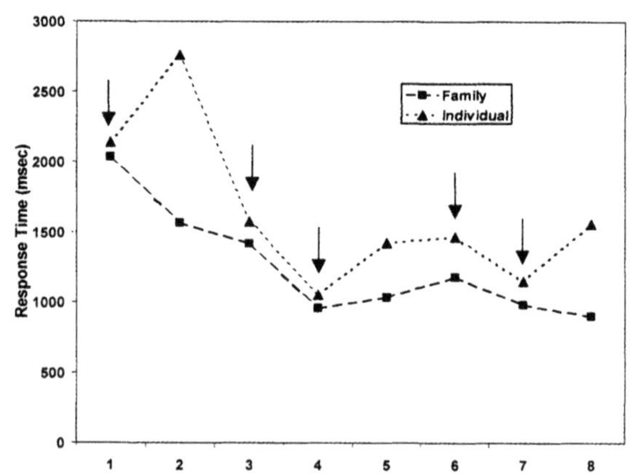

Figure 15. *Comparison of Edward's response times for individual verification trials and family verification trials. In particular, the responses were drawn from trials in which the label and greeble were consistent, and the subject responded correctly. The arrows point to sessions in which Edward's response times for the two trial types were not significantly different.*

three tasks assessing greeble knowledge, and his response times were comparable to those of the control subjects. He also met the criterion for expertise involving response time. This contrasts sharply with his face recognition abilities. Despite a lifetime of experience with upright faces, he appears to have not developed any expertise with them.

In our discussion of the interpretation of these results (Duchaine et al., 2004), we considered two explanations. One possibility is that Edward was able to acquire expertise with the greebles with the same speed as that of the control subjects. On this account, expertise with greebles and expertise with faces rely on separate mechanisms. Both types of mechanism operate normally in the control subjects, but for Edward only the mechanisms used with greebles operate normally. However, we favour a second interpretation, because we do not believe that past research has demonstrated that subjects process greebles in a qualitatively different fashion after training (Duchaine et al., 2004; McKone & Kanwisher, 2005). We believe that neither Edward nor the controls developed face-like expertise in the greeble training.

Past discussions of greeble expertise have relied on a number of different measures to argue for the presence of expertise. While Gauthier and colleagues have considered the response time comparison an important measure of expertise, we have empirical and theoretical concerns about it. In the only paper displaying individual data during greeble training (Gauthier et al., 1998), the session at which each of the 12 subjects met this criterion was highlighted; 2 met it in the fourth session, 2 in the third, 1 in the second, and 1 in the first session. Edward met it in the first session. Thus, many subjects achieve the criterion after very little training. Furthermore, regardless of the object classes used, response time with the two types of verification will surely depend on the amount of practice with each type and the similarity between individuals and between families. With more practice with individual identification, one would expect that subjects would more quickly meet the criterion while more practice with family identification would cause them to reach it more slowly. When we consider similarity it is apparent that if the individual greebles were more similar to one another, then individual response times would be increased, and the criterion would have been more difficult to meet whereas decreased similarity would have the opposite effect. Thus this criterion is strongly influenced by the parameters of the experiment, and so it is a very questionable measure of a qualitative shift in recognition processes.

Previous results from behavioural experiments purportedly showing configural processing after training are also unpersuasive (McKone & Kanwisher, 2005). While some experiments have shown the predicted effects, other experiments have shown null effects or effects in the opposite-to-predicted direction. A thorough discussion of each experiment investigating configural effects after greeble training is presented in McKone and Kanwisher (2005). Also, as mentioned earlier, there is no evidence that training leads to inversion effects for greebles nor is there clear evidence that training improves performance with new sets of greebles. The neural effects that are claimed to indicate that greeble training leads to expertise are also not convincing (McKone & Kanwisher, 2005). It has not been shown that training leads to increased fusiform activations in functional magnetic resonance imaging. Training also does not increase the magnitude of the N170 in face-selective electrodes (Rossion, Curran, & Gauthier, 2002), and training appears to affect left- but not right-lateralized processes whereas face-selective ERPs tend to be right lateralized or bilateral (Bentin, McCarthy, Perez, Puce, & Allison, 1996).

Because the evidence does not demonstrate that training activates different mechanisms, there is little reason to believe that Edward or the controls have greeble expertise (Duchaine et al., 2004). Instead, they simply used object recognition mechanisms throughout the training. Percent correct did improve during the training, but it is not surprising that practice with the task and the object–name pairs improved performance. Given

Edward's normal performance with objects in other experiments, we would not expect him to have any difficulties with the greebles if greeble performance relies solely on object recognition mechanisms. Regardless of which interpretation of Edward's results is correct, the results are clearly inconsistent with the rapid expertise hypothesis.

Matching across different views: Upright bodies and human faces

The greeble training demonstrates that the rapid-expertise explanation cannot account for Edward's prosopagnosia, but the results do not bear on the other version of the expertise explanation. The extended expertise explanation suggests that the acquisition of expertise with a class requires years of experience with it (Carey, 1992; Diamond & Carey, 1986). However, despite the prominence of this hypothesis, it remains unclear what nonface classes are processed with such mechanisms so testing this explanation is challenging.

Above, we discussed the many lines of evidence that are consistent with the view that upright faces are processed by face-specific mechanisms. This evidence includes behavioural experiments with normal subjects using a wide variety of methods including the inversion effect (Diamond & Carey, 1986; Yin, 1969), composite effect (Hole, 1994; Young et al., 1987), part–whole effect (Tanaka & Farah, 1993; Tanaka & Sengco, 1997), and similarity ratings (Leder & Bruce, 1998). The extended expertise explanation predicts that expert categories will also show these effects, but among these many effects, only inversion effects in recognition memory have been found with experts. Diamond and Carey (1986) found that dog show judges showed face-sized inversion effects. However, a recent study of Labrador experts did not replicate this effect. The Labrador experts had an average of 21 years of experience, but experts and novices showed comparably sized, small inversion effects, and neither group showed a composite effect (Robbins & McKone, 2005). This effect has not been found with any other classes. In addition, inversion effects do not provide a direct test of whether a class is being processed in a configural or holistic manner, and memory in general tends to be better when subjects are familiar with the memoranda (McKone & Kanwisher, 2005). In the only published, direct test of configural processing in experts, experts did not show part–whole effects for biological cells, Rottweilers, or cars (Tanaka, 1996; cited in Tanaka & Gauthier, 1997). Hence, there is little behavioural support for the expertise hypothesis.

However, a recent paper showed comparably sized inversion effects for faces and the positions of body parts in a same–different paradigm (Reed, Stone, Bozova, & Tanaka, 2003). In addition, bodies, like faces, produce selective activation in visual cortex (Downing, Jiang, Shuman, & Kanwisher, 2001; Peelen & Downing, 2005) and are more likely than most objects to capture attention (Downing, Bray, Rogers, & Childs, 2004). Expert processing for bodies appears reasonable given the conditions under which extended expertise is hypothesized to be acquired. Humans are, of course, constantly exposed to bodies, and bodies, like faces, are used to assess identity, gender, age, attractiveness, emotion, and intention. Second, bodies, like faces, share a common first-order configuration. Thus, bodies are currently the leading nonface candidate class to be processed by mechanisms used for extended expertise, and so we investigate Edward's ability to process bodies. To make the task analogous to a face matching task, the subjects are asked to match the identity of bodies that differ in terms of shape. The extended expertise explanation predicts that he will show impairments with bodies. Because bodies have curved surfaces the results are relevant to the curvature explanation, and because the matching requires individual recognition the results bear on the individuation explanation.

Control participants

A total of 10 participants (8 females, age range: 18–35 years) took part in the experiment.

Stimuli

Faces. Four photographs of four different men's faces were used in the experiment. Each face was presented in four different head rotations ranging from profile to three-quarter view. The outline of the face and the hair were covered to conceal nonfacial cues that might be used for recognition.

Bodies. Four headless male bodies were generated using Poser 4.0. The width and height of the torsos differed for each body, but the snug clothing was identical for all bodies. Four different trunk rotations were created for each body (see Figure 16).

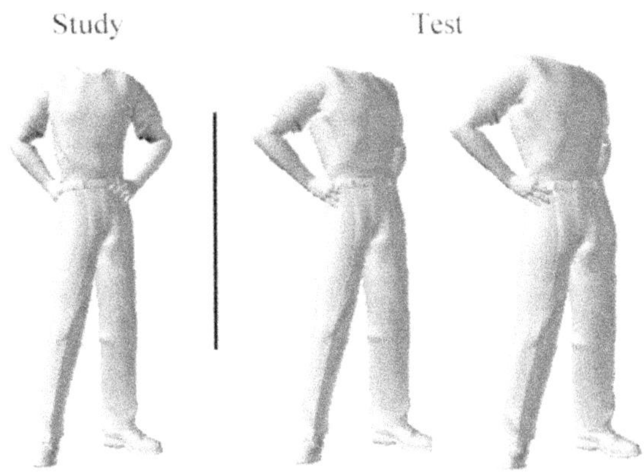

Figure 16. *Examples from the body-matching test. Subjects briefly viewed the study body and then chose the test body that matched the study body.*

Procedure

Subjects performed a two-alternative forced-choice task with either faces or bodies.

Faces and bodies were presented in different blocks. In both tasks, a stimulus was presented at the centre of the screen for 250 ms followed by two stimuli presented side by side with similar orientations. The orientations of the test stimuli always differed from the study image, but one of the stimuli matched the first stimulus on identity. Thus, subjects had to match the first and second stimuli based on identity across rotations. The two stimuli were presented on the screen until a response was made.

Results

The results for the face and body matching tasks are displayed in Figure 17. As expected, Edward had great difficulty with the face matching task. His score of 69.4% correct is 3 standard deviations below the control average of 90.4% ($SD = 6.1$). In contrast, his percent correct with bodies was the second best among all subjects. Edward's percent correct was 93.1%, and the control average was 89.2% ($SD = 3.7$). His response times for both faces and bodies were in the normal range. With faces, controls averaged 1,018 ms ($SD = 309$) while Edward averaged 1,271 ms; with bodies, controls averaged 957 ms ($SD = 286$), and Edward averaged 1,062.

Comment

Edward showed a clear dissociation between impaired face matching and normal body matching. His normal body perception is consistent with his report that he often uses body shape to determine identity and his avid interest in gymnastics and figure skating. Because human bodies are a good candidate for the application of visual expertise, Edward's results appear to be inconsistent with the extended expertise explanation. The results are consistent with other cases demonstrating that face recognition and nonface expert recognition are neuropsychologically dissociable. RM, who had extensive experience with cars, maintained his ability with cars after losing his face recognition abilities and was able to identify the makes and models of more cars than could any controls (Sergent & Signoret, 1992). Conversely, CK, an object agnosic with normal face recognition, was an expert with toy soldiers and planes yet he lost his abilities with these classes (Moscovitch et al., 1997). Perhaps most troubling for expertise explanations is that there are no cases with a selective association between face recognition and nonface expert recognition. In summary, there is currently no neuropsychological support for a common mechanism for faces and nonface expert categories.

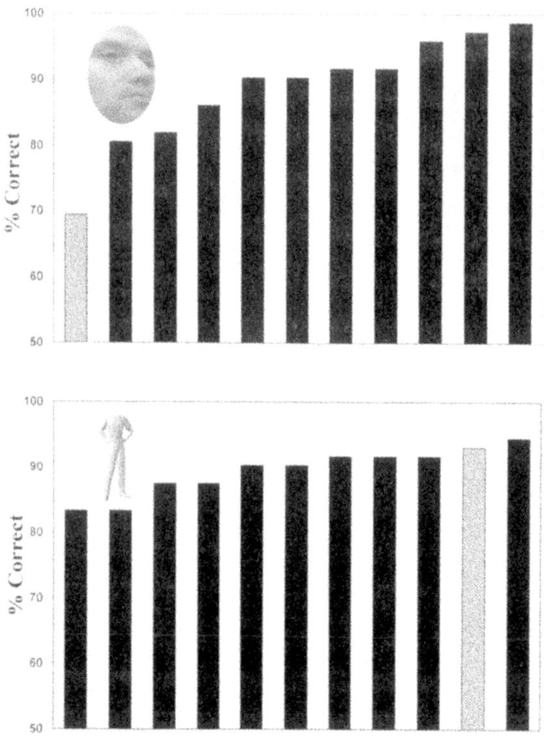

Figure 17. *Percent correct for each subject for face and body matching. Black columns are controls, and the hashed column is Edward.*

GENERAL DISCUSSION

We have tested all of the alternative explanations of prosopagnosia in a man with severe developmental prosopagnosia. Our experiments have shown that Edward has impairments with many types of face processing ability (identity, emotions, gender, attractiveness), yet he performed normally on nearly every test of nonface recognition with which we assessed him. These tests were designed to test the different accounts of prosopagnosia, and in Table 1 we present a list of the tests conducted with Edward. His results were inconsistent with all of the alternative explanations. As a result, it appears that none of the existing alternative explanations of prosopagnosia can account for Edward's prosopagnosia. Note that these results do not demonstrate that these explanations could not account for other cases of prosopagnosia, but they do demonstrate that they cannot explain his case.

Edward performed normally with face detection and showed a typical inversion effect so it appears that he has no trouble categorizing a visual stimulus as a face. However, his impairment affects a wide range of later face processing tasks. Thus, his processing difficulties are early in the face processing stream after face categorization but before face representations are processed by the separate mechanisms that have been hypothesized to underlie our ability to perform different face processing tasks (Bruce & Young, 1986). In Bruce and Young's influential model, Edward's impairment would be in the structural encoding stage.

When acquired prosopagnosics have defective structural encoding, it results from damage to the mechanisms normally performing this encoding. However, in Edward's case, this explanation seems unlikely. Because his performance with upright and inverted faces was nearly identical in the matching task, it appears that he processes

Table 1. *Evidence against the explanations for prosopagnosia*

	Individuation	*Curvature*	*Holistic*	*Configural*	*Rapid exp.*	*Expanded exp.*
Old–new discriminations	X	X	X			
Inverted face matching	X	X	X			
Tests of visual closure				X		
House discrimination	X		X	X		
Greeble training					X	
Body matching	X	X			X	X

Note: An X indicates that the results from an experiment were inconsistent with an explanation. Exp. = expertise.

these two classes with the same mechanisms. His inverted performance was in the normal range, and so it seems that his recognition systems treat upright faces in the same way that normal subjects treat inverted faces. He simply never developed the mechanisms that normally perform this special structural encoding. Instead Edward's visual system processes both orientations with more general-purpose recognition mechanisms that operate in a less configural manner than the mechanisms processing upright faces.

In the Introduction, we discussed the many architectures potentially involved with face recognition and visual recognition more generally. Consideration of both Edward's results and CK's results (Moscovitch & Moscovitch, 2000; Moscovitch et al., 1997) demonstrate the importance of face-specific mechanisms for face recognition. CK can identify faces as well as normal subjects can despite severe damage to the mechanisms used with nonface objects. Conversely, Edward's famous face performance indicates that he has almost no ability to identify faces despite the fact that the mechanisms that he uses for object recognition appear to be normal. Their cases suggest that face recognition is not the product of a number of mechanisms, one of which is face specific, but instead it is carried out entirely or nearly entirely by face-specific mechanisms.

Theorists discussing domain-specific mechanisms have often pointed to face recognition as an ability likely to be carried out by domain-specific mechanisms (Cowie, 1998; Fodor, 1983; Jackendoff, 1992; Tooby & Cosmides, 1992), and our findings with Edward provide firm support for this notion. However, these mechanisms can be characterized in a more precise fashion. A number of the alternative explanations for prosopagnosia tested with Edward are also domain-specific hypotheses. The holistic explanation suggested that objects that are difficult to decompose into parts are processed by mechanisms specialized for processing such objects. Similarly, the curvature explanation proposed specialized mechanisms for objects with significant curved surfaces. Neither nondecomposable objects nor curved objects are categories that we naturally carve the world into, but they are domains nonetheless. In contrast, faces are a category used in everyday categorization. To capture this distinction between types of domain, we can say that Edward's results provide evidence for a cognitive specialization for a natural category. That some cognitive mechanisms are specialized to process natural categories makes biological sense. We use these natural categories in everyday thought, because these are categories that affect our functioning in an enduring, systematic manner. In other words, they matter to us so we think about them. Cognitive mechanisms are created, whether phylogenetically or ontogenetically, in response to categories that matter, so it seems likely that other cognitive specializations are also consistent with our natural categories.

Developmental inferences

The existence of face-specific mechanisms leaves open the important question of the developmental mechanisms that give rise to these mechanisms. Previous cases of developmental prosopagnosia have indicated that face, object, and scene recognition are developmentally dissociable (Duchaine & Nakayama, 2005; Lerner et al., 2003; Nunn et al., 2001), but the nature of the disorder was unclear in the previous cases. In Edward's case, the evidence implicates a face-specific impairment and so indicates that he failed to develop these mechanisms despite developing normal object recognition mechanisms. Although face and object mechanisms may share a number of developmental mechanisms, Edward's developmental dissociation indicates that their construction involves different developmental mechanisms. However, Edward's results reveal little about how these developmental processes work, because retrospectively it is difficult to determine where the developmental process went awry in congenital cases. Prospective studies of children from families with genetic prosopagnosia and face perception problems caused by early brain damage, cataracts, and other known etiologies hold more promise. In addition, developmental cases similar to CK's agnosia without prosopagnosia would be highly informative. Given that there appear to be a number of specialized visual recognition mechanisms (Aguirre et al., 1998; Downing et al., 2001; Epstein, DeYoe, Press, Rosen, & Kanwisher, 2001; Epstein & Kanwisher, 1998; Grossman et al., 2000; Peelen & Downing, 2005), it will be interesting to see how these fractionate developmentally.

These developmental questions are central issues, but they are difficult to approach. Although congenital prosopagnosia and other congenital agnosias are likely to be powerful means to understand visual recognition mechanisms and their developmental basis, this approach depends on fortuitous dissociations caused by uncertain developmental events. Another converging method to examine these questions involves studying nonhuman primates raised under controlled conditions, and this approach circumvents some of the limitations of human developmental neuropsychology. For example, Mineka and colleagues found that laboratory-raised macaques develop intense fears to objects with reptilian properties (e.g., snakes, crocodiles) when they view another macaque behaving fearfully in the presence of the object (Cook & Mineka, 1989; Mineka & Cook, 1993). In contrast, they do not develop intense fears under identical conditions when an object does not have reptilian properties (e.g., flower, rabbit). Macaques were also used in a study that looked at the responses of monkeys raised in isolation to a variety of still images (Sackett, 1966). While the infants did not respond differentially to some images of monkeys (neutral adults, fearful adults, withdrawing adults) or control stimuli, they made revealing responses to photographs of threatening adults and neutral infants. In particular, the infants showed high rates of disturbance behaviours when presented with images of threatening adults. They also played significantly more when presented with threatening adults or infants. Because the macaques in these two experiments had no experience with snakes or other monkeys, it seems that their responses must result from the operation of evolved specializations coupled to motivational mechanisms. Though rarely used by vision researchers, similar methods hold great promise as a means of understanding the computational and developmental organization of recognition mechanisms.

In the Introduction, we mentioned the debate concerning developmental cognitive disorders and whether specific developmental cognitive disorders exist. Thomas and Karmiloff-Smith (2002) contend that specific developmental disorders should not exist, because developmental impairments to one system will necessarily affect the operation of other mechanisms. Because neighbouring brain regions perform object recognition and face recognition (Grill-Spector, 2004), they are especially likely to be developmentally interdependent. Nevertheless, Edward's normal object recognition and impaired face recognition indicate that developmental visual disorders can be quite specific, and defective developmental processes affecting particular visual mechanisms do not necessarily influence the development of other visual mechanisms. This is contrary to theoretical arguments against residual normality and consistent with other cases showing selective dissociations in developmental disorders and early brain damage such as dyslexia (Ramus, 2002; Ramus et al., 2003), semantic memory dysfuntion (Temple & Richardson, 2004), acalculia (Landerl et al., 2004), and episodic memory dysfunction (Vargha-Khadem et al., 1997; Vargha-Khadem et al., 2001).

Summary

We have addressed all of the existing alternative explanations of prosopagnosia, and we have rejected each of these accounts. Edward's remarkably restricted impairment with upright faces is best accounted for by the face-specific explanation, which claims that prosopagnosia results from defective face-specific mechanisms. This explanation for prosopagnosia is consistent with evidence from behavioural experiments, neuroimaging, neuropsychology, and neurophysiology that also suggests that the human brain contains face-specific mechanisms. Furthermore, because his case is developmental in nature, it indicates that face and nonface mechanisms are created, at least in part, by different developmental processes.

PrEview proof published online 13 February 2006

REFERENCES

Aguirre, G. K., Zarahn, E., & D'Esposito, M. (1998). An area within human ventral cortex sensitive to "building" stimuli: Evidence and implications. *Neuron, 21*, 373–383.

Ariel, R., & Sadeh, M. (1996). Congenital visual agnosia and prosopagnosia in a child: A case report. *Cortex, 32*, 221–240.

Baron-Cohen, S., Wheelwright, S., Hill, J., Raste, Y., & Plumb, I. (2001). The "Reading the Mind in the Eyes" test revised version: A study with normal adults, and adults with Asperger syndrome or high-functioning autism. *Journal of Child Psychology and Psychiatry, 42*, 241–251.

Barton, J. J., Cherkasova, M. V., Hefter, R., Cox, T. A., O'Connor, M., & Manoach, D. S. (2004). *Brain, 127*, 1706–1716.

Barton, J. J., Cherkasova, M. V., Press, D. Z., Intrilligator, J. M., & O'Connor, M. (2003). Developmental prosopagnosia: A study of three patients. *Brain & Cognition, 51*, 12–30.

Barton, J. J., Press, D. Z., Keenan, J. P., & O'Connor, M. (2002). Lesions of the fusiform face area impair perception of facial configuration in prosopagnosia. *Neurology, 58*, 71–78.

Behrmann, M., Avidan, G., Marotta, J. J., & Kimchi, R. (2005). Detailed exploration of face-related processing in congenital prosopagnosia: 1. Behavioral findings. *Journal of Cognitive Neuroscience, 17*, 1130–1149.

Bentin, S., Deouell, L., & Soroker, N. (1999). Selective streaming of visual information in face recognition: Evidence from congenital prosopagnosia. *NeuroReport, 10*, 823–827.

Bentin, S., McCarthy, G., Perez, E., Puce, A., & Allison, T. (1996). Electrophysiological studies of face perception in humans. *Journal of Cognitive Neuroscience, 8*, 551–565.

Bruce, V., & Young, A. W. (1986). Understanding face recognition. *British Journal of Psychology, 77*, 305–327.

Bruce, V., & Young, A. W. (1998). *In the eye of the beholder: The science of face perception*. Oxford, UK: Oxford University Press.

Burghardt, G. (1990). Cognitive ethology and critical anthropomorphism: A snake with two heads and hog-nosed snakes that play dead. In C. Ristau (Ed.), *Cognitive ethology: The minds of other animals* (pp. 53–90). Hillsdale, NJ: Lawrence Erlbaum Associates, Inc.

Calder, A. J., Young, A. W., Perrett, D. I., Etcoff, N. L., & Rowland, D. (1996). Categorical perception of morphed facial expressions. *Visual Cognition, 3*, 81–117.

Caramazza, A., & Mahon, B. Z. (2003). The organization of conceptual knowledge: The evidence from category-specific semantic deficits. *Trends in Cognitive Science, 7*, 354–361.

Caramazza, A., & Shelton, J. R. (1998). Domain-specific knowledge systems in the brain: The animate–inanimate distinction. *Journal of Cognitive Neuroscience, 10*, 1–34.

Carey, S. (1992). Becoming a face expert. *Philosophical Transactions of the Royal Society of London, 335*, 95–103.

Carlesimo, G. A., Fadda, L., Turriziani, P., Tomaiuolo, F., & Caltragirone, C. (2001). Selective sparing of face learning in a global amnesic patient. *Journal of Neuropsychology, Neurosurgery, and Psychiatry, 71*, 340–346.

Chomsky, N. (1980). *Rules and representations*. New York: Columbia University Press.

Cipolotti, L., Robinson, G., Blair, J., & Frith, U. (1999). Fractionation of visual memory: Evidence from a case with multiple neurodevelopmental impairments. *Neuropsychologia, 37*, 455–465.

Cook, M., & Mineka, S. (1989). Observational conditioning of fear to fear-relevant versus fear-irrelevant stimuli in rhesus monkeys. *Journal of Abnormal Psychology, 98*, 448–459.

Cowie, F. (1998). *What's within: Nativism reconsidered*. Oxford, UK: Oxford University Press.

Damasio, A. R., Damasio, H., & Van Hoesen, G. W. (1982). Prosopagnosia: Anatomic basis and behavioral mechanisms. *Neurology, 32*, 331–341.

Darwin, C. (1872). *The expression of emotions in man and animals*. Chicago: University of Chicago Press.

Davidoff, J. (1986). The mental representation of faces: Spatial and temporal factors. *Perception and Psychophysics, 40*, 391–400.

de Gelder, B., & Rouw, R. (2000). Configural face processes in acquired and developmental prosopagnosia: Two separate face systems? *NeuroReport, 11*, 3145–3150.

de Haan, E. (1999). A familial factor in the development of face recognition deficits. *Journal of Clinical and Experimental Neuropsychology*, *21*, 312–315.

de Haan, E. H., & Campbell, R. (1991). A fifteen year follow-up of a case of developmental prosopagnosia. *Cortex*, *27*, 489–509.

Diamond, R., & Carey, S. (1986). Why faces are and are not special: An effect of expertise. *Journal of Experimental Psychology*, *115*, 107–117.

Downing P. E., Bray, D., Rogers, J., & Childs, C. (2004). Bodies capture attention when nothing is expected. *Cognition*, *93*, 603–608.

Downing, P., Jiang, Y., Shuman, M., & Kanwisher, N. (2001). A cortical area selective for visual processing of the human body. *Science*, *293*, 2470–2473.

Duchaine, B. (2000). Developmental prosopagnosia with normal configural processing. *Neuroreport*, *11*, 79–83.

Duchaine, B., Dingle, K., Butterworth, E. B., & Nakayama, K. (2004). *Neuron*, *43*, 469–473.

Duchaine, B., & Nakayama, K. (2005). Dissociations of face and object recognition in developmental prosopagnosia. *Journal of Cognitive Neuroscience*, *17*, 249–261.

Duchaine, B., & Nakayama, K. (2006). The Cambridge Face Memory Test: Results for neurologically intact individuals and an investigation of its validity using inverted face stimuli and prosopagnosic patients. *Neuropsychologia*, *44*, 576–585.

Duchaine, B., Nieminen-von Wendt, T., New, J., & Kulomaki, T. (2003a). Dissociations of visual recognition in a developmental prosopagnosic: Evidence for separate developmental processes. *Neurocase*, *9*, 380–389.

Duchaine, B., Parker, H., & Nakayama, K. (2003b). Normal emotion recognition in a prosopagnosic. *Perception*, *32*, 827–838.

Ekman, P., & Friesen, W. V. (1976). *Pictures of facial affect*. Palo Alto, CA: Consulting Psychologists Press.

Ekstrom, R., French, J. W., & Harman, H. H. (1976). *Manual for kit of factor-referenced cognitive tests*. Princeton, NJ: Educational Testing Services.

Epstein, R., DeYoe, E. A., Press, D. Z., Rosen, A. C., & Kanwisher, N. (2001). Neuropsychological evidence for a topographical learning mechanism in parahippocampal cortex. *Cognitive Neuropsychology*, *18*, 481–508.

Epstein, R., & Kanwisher, N. (1998). A cortical representation of the local visual environment. *Nature*, *392*, 598–601.

Farah, M. J. (1990). *Visual agnosia*. Cambridge, MA: MIT Press.

Farah, M. J. (1996). Is face recognition "special"? Evidence from neuropsychology. *Behavioural Brain Research*, *76*, 181–189.

Farah, M. J., McMullen, P. A., & Meyer, M. M. (1991). Can recognition of living things be selectively impaired? *Neuropsychologia*, *29*, 185–193.

Farah, M. J.,Wilson, K. D., Drain, H. M., & Tanaka, J. R. (1995). The inverted face inversion effect in prosopagnosia: Evidence for mandatory, face-specific perceptual mechanisms. *Vision Research*, *35*, 2089–2093.

Fodor, J. (1983). *The modularity of mind*. Cambridge, MA: MIT Press.

Fox, A. (1997, June). *The assessment of fighting ability in humans*. [Abstract]. Paper presented at the meeting of the Human Behavioral and Evolution Society, Tucson, AZ, USA.

Freire, A., Lee, K., & Symons, L. A. (2000). The face-inversion effect as a deficit in encoding of configural information: Direct evidence. *Perception*, *29*, 159–170.

Gauthier, I., Behrmann, M., & Tarr, M. J. (1999). Can face recognition really be dissociated from object recognition? *Journal of Cognitive Neuropsychology*, *11*, 349–370.

Gauthier, I., Skudlarski, P., Gore, J. C., & Anderson, A. W. (2000). Expertise for cars and birds recruits brain areas involved in face recognition. *Nature Neuroscience*, *3*, 191–197.

Gauthier, I., & Tarr, M. J. (1997). Becoming a "greeble" expert: Exploring mechanisms for face recognition. *Vision Research*, *37*, 1673–1682.

Gauthier, I., & Tarr, M. J. (2002). Unraveling mechanisms for expert object recognition: Bridging brain activity and behavior. *Journal of Experimental Psychology: Human Perception and Performance*, *28*, 431–446.

Gauthier, I., Williams, P., Tarr, M. J., & Tanaka, J. (1998). Training "greeble" experts: A framework for studying expert object recognition processes. *Vision Research*, *38*, 2401–2428.

Grill-Spector, K. (2004). The functional organization of the ventral visual pathway and its relationship to object recognition. In N. Kanwisher & J. Duncan (Eds.), *Attention & performance XX: Functional neuroimaging of visual cognition*. Oxford, UK: Oxford University Press.

Grossman, E. D., Donnelly, M., Price, P., Morgan, V., Pickens, D., & Neighbor, G. et al. (2000). Brain areas involved in perception of biological motion. *Journal of Cognitive Neuroscience*, *12*, 711–720.

Harris, A., Duchaine, B., & Nakayama, K. (2005). Normal and abnormal face selectivity in developmental prosopagnosics. *Neuropsychologia, 43*, 2125–2136.

Henke, K., Schweinberger, S. R., Grigo, A., Klos, T., & Sommer, W. (1998). Specificity of face recognition: Recognition of exemplars of non-face objects in prosopagnosia. *Cortex, 34*, 289–296.

Hirschfeld, L. A., & Gelman, S. A. (1994). *Mapping the mind: Domain-specificity in cognition and culture.* New York: Cambridge University Press.

Hole, G. J. (1994). Configurational factors in the perception of unfamiliar faces. *Perception, 23*, 65–74.

Incisa della Rocchetta, A., Cipolotti, L., & Warrington, E. K. (1996). Topographical disorientation: Selective impairment of locomotor space? *Cortex, 32*, 727–735.

Jackendoff, R. (1992). *Languages of the mind.* Cambridge, MA: MIT Press.

Jones, R. D., & Tranel, D. (2001). Severe developmental prosopagnosia in a child with superior intellect. *Journal of Clinical and Experimental Neuropsychology, 23*, 265–273.

Kanwisher, N., McDermott, J., & Chun, M. M. (1997). The fusiform face area: A module in human extrastriate cortex specialized for face perception. *Journal of Neuroscience, 17*, 4302–4311.

Klinnert, M. D., Campos, J. J., Sorce, J. F., Emde, R. N., & Svejda, M. (1983). Emotions as behavior regulators: Social referencing in infancy. In R. Plutchik & H. Kelleman (Eds.), *Emotion: Theory, research and experience: Vol. 2. Emotions in early development* (pp. 57–86). New York: Academic Press.

Kosslyn, S., Hamilton, S., & Bernstein, J. (1995). The perception of curvature can be selectively disrupted in prosopagnosia. *Brain and Cognition, 27*, 36–58.

Kracke, I. (1994). Developmental prosopagnosia in Asperger syndrome: Presentation and discussion of an individual case. *Developmental Medicine and Child Neurology, 36*, 873–886.

Kreiman, G., Koch, C., & Fried, I. (2000). Category-specific visual responses of single neurons in the human medial temporal lobe. *Nature Neuroscience, 3*, 946–953.

Laeng, B., & Caviness, V. S. (2001). Prosopagnosia as a deficit in encoding curved surface. *Journal of Cognitive Neuroscience, 13*, 556–576.

Landerl, K., Bevan, A., & Butterworth, B. (2004). Developmental dyscalculia and basic numerical capacities: A study of 8–9-year-old students. *Cognition, 93*, 99–125.

Landis, T., Cummings, J. L., Christen, L., Bogen, J. E., & Imhof, H. G. (1986). Are unilateral right posterior cerebral lesions sufficient to cause prosopagnosia? Clinical and radiological findings in six additional patients. *Cortex, 22*, 243–252.

Leder, H., & Bruce, V. (1998). Local and relational aspects of face distinctiveness. *Quarterly Journal of Experimental Psychology, 51A*, 449–473.

Le Grand, R., Mondloch, C. J., Maurer, D., & Brent, H. P. (2001). Early visual experience and face processing. *Nature, 412*, 786.

Le Grand, R., Mondloch, C. J., Maurer, D., & Brent, H. P. (2003). Expert face processing requires visual input to the right hemisphere during infancy. *Nature Neuroscience, 6*, 1108–1112.

Lerner, Y., Pianka, P., Azmon, B., Leiba, H., Stolovitch, C., Loewenstein, A., et al. (2003). Area-specific amblyopic effects in human occipitotemporal object representations. *Neuron, 40*, 1023–1029.

Levine, D. N., & Calvanio, R. (1989). Prosopagnosia: A defect in configural processing. *Brain and Cognition, 10*, 149–170.

Macmillan, N. A., & Creelman, C. D. (1991). *Detection theory: A user's guide.* New York: Cambridge University Press.

Maurer, D., Le Grand, R., & Mondloch, J. (2002). The many faces of configural processing. *Trends in Cognitive Sciences, 6*, 255–260.

McCarthy, G., Puce, A., Belger, A., & Allison, T. (1999). Electrophysiological studies of human face perception: II. Response properties of face-specific potentials generated in occipitotemporal cortex. *Cerebral Cortex, 9*, 431–444.

McCarthy, G., Puce, A., Gore, J., & Allison, T. (1997). Face-specific processing in the human fusiform gyrus. *Journal of Cognitive Neuroscience, 9*, 605–610.

McConachie, H. R. (1976). Developmental prosopagnosia: A single case report. *Cortex, 12*, 76–82.

McKone, E., & Kanwisher, N. (2005). Does the human brain process objects of expertise like faces? A review of the evidence. In S. Dehaene, J. R. Duhamel, M. Hauser, & G. Rizzolatti (Eds.), *From monkey brain to human brain.* Cambridge, MA: MIT Press.

McKone, E., Martini, P., & Nakayama, K. (2001). Categorical perception of face identity in noise isolates configural processing. *Journal of Experimental Psychology: Human Perception and Performance, 27*, 573–599.

McMullen, P., Fisk, J. D., & Phillips, S. (2000). Apperceptive agnosia and face recognition. *Neurocase, 6*, 403–414.

Michelon, P., & Biederman, I. (2003). Less impairment in face imagery than face perception in early prosopagnosia. *Neuropsychologia, 41*, 421–441.

Mineka, S., & Cook, M. (1993). Mechanisms involved in the observational conditioning of fear. *Journal of Experimental Psychology: General, 122*, 23–38.

Moscovitch, M., & Moscovitch, D. A. (2000). Super face-inversion effects for isolated internal or external features and for fractured faces. *Cognitive Neuropsychology, 18*, 201–220.

Moscovitch, M., Winocur, G., & Behrmann, M. (1997). What is special about face recognition? Nineteen experiments on a person with visual object agnosia and dyslexia but normal face recognition. *Journal of Cognitive Neuroscience, 9*, 555–604.

Navon, D. (1977). Forest before trees: The precedence of global features in visual perception. *Cognitive Psychology, 9*, 353–383.

Nunn, J. A., Postma, P., & Pearson, R. (2001). Developmental prosopagnosia: Should it be taken at face value? *Neurocase, 7*, 15–27.

Papousek, H., & Papousek, M. (1979). Early ontogeny of human social interaction: Its biological roots and social dimensions. In M. von Cranach, K. Foppa, W. Lepenies, & D. Ploog (Eds.), *Human ethology: Claims and limits of a new discipline*. Cambridge, UK: Cambridge University Press.

Peelen, M., & Downing, P. (2005). Selectivity for the human body in the fusiform gyrus. *Journal of Neurophysiology, 93*, 603–608.

Pelli, D. G., Robson, J. G., & Wilkins, A. J. (1988) The design of a new letter chart for measuring contrast sensitivity. *Clinical Vision Sciences, 2*, 187–199.

Perrett, D. I., & Mistlin, A. J. (1990). Perception of facial characteristics by monkeys. In W. C. Stebbins & M. A. Berkley (Eds.), *Comparative perception* (Vol. II, pp. 187–215). New York: Wiley.

Pinker, S. (1994). *The language instinct*. New York: Morrow.

Pylyshyn, Z. W., & Storm, R. W. (1988). Tracking multiple independent targets: Evidence for a parallel tracking mechanism. *Spatial Vision, 3*, 1–19.

Quinn, P. C., Yahr, J., Kuhn, A., Slater, A., & Pascalis, O. (2002). Representation of the gender of human faces by infants: A preference for female. *Perception, 31*, 1109–1121.

Ramus, F. (2002). Evidence for a domain-specific deficit in developmental dyslexia. *Behavioral and Brain Sciences, 25*, 767–768.

Ramus, F., Rosen, S., Dakin, S. C., Day, B. L., Castellote, J. M., White, S., et al. (2003). Theories of developmental dyslexia: Insights from a multiple case study of dyslexic adults. *Brain, 126*, 841–865.

Reed, C. L., Stone, V., Bozova, S., & Tanaka, J. (2003). The body inversion effect. *Psychological Science, 14*, 302–308.

Riddoch, M. J., & Humphreys, G. W. (1993). *BORB: Birmingham Object Recognition Battery*. Hove, UK: Lawrence Erlbaum Associates Ltd.

Ristau, C. (1991). Aspects of the cognitive ethology of an injury-feigning bird, the piping plover. In C. Ristau (Ed.), *Cognitive ethology: The minds of other animals* (pp. 91–126). Hillsdale, NJ: Lawrence Erlbaum Associates, Inc.

Robbins, R., & McKone, E. (2005). *No face-like processing for objects-of-expertise in three behavioural tasks*. Manuscript submitted for publication.

Rosch, E., Mervis, C. B., Gray, W. D., Johnson, D. M., & Bayes-Braem, P. (1976). Basic objects in natural categories. *Cognitive Psychology, 8*, 382–439.

Rossion, B., Curran, T., & Gauthier, I. (2002). A defense of the subordinate-level expertise account for the N170 component. *Cognition, 85*, 189–196.

Rubenstein, A. J., Langlois, J. H., & Kalakanis, L. (1999). Infant preferences for attractive faces: A cognitive explanation. *Developmental Psychology, 35*, 848–855.

Sackett, G. P. (1966). Monkeys reared in isolation with pictures as visual input: Evidence for an innate releasing mechanism. *Science, 154*, 1468–1473.

Sadr, J., Duchaine, B. C., & Nakayama, K. (2004). *The perception of facial attractiveness in prosopagnosia*. Proceedings of the Vision Sciences Society annual meeting, Sarasota, FL, USA.

Sartori, S., & Job, R. (1988). The oyster with four legs: A neuropsychological study on the interaction of visual and semantic information. *Cognitive Neuropsychology, 5*, 105–132.

Schweich, M., & Bruyer, R. (1993). Heterogeneity in the cognitive manifestations of prosopagnosia: The study of a group of single cases. *Cognitive Neuropsychology, 10*, 529–547.

Sergent, J., & Signoret, M. (1992). Implicit access to knowledge derived from unrecognised faces in prosopagnosia. *Cerebral Cortex, 2*, 389–400.

Snodgrass, J. G., & Vanderwart, M. (1980). *Journal of Experimental Psychology: Human Learning and Memory, 6*, 174–215.

Tanaka, J. W. (2001). The entry point of face recognition: Evidence for face expertise. *Journal of Experimental Psychology: General, 130*, 534–543.

Tanaka, J. W., & Farah, M. J. (1993). Parts and wholes in face recognition. *Quarterly Journal of Experimental Psychology, 46A*, 225–245.

Tanaka, J., & Gauthier, I. (1997). Expertise in object and face recognition. *The Psychology of Learning and Motivation, 36*, 83–125.

Tanaka, J. W., & Sengco, J. A. (1997). Features and their configuration in face recognition. *Memory and Cognition, 25*, 583–592.

Tanaka, J. W., & Taylor, M. (1991). Object categories and expertise: Is the basic level in the eye of the beholder? *Cognitive Psychology, 23*, 457–482.

Temple, C., & Richardson, P. (2004). Developmental amnesia: A new pattern of dissociation with intact episodic memory. *Neuropsychologia, 42*, 764–781.

Thomas, M., & Karmiloff-Smith, A. (2002). Are developmental disorders like cases of adult brain damage? Implications from connectionist modelling. *Behavioral and Brain Sciences, 25*, 727–750.

Tooby, J., & Cosmides, L. (1992). The psychological foundations of culture. In J. Barkow, L. Cosmides, & J. Tooby (Eds.), *The adapted mind: Evolutionary psychology and the generation of culture.* New York: Oxford University Press.

Vargha-Khadem, F., Gadian, D. G., & Mishkin, M. (2001). Dissociations in cognitive memory: The syndrome of developmental amnesia. *Philosophical Transactions of the Royal Society of London B, 356*, 1435–1440.

Vargha-Khadem, F., Gadian, D. G., Watkins, K. E., Connelly, A., Van Paesschen, W., & Mishkin, M. (1997). Differential effects of early hippocampal pathology on episodic and semantic memory. *Science, 277*, 376–380.

Waitt, C., Little, A. C., Wolfensohn, S., Honess, P., Brown, A. P, Buchanan-Smith, H. M. et al. (2003). Evidence from rhesus macaques suggests that male coloration plays a role in female primate mate choice. *Proceedings of the Royal Society of London B, 270*, 144–146.

Whiteley, A., & Warrington, E. K. (1978). Selective impairment of topographical memory: A single case study. *Journal of Neurology, Neurosurgery, & Psychiatry, 41*, 575–578.

Yin, R. (1969). Looking at upside-down faces. *Journal of Experimental Psychology, 81*, 141–145.

Yin, R. (1970). Face recognition by brain-injured patients: A dissociable ability. *Neuropsychologia, 8*, 395–402.

Young, A. W., Hellawell, D., & Hay, D. (1987). Configurational information in face perception. *Perception, 16*, 747–759.

Yovel, G., & Duchaine, B. C. (in press). Specialized face perception mechanisms extract both part and spacing information from faces: Evidence from developmental prosopagnosia. *Journal of Cognitive Neuroscience.*

Yovel, G., Duchaine, B., Nakayama, K., & Kanwisher, N. (2005, November). *The fusiform face areas in prosopagnosic subjects do not discriminate between faces.* Paper presented at the 35th Annual Meeting of the Society for Neuroscience [Program No. 362.3], Washington, DC, USA.

Yovel, G., & Kanwisher, N. (2004). Face perception: Domain-specific, not process-specific. *Neuron, 44*, 889–898.

Yovel, G., & Kanwisher, N. (2005). *A common mechanism for processing part and spacing information for only upright faces: Evidence from individual differences.* Manuscript submitted for publication.

COGNITIVE NEUROPSYCHOLOGY, 2006, 23 (5), 748–761

Psychology Press
Taylor & Francis Group

A double dissociation between sensorimotor impairments and reading disability: A comparison of autistic and dyslexic children

Sarah White and Uta Frith
Institute of Cognitive Neuroscience, University College London, London, UK

Elizabeth Milne
University of Sheffield and Department of Human Communication Science, University College London, London, UK

Stuart Rosen
Department of Phonetics and Linguistics, University College London, London, UK

John Swettenham
Department of Human Communication Science, University College London, London, UK

Franck Ramus
Institute of Cognitive Neuroscience, University College London, London, UK, and Laboratoire de Sciences Cognitives et Psycholinguistique, EHESS/CNRS/ENS, Paris, France

Does sensorimotor dysfunction underlie reading impairment? To investigate this question, a battery of literacy, phonology, auditory, visual, and motor tests were administered to age- and ability-matched groups of dyslexic, autistic, and control children. As in previous studies, only a subset of the dyslexic children had sensory and/or motor impairments, whilst some dyslexics were entirely spared, suggesting that sensorimotor impairments are not necessary to cause reading disability. A subset of autistic children was also found to have sensorimotor impairments; however, some of these children did not have reading problems, suggesting that sensorimotor impairments are not sufficient to cause reading disability. We conclude that sensorimotor and reading impairments are doubly dissociable. Sensorimotor impairments do not seem to be the cause of reading disability, but can be seen as nonspecific markers for developmental disorder.

Correspondence should be addressed to Sarah White, Institute of Cognitive Neuroscience, University College London, 17 Queen Square, London WC1N 3AR, UK (Email: s.white@ucl.ac.uk).

We are grateful to Peter Hansen (Department of Physiology, Oxford University) for supplying the visual tasks. We would also like to thank the following: all the children who took part, and their parents, for their time, effort, and cooperation; All Saints Benhilton Primary School, the Autism Unit at Axton Chase School, Hillingdon Manor School, and the Marlborough Unit at Byron School for their patience and assistance; and Martin Turner for his help with recruiting participants. This study was funded by a Marie Curie fellowship of the European Community programme Quality of Life (QLGI-CT-1999–51305; F.R.), and by a Medical Research Council grant (G9617036; U.F.).

http://www.psypress.com/cogneuropsychology DOI:10.1080/02643290500438607

Developmental disorders are complex and often appear to be very heterogeneous; it is therefore difficult to identify the causes of the main symptoms. Indeed, the aetiology of developmental dyslexia is currently the subject of a debate between two main opposing views. One view proposes that reading disability is due to a cognitive impairment specific to phonological processing (Snowling, 2000; Vellutino, 1979), arising from a dysfunction of certain left-hemisphere peri-sylvian brain areas (McCandliss & Noble, 2003; Paulesu et al., 2001; Shaywitz et al., 1998). The other view recognizes the role played by the phonological deficit but sees it as only one consequence of a more general sensorimotor syndrome, including auditory, visual, and motor dysfunctions. If so, the biological origin of this syndrome might be a pan-sensory magnocellular dysfunction with secondary disruption to the cerebellum and hence motor systems (Stein, 2001; Stein & Walsh, 1997), or a general learning disability based on cerebellar dysfunction (Nicolson, Fawcett, & Dean, 2001). Recently, this view has been challenged by evidence suggesting that sensorimotor dysfunction affects only a fraction of dyslexics, questioning its causal contribution to reading failure (see Ramus, 2003, for a recent review).

Nevertheless, although sensorimotor impairments may not be necessary to cause reading disability, they may be sufficient; they might provide a valid explanation of reading disability for the subset of affected dyslexics. This would predict that reading disability would occur whenever an individual was affected by such sensorimotor impairments. This prediction is particularly interesting since the sensorimotor impairments documented in dyslexia are not restricted to the dyslexic population. Visual magnocellular deficits have been found in autism (Gepner & Mestre, 2002; Milne et al., 2002; Spencer et al., 2000) and Williams syndrome (Atkinson et al., 1997), auditory deficits have been found in specific language impairment (SLI; Tallal & Piercy, 1973; Wright et al., 1997) and autism (Oram Cardy, Flagg, Roberts, Brian, & Roberts, 2005), and motor deficits have been found in autism (Courchesne, 1997; Hallett et al., 1993; Noterdaeme, Mildenberger, Minow, & Amorosa, 2002), Williams syndrome (Jones et al., 2002), SLI (Hill, 2001), and of course developmental coordination disorder (DCD; Hill, 1998).

Sensorimotor impairments therefore seem to be more generally found in a large variety of developmental disorders, in which reading disability is not necessarily a characteristic feature. However, assessments of the reading abilities of such populations are not routinely performed. In the case of autism, reading ability varies widely from none to hyperlexic (Whitehouse & Harris, 1984) and therefore presents a suitable testing ground for the hypothesis that sensorimotor impairments have the same putative effects on reading outside the "official" dyslexic population. The present study therefore compares literacy, phonology, auditory, visual, and motor skills between dyslexic and autistic children, with the aim of evaluating the relationship between sensorimotor dysfunction and reading disability.

Method

The present study reports novel analyses of data that have been partially published before. More specifically, the data obtained on dyslexic and control children were reported by White et al. (2006), while the visual and motor data obtained on autistic children were reported by Milne et al. (in press). Literacy, phonology, and auditory data from the autistic children have not been reported before. The originality of the present paper is in the comparison between the dyslexic and autistic populations across the whole range of abilities.

Participants

In total, 22 autistic children were compared to 23 dyslexic and 22 control children. The groups were chosen to be matched on their range of ages and nonverbal IQs: age, $F(2, 64) = 1.02$; nonverbal IQ, $F(2, 64) = 1.93$. All children were aged between 8 and 12 years and had nonverbal IQs of at least 85, with the exception of 4 high-functioning and able autistic children with nonverbal IQs of 70, 73, 79, and 84, as measured by

Raven's Standard Progressive Matrices (Raven, Court, & Raven, 1988); raw scores were converted to standardized scores by interpolation and extrapolation from percentile scores given in the manual. The autistic children had all independently received a diagnosis of autism, autistic spectrum disorder, or Asperger syndrome and were recruited through special schools for children with such diagnoses. The majority of the dyslexic children were referred from the Dyslexia Institute and had therefore received the same neuropsychological assessment from the same highly experienced educational psychologist. All participants had pure-tone detection thresholds below 25 dB in both ears across a range of frequencies (0.5–8 Hz).

Procedure

The study obtained ethical approval from the Joint UCL/UCLH Committees on the Ethics of Human Research, and informed consent to participate was given by both parent and child. Children were tested individually in a quiet room at their home, at their school, or at the Institute of Cognitive Neuroscience. Testing was divided into three sessions of approximately an hour each, and every child completed a battery of tasks assessing literacy, phonology, auditory, visual, and motor abilities. The sensorimotor tests were chosen to reflect those currently in use by the proponents of each theory and on which they have found significant group differences. Further methodological details can be found in White et al. (2006).

Literacy tests

The children were tested on the Wide Range Achievement Test (WRAT3; Wilkinson, 1993), a standardized literacy assessment, to provide a measure of their single-word reading and spelling skills.

Phonology tests

The Phonological Assessment Battery (PhAB; Frederickson, Frith, & Reason, 1997), another standardized assessment, was used to assess skill at processing and manipulating speech sounds. The rhyme, spoonerisms, nonword reading, rapid automatic naming (two tests), and fluency (three tests) subtests were all administered according to the test manual. It should be noted that one of the fluency tasks (semantic fluency) is a nonphonological control task.

Auditory tests

All auditory tasks were run on a laptop computer using calibrated headphones. Two tasks involving the categorization of phonemes were presented, using single stimuli from the speech sound continua /ba/–/da/ and *coat–goat*. A further task using the /ba/–/da/ continuum involved the discrimination of a pair of identical sounds from a pair of differing sounds, and a nonspeech version of this task was also administered, using only the second formant (tasks as in Ramus et al., 2003, and Rosen & Manganari, 2001). Finally, the children were required to detect which of two tones was frequency modulated (FM) at 2 Hz (task inspired from Witton et al., 1998). Each task was performed twice, and the best performance was recorded.[1]

Visual tests

Both the motion coherence and form coherence tasks were run on a laptop computer (tasks as in Hansen et al., 2001). In both tasks, participants viewed two panels on the screen and judged which contained the coherent signal. In the critical condition, dots moving coherently from side to side were presented in one panel, and in the control condition, a coherent circular form made up of line elements was presented in one panel. The second panel always contained a random

[1] Reliability analysis indicated that performance between the two trials of each task was inconsistent, more so for some tasks than others (Cronbach's alpha: /ba/–/da/ = .24, *coat–goat* = .33, FM 2 Hz = .65, speech formant discrimination = .35, nonspeech formant discrimination = .56). Such inconsistency may indicate additional task demands required to perform these tasks well; indeed, we believe that these tasks have a particularly high attentional load. We therefore took the best performance on a particular task as the most reliable measure of a child's auditory abilities, independent of other task demands.

signal: dots moving in random directions or line elements in random orientations. A weighted adaptive staircase procedure was used to present different levels of coherence in the signal, from which a detection threshold was calculated. Catch trials were also included to check that the children understood the task and were attending to its demands. Each condition was performed twice, and the average detection threshold was calculated.[2]

Motor tests

Motor skill was assessed using two manual dexterity and two balance tasks. As measures of manual dexterity, the child was required to thread beads onto a string (Fawcett & Nicolson, 1996) and also to perform a task known as finger and thumb (Dow & Moruzzi, 1958), involving rotation of the hands with thumb and index finger of opposite hands touching. Both balance tasks were taken from the Movement Assessment Battery for Children (Henderson & Sugden, 1992): a one-legged balance task (stork balance) and heel-to-toe (walking along a line with heel and toe touching). All tasks were performed twice, and average performance was recorded.[3]

Results

ANOVAs were used to assess differences between groups, unless otherwise stated; due to multiple comparisons, we chose to set our alpha level to $p = .01$. As well as group differences, individual differences in performance were studied, and outliers with abnormally low performance were identified as lying more than 1.65 standard deviations (*SD*s) below the control mean, equivalent to the bottom 5% of a normal distribution (procedure as in Ramus et al., 2003). Summary factors, accounting for all tasks in a given modality, were also calculated by averaging z-scores (calculated in relation to control performance) for each participant across tasks in each modality.

Literacy tests

As expected, the groups differed on reading, $F(2, 64) = 28.60$, $p < .001$, and spelling tasks, $F(2, 64) = 28.51$, $p < .001$. However, pairwise comparisons revealed not only that the dyslexic group performed worse than the control group on both tasks ($p < .001$) but that the autistic group also did ($p < .001$). A very marginal difference existed between the dyslexic and autistic groups (read $p = .092$; spell $p = .064$), indicating that, as a group, the autistic children were not quite as impaired as the dyslexics on the reading and spelling tasks. The nonword reading test revealed the same pattern of differences between groups, $F(2, 64) = 20.88$, $p < .001$, with both dyslexic ($p < .001$) and autistic children ($p = .003$) performing more poorly than controls, and dyslexic children performing slightly more poorly than autistic children ($p = .013$). (See Table 1.)

A literacy factor was calculated by combining reading, spelling, and nonword reading scores. A total of 96% of dyslexic children were outliers on this factor, while 59% of autistic children and 18% of controls were. This factor was found to be weakly correlated to nonverbal IQ in the whole sample ($r = .26$, $p = .037$) and more strongly in the control and dyslexic groups (control, $r = .57$, $p = .006$; dyslexic, $r = .55$, $p = .006$) but not in the autistic group ($r = .06$). Given the overall IQ–literacy correlation, individual differences in nonverbal IQ were taken into account by entering each summary factor as the dependent variable in a regression analysis with nonverbal IQ as the independent variable. Unstandardized residuals for each participant were recorded from this analysis as the corrected

[2] Reliability analysis indicated that performance between the two trials of each task was consistent; Cronbach's alpha: motion (ranked data as not normally distributed) = .74, form = .6. We therefore took the average performance to be the most reliable measure of a child's abilities.

[3] Reliability analysis indicated that performance between the two trials of each task was highly consistent; Cronbach's alpha: bead threading (ranked data) = .84, finger and thumb = .87, heel-to-toe (ranked data) = .88, stork balance (ranked data) = .84. We therefore took the average performance to be the most reliable measure of a child's abilities.

Table 1. *Background and literacy test means*

	Control	*Dyslexic*	*Autistic*		
			All	*Good reader*	*Poor reader*
Number	22	23	22		
Male:female	9:13	14:9	20:2		
Age[a]	123.82 (13.73)	126.04 (15.01)	119.27 (19.36)		
Nonverbal IQ	102.95 (13.88)	102.13 (13.21)	95.59 (13.83)		
Reading***	112.64 (10.57)	85.78*** (11.86)	93.55*** (13.98)		
Spelling***	113.23 (12.94)	84.83*** (9.27)	93.64*** (15.74)		
Nonword reading***	114.95 (12.68)	93.39*** (6.74)	103.18** (13.18)		
Original literacy factor***	0.00 (1.00)	− 2.42*** (0.78)	− 1.60*** (1.22)		
Corrected literacy factor***	0.00 (1.00)	− 2.83*** (0.77)		− 0.20 (0.89)	− 2.67*** (0.92)

Note: Test scores are standardized scores. Literacy factor scores are based on averaged z-scores. Stars next to the test name indicate an overall group difference. Stars within the table indicate differences between that group and the control group. Standard deviations in parentheses.

[a]In months.

$^{**}p < .01$; $^{***}p < .001$.

summary factor. The literacy factor was therefore recalculated, group difference, $F(2, 64) = 25.02$, $p < .001$, and all 23 dyslexics were found to be outliers. The literacy scores of the autistic children were extremely wide ranging and were therefore divided into two groups of good and poor readers, resulting in 9 children falling above (good readers) and 13 children falling below (poor readers) the outlier threshold. This division does not make the assumption that the autistic poor readers were dyslexic (as they may have other reasons to read poorly); rather it rules out the possibility that any of the autistic good readers had a reading disability. These two groups of autistic children were entered separately into all further analyses. Two controls were also literacy outliers and were therefore removed from all further analysis as it could not be assumed that their literacy development was normal.

Phonology

Group differences were found on all of the PhAB subtests ($F > 4$, $p \leq .008$) except alliteration fluency, $F(3, 61) = 0.302$, $p = .824$, on which the control group performed worse than expected, given the scores on the other subtests. Pairwise comparisons revealed that the dyslexics had severe phonological problems, performing worse than controls on all the phonological subtests ($p \leq .001$, except rhyme fluency where $p = .028$). Similarly, the autistic poor readers performed worse than controls on these same tasks ($p \leq .002$) except for rapid automatic picture naming ($p = .238$). However, unlike the dyslexics, both autistic groups also performed marginally worse than controls on the nonphonological semantic fluency task (poor readers, $p = .025$; good readers, $p = .023$) despite the autistic good readers performing as well as the controls on all the phonological tasks. This is likely to be due to the presence of poor semantic skills in autism.

The scores from the six phonological tasks were combined to give a phonology factor, and after accounting for nonverbal IQ, 48% of the dyslexic children, 38% of the autistic poor readers, and 33% of the autistic good readers[4] were found to be outliers (no control outliers), $F(3, 61) = 10.121$, $p < .001$ (see Table 2).

[4] It should be noted that the phonological measures used here may tap other abilities, particularly general processing speed in the rapid automated naming tests. We include these tests as they have been shown to be sensitive to the phonological impairment in dyslexia (see Frederickson et al., 1997). However, it is possible that some autistic children may therefore be defined as phonological outliers for nonphonological reasons.

Table 2. *Phonology test means*

	Control	Dyslexic	Autistic: Good reader	Autistic: Poor reader
Rhyme***	112.30 (11.89)	96.26** (14.09)	98.33 (15.54)	89.77*** (13.38)
Spoonerisms***	112.80 (11.08)	98.00*** (9.19)	110.56 (3.00)	97.00*** (14.46)
Rapid automatic picture naming**	108.75 (12.93)	92.22** (12.76)	100.44 (16.69)	99.25 (14.28)
Rapid automatic digit naming***	109.25 (12.51)	88.83*** (9.67)	101.00 (18.5)	91.00** (17.26)
Alliteration fluency	100.05 (7.98)	99.61 (10.66)	100.00 (14.11)	96.62 (13.44)
Rhyme fluency**	114.55 (10.82)	101.70* (11.93)	103.33 (14.47)	92.85*** (18.58)
Semantic fluency**	107.10 (11.06)	100.65 (15.29)	90.00* (13.92)	92.08* (17.68)
Phonology factor***	0.00 (1.00)	− 1.62*** (0.96)	− 0.69 (1.50)	− 1.89*** (1.47)

Note: Test scores are standardized scores. Phonology factor scores are based on averaged z-scores. Stars next to the test name indicate an overall group difference. Stars within the table indicate differences between that group and the control group. Standard deviations in parentheses.
$^{**}p < .01$; $^{***}p < .001$.

Auditory tasks

The full auditory data from one autistic child was lost, whilst 3 dyslexics and 4 controls were without data for the /ba/−/da/ and *coat−goat* tasks due to the use of incorrect task parameters. The only task to produce a significant group difference was the FM at 2 Hz task, $F(3, 60) = 7.19$, $p < .001$, and this was due to both autistic groups performing more poorly than controls (poor readers, $p = .014$; good readers, $p = .001$) and the good readers performing worse than the dyslexics ($p = .007$; see Table 3). Individual performance on all tasks appeared to follow little pattern, with different children having difficulties on different tasks. On combining the results from the five experimental tasks into an auditory factor and accounting for age as well as nonverbal IQ (as none of the sensorimotor tasks was standardized for age, unlike the literacy and phonological tasks), a marginal group difference was found, $F(3, 60) = 2.928$, $p = .041$, with the autistic poor readers performing slightly worse than controls ($p = .055$). A total of 30% of dyslexics, 38% of autistic poor readers, and 50% of autistic good readers were found to be outliers (10% control outliers).

Table 3. *Auditory test means*

	Control	Dyslexic	Autistic: Good reader	Autistic: Poor reader
/ba/−/da/	3.49 (4.38)	3.99 (4.73)	4.16 (3.77)	3.21 (3.98)
coat−goat	2.99 (1.13)	5.05 (5.31)	7.08 (7.76)	8.38 (7.30)
FM 2 Hz***	1.98 (2.15)	2.64 (2.44)	6.53** (3.71)	5.11* (3.62)
Formant (speech) discrimination	6.63 (3.31)	6.27 (4.88)	9.23 (6.05)	8.31 (5.41)
Formant (nonspeech) discrimination	6.33 (3.83)	6.05 (4.03)	7.00 (4.76)	7.56 (4.85)
Auditory factor*	0.00 (1.00)	−0.52 (1.74)	−1.60 (2.61)	−1.71 (2.44)

Note: Test scores are quoted as just-noticeable-differences/modulation indexes for FM tasks (low scores indicate good performance). Auditory factor scores are based on averaged z-scores. Stars next to the test name indicate an overall group difference. Stars within the table indicate differences between that group and the control group. Standard deviations in parentheses.
$^{*}p < .05$; $^{**}p < .01$; $^{***}p < .001$.

Visual tasks

A minority of children failed more than one catch trial across both measurements for each condition. Subsequently, the data for any child who failed more than 20% of catch trials on a measurement were removed from the analysis. This meant that 5 autistic children on the motion coherence task and 1 autistic child on the form coherence task had a test score based on one rather than two measurements. One further autistic child had extremely poor catch trial performance on the motion coherence task, failing 38% and 43% of catch trials on the two measurements, as well as poor motion coherence thresholds, and appeared to find the task extremely difficult. However, his good catch trial performance on the form coherence task as well as his general high levels of motivation during testing indicated that he had a specific problem with motion coherence rather than a general attention problem. His results were therefore not excluded. In addition, the motion coherence task data were lost for one dyslexic child due to technical problems.

The motion coherence task produced a borderline significant difference between the groups, $F(3, 60) = 2.570$, $p = .063$, whereas the control form coherence task did not, $F(3, 61) = 2.116$; see Table 4). Pairwise comparisons revealed no significant group differences on either task. After accounting for both nonverbal IQ and age, 13% of dyslexics, 31% of autistic poor readers, and 33% of autistic good readers were outliers on the motion task (10% control outliers) while 17% of dyslexics, 23% of autistic poor readers, and 22% of autistic good readers were outliers on the form task (5% control outliers). However, 3 autistic children (1 good reader and 2 poor readers) had poor performance far out of the range of either the dyslexics or controls on the motion task. These children appeared to have such severe problems with motion detection that they could hardly perform the task at all, whilst only one of these children also had problems with form coherence detection.

The two visual tasks were not combined to create a single visual factor as they are believed to tap different aspects of visual processing.

Table 4. *Visual test means*

			Autistic	
	Control	*Dyslexic*	*Good reader*	*Poor reader*
Motion	10.17	10.53	18.78	15.91
	(4.28)	(3.30)	(15.66)	(16.13)
Form	27.08	27.58	29.52	32.39
	(4.10)	(7.43)	(3.10)	(9.90)

Note: All comparisons are nonsignificant. Test scores are coherence thresholds (low scores indicate good performance). Standard deviations in parentheses.

Motor tasks

The data from all the motor tasks were found to have distributions significantly different from the normal distribution (Shapiro–Wilk's test) so nonparametric analysis was required (Kruskal–Wallis H-test, approximated to the χ^2 distribution). Group differences were found on all four motor tests, although the balance tasks were more marginal than the manual dexterity tasks (bead threading, $\chi^2 = 12.711$, $p = .005$; finger & thumb, $\chi^2 = 17.075$, $p = .001$; heel-to-toe, $\chi^2 = 9.777$, $p = .021$; stork balance, $\chi^2 = 10.295$, $p = .016$). The dyslexics were marginally worse than controls only at the stork balance task ($p = .030$) while the autistic poor readers were marginally worse at both balance tasks (heel-to-toe, $p = .054$; stork balance, $p = .024$), and the autistic good readers were marginally worse at the finger and thumb and the heel-to-toe task (finger and thumb, $p = .012$; heel-to-toe, $p = .012$; see Table 5). A motor variable, accounting for both nonverbal IQ and age, was produced by combining scores over all these tasks, and a group difference was found on this factor, $F(3, 63) = 6.43$, $p = .001$, with both autistic groups performing worse than controls (good readers, $p < .001$, poor readers, $p = .005$). A total of 17% of dyslexics, 38% of autistic poor readers, and 56% of autistic good readers were found to be outliers (no control outliers). Again, a number of the autistic children had poor performance well outside the range of the dyslexics and controls.

Table 5. *Motor test means*

			Autistic	
	Control	*Dyslexic*	*Good reader*	*Poor reader*
Bead threading[a]**	55.53 (6.84)	54.50 (13.14)	78.84 (24.83)	61.85 (11.88)
Finger & thumb[a]**	8.70 (2.95)	8.33 (1.57)	26.20* (18.33)	19.98 (17.42)
Heel-to-toe[b]*	15.00 (0.00)	13.57 (3.60)	10.89* (5.16)	12.69 (4.52)
Stork balance[a,c]*	19.33 (2.28)	16.88* (5.20)	17.37 (5.80)	13.72* (6.58)
Motor factor**	0.00 (1.00)	−0.47 (1.60)	−3.47 (3.98)	−2.27 (3.46)

Note: Low scores in bead threading and finger and thumb indicate good performance; high scores in heel-to-toe and stork balance indicate good performance. Motor factor scores are based on averaged z-scores. Stars next to the test name indicate an overall group difference. Stars within the table indicate differences between that group and the control group. Standard deviations in parentheses.

[a]In s. [b]No. of steps, 15 max. [c]20 max.

$^{*}p < .05$; $^{**}p < .01$; $^{***}p < .001$.

Correlates of reading ability

In order to study the extent to which the different impairments are able to predict literacy ability, correlations between the corrected summary variables were performed. As the sensorimotor variables were not normally distributed, they were first rank ordered. As can be seen from Figure 1, phonology is a good predictor of literacy skill, as a strong correlation was found between the literacy and phonology factors in the whole sample ($r = .716$, $p < .001$), as well as within each of the groups (control, $r = .484$, $p = .031$; dyslexic, $r = .851$, $p = .004$; autistic poor readers, $r = .650$, $p = .016$; autistic good readers, $r = .670$, $p = .048$). Other marginal correlations were found in the whole sample between the phonology factor and visual motion ($r = .265$, $p = .034$) and motor ($r = .283$, $p = .022$) factors, as well as between the auditory, visual motion, and motor factors (auditory and visual, $r = .337$, $p = .007$; auditory and motor, $r = .461$, $p < .001$; visual and motor, $r = .379$, $p = .002$). However, these correlations only held within the control group. No other correlations were significant.

A multiple linear step-wise regression was performed to investigate which factors, from phonology, auditory, visual motion, and motor, could predict the variance in literacy performance (sensorimotor factors rank ordered). The phonology factor accounted for 52% of the variance in literacy performance, $F(1, 61) = 67.2$, $p < .001$, whilst none of the other factors was found to be a significant predictor of literacy. This was also found to be true when regressions were performed for each group separately. Literacy skill can therefore be explained in the majority of cases by phonological skill alone, after accounting for age and general ability.

Occurrence of impairments

Figure 2 shows all the children grouped by their deviant performance on different tasks. In total, 48% of dyslexics, 54% of autistic poor readers, and 67% of autistic good readers had one or more sensorimotor impairments, as did 15% of controls. Although the autistic good readers performed much better than the dyslexics on the literacy factor, $t(30) = 8.347$, $p < .001$, and marginally so on the phonology factor, $t(30) = 2.087$, $p = .045$, they did not differ on the auditory, $t(29) = 1.298$, and visual motion, $t(8.3) = 1.496$, factors and were marginally worse than the dyslexics on the motor factor, $t(9.0) = 2.197$, $p = .056$. Similarly, although autistic good readers performed better than autistic poor readers on the literacy factor, $t(20) = 6.288$, $p < .001$, and marginally better on the phonology factor, $t(20) = 1.860$, $p = .078$, they did not differ on any sensorimotor factor ($t < 0.8$). Furthermore, those dyslexics with sensorimotor impairments were no worse than those without

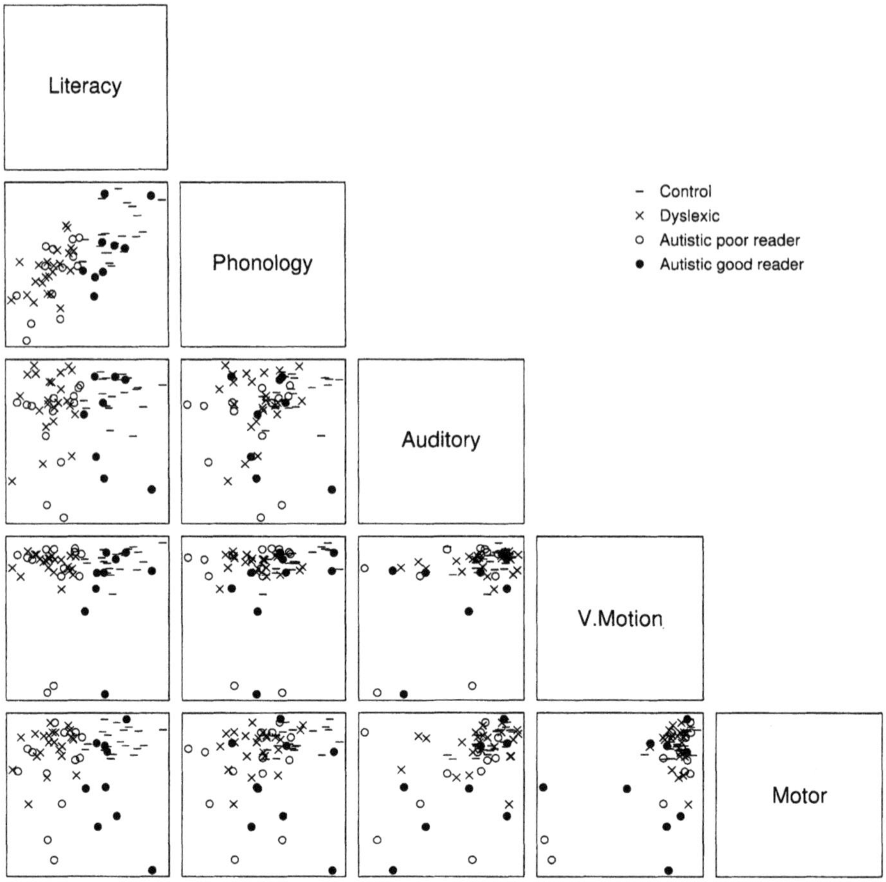

Figure 1. *Summary of correlations between literacy, phonology, auditory, visual motion, and motor factors. Good scores for each plot are in the top right corner, poor scores in the bottom left. The x-axis is denoted by the label above for each plot, the y-axis by the label to the right. The axes' scales are determined by the range of values present in the data set; the range within the control group should therefore be used as a basis for comparison to determine normal performance on each measure.*

on both phonology and literacy measures: literacy, $t(15.2) = 0.888$; phonology, $t(21) = 0.982$. Together, these comparisons suggest that differences in reading ability are not paralleled by differences in sensorimotor function.

Double dissociations

Figure 2 indicates not only that there is no relationship between sensorimotor and reading impairments, but also that there are complete double dissociations between the two domains. Indeed, it can be seen that 6 autistic children (as well as 3 controls) achieve normal reading skills despite one or several sensorimotor impairments.[5] Even with a full combination of visual, auditory, and motor impairments, 2 autistic children manage to read normally. This contrasts with 12 dyslexics who have a clear reading deficit without any evidence of sensorimotor impairment. For a more detailed illustration of

[5] Furthermore, of the 3 autistic and 2 control children who were outliers on the visual motion task but had good reading, only 1 of the autistic children was also an outlier on the control form task indicating that, for the majority, their sensorimotor impairments were specific rather than attributable to more general factors such as attention.

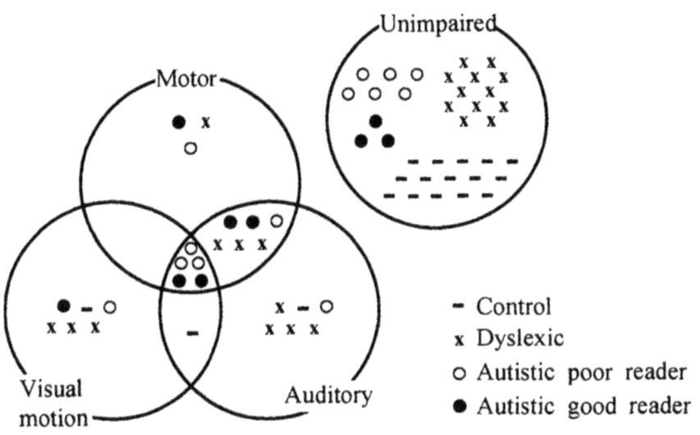

Figure 2. *Classification of all children by modality of impairment, when impairment is defined as more than 1.65 standard deviations below the control mean.*

these double dissociations, individual profiles of some of the most contrasted cases are provided in Figure 3.

The double dissociation logic can be criticized for setting arbitrary deviance thresholds and artificially splitting the subjects into impaired and intact categories, while there might be little difference between subjects whose scores are just above or below the thresholds. However, examination of Figure 3 shows that the present double dissociations are no artefact of deviance thresholds. Indeed, most subjects shown here have scores well beyond the thresholds chosen: Several severe dyslexics show average or superior performance in all sensorimotor domains (e.g., AF, RE, and TS), while several autistic good readers have extremely poor sensorimotor skills (indeed poorer than the poorest dyslexics; e.g., AR, IH, and JM). Furthermore the numbers involved here on each side of the dissociation (6 vs. 12) make it difficult to dismiss such cases as unrepresentative exceptions.

Discussion

Previous research has shown that dyslexics, as a group, present a variety of sensory and/or motor impairments (e.g., Nicolson et al., 2001; Stein & Walsh, 1997). Such evidence has been used to propose that the underlying cause of developmental dyslexia is to be found in general sensorimotor impairments (for instance, general magnocellular or cerebellar dysfunction) rather than in a specific phonological deficit. However, only a fraction of dyslexics seem to be affected by such sensorimotor impairments, as demonstrated by recent studies (Ramus et al., 2003; White et al., in press) and meta-analyses of the published literature (Ramus, 2003). It therefore seems that sensorimotor impairments can be the cause of reading disability in at best a subset of dyslexic children. But are they, really?

If they are, then one prediction is that all children who exhibit similar sensorimotor impairments should also be reading disabled. Building on previous research showing that at least a subset of autistic children has similar auditory, visual, and motor impairments, we have systematically investigated sensorimotor and reading impairments in matched groups of dyslexic, autistic, and control children.

We found that a subset of both dyslexic and autistic populations do indeed show sensorimotor impairments. Such impairments are rather more prevalent in the autistic than in the dyslexic population. However, sensorimotor impairments occurred in a pattern that was entirely independent of the occurrence of reading disability. Indeed, sensorimotor variables explained no variance in literacy. Neither dyslexics nor autistic poor readers showed more sensorimotor impairments than autistic good readers. Furthermore, many dyslexic and autistic children had neither sensory nor motor problems but still had poor literacy and phonology scores, indicating that sensorimotor deficits are not a necessary cause of reading impairment. Similarly, many autistic good readers had sensorimotor problems whilst displaying preserved literacy and phonological abilities, indicating that sensorimotor impairments are not sufficient to result in reading difficulties. These parallel findings of dyslexics without sensorimotor impairment, and autistic children without reading problems but with sensorimotor impairment, indicate that sensorimotor and reading impairments are doubly dissociable. Overall we find no relationship whatsoever between sensorimotor and reading impairments.

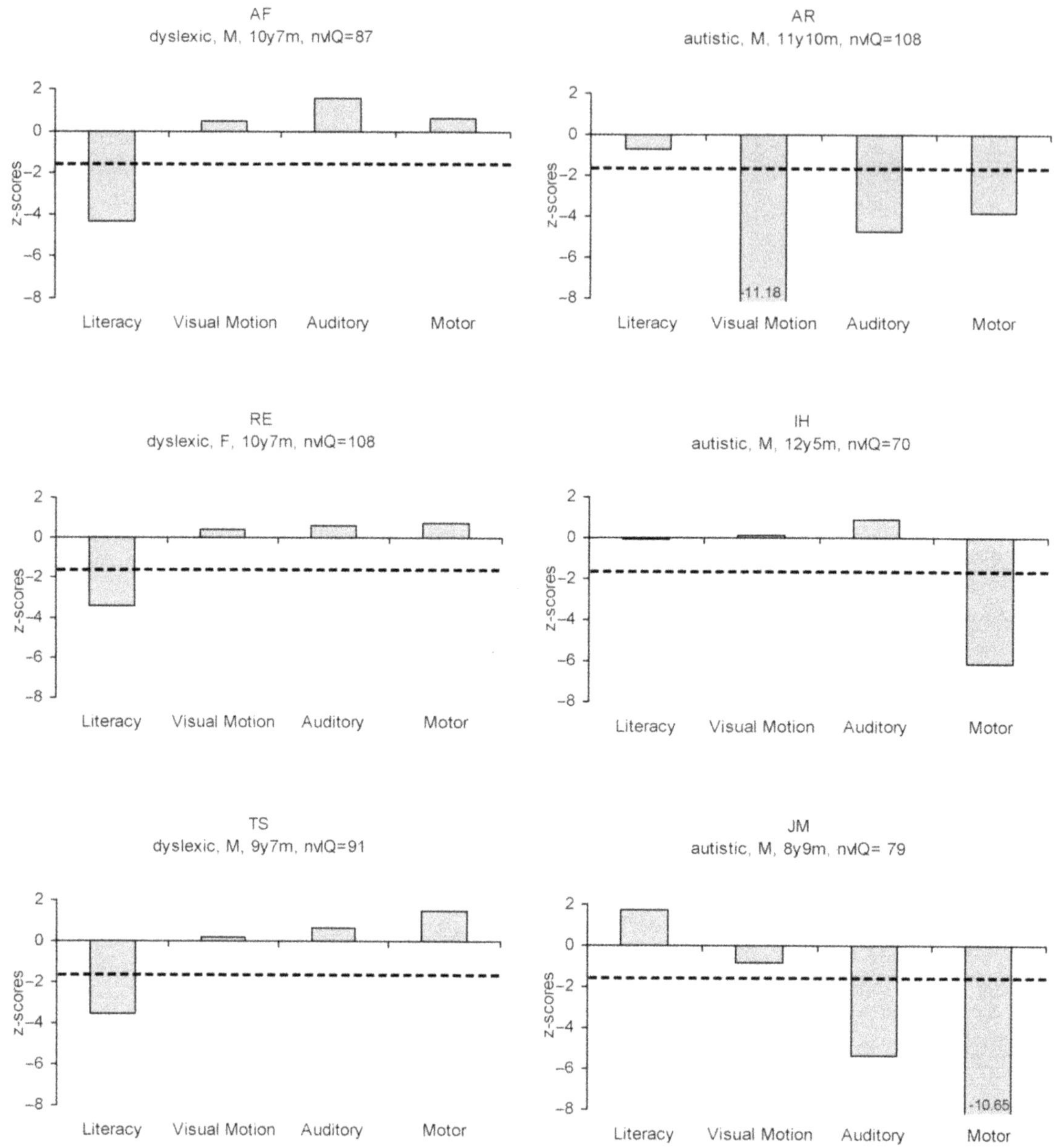

Figure 3. *Profiles for 6 participants illustrating the double dissociation between reading and sensorimotor impairments. The x-axis denotes z-scores based on the control group, and the dotted line indicates performance at 1.65 standard deviations below the control mean.*

While sensory and/or motor theories of dyslexia are sometimes presented as unifying theories explaining all cases (Stein & Walsh, 1997), more realistic versions of these theories acknowledge the possible existence of subtypes within the populations and claim to account for only some affected individuals (Tallal, 2004). In that case, our focusing on a few cases not affected by sensorimotor deficits might seem unfair and irrelevant to these theories. Yet even these weaker versions would predict that when a sensorimotor deficit of the specified type is present, it does cause a reading impairment. This prediction runs against our finding of cases with sensorimotor deficits but without reading impairment. That is, even accounting for different subtypes of dyslexia with different aetiology, the pattern of double dissociations that we have observed is generally inconsistent with sensorimotor theories.

Obviously, double dissociations should be interpreted more cautiously in developmental than in acquired disorders (Paterson, Brown, Gsödl, Johnson, & Karmiloff-Smith, 1999). The pattern of impairments may indeed change throughout development, so that the cross-sectional picture that we have taken here might not reflect the pattern of impairments at an earlier stage of development more relevant to language and reading acquisition. But what are the alternative interpretations of the present data? An interpretation consistent with a sensorimotor theory of dyslexia would need to assume: (a) that sensorimotor impairments are present in all dyslexics at birth, but recover in most of them before the time of testing; and (b) either that the sensorimotor impairments observed in autistic children are acquired at a stage when they do not impact on reading acquisition anymore, or that they are in fact of a different nature from those observed in dyslexic children, so that they do not have the same secondary effects on reading. This is certainly a possibility but in the absence of supportive evidence this does not appear to be the most parsimonious explanation.

How likely is it that sensorimotor impairments observed in autistic children are of a different nature from those observed in dyslexic children? It should be recalled that the tasks used here do not tap random aspects of sensorimotor function, but have been chosen precisely because of their presumed capacity to reveal deficits conducive to reading disability according to sensorimotor theories of dyslexia, and because dyslexics have been repeatedly shown to be poor at those tasks. Certainly there are several ways to fail a given task. In the case of autistic children, one might want to argue that they fail because of general intellectual disability, poor task comprehension, or poor executive function that might lead to an inability to concentrate on the sensorimotor tasks. Yet this would not predict the observed pattern, with only a subset of autistic children affected across the whole range of IQ scores and with selective impairments for certain tasks but not others (e.g., motion but not form detection). Furthermore this would beg the question of why those factors that might explain poor autistic performance in sensorimotor tasks would not affect reading ability in the same way.

Sensorimotor impairments may not be able by themselves to explain dyslexia or autism, but it is quite remarkable that they were much more prevalent in both the dyslexic and the autistic than in the control population. Why this is so remains unknown. One possibility is that, rather than being causes of reading (or any other specific cognitive) disability, sensorimotor impairments are more general nonspecific markers of neurodevelopmental disorders. This hypothesis is consistent with the model proposed by Ramus (2004), in which specific cognitive deficits (like dyslexics' phonological deficit) are caused by abnormalities in specific cortical areas, while sensorimotor disorders are secondary, occasional consequences of cortical abnormalities, regardless of their location (hence regardless of the nature of the cognitive deficit). Such a model would seem to be able to explain both the prevalence of sensorimotor impairments in all neurodevelopmental disorders and the absence of any reliable relationship between them and any specific cognitive deficit.

PrEview proof published online 24 February 2006

REFERENCES

Atkinson, J., King, J., Braddick, O., Nokes, L., Anker, S., & Braddick, F. (1997). A specific deficit of dorsal stream function in Williams' syndrome. *Neuroreport, 8*, 1919–1922.

Courchesne, E. (1997). Brainstem, cerebellar and limbic neuroanatomical abnormalities in autism. *Current Opinions in Neurobiology*, 7, 269–278.

Dow, R., & Moruzzi, G. (1958). *The physiology and pathology of the cerebellum.* Minneapolis, MN: University of Minnesota Press.

Fawcett, A., & Nicolson, R. (1996). *The Dyslexia Screening Test.* London: The Psychological Corporation.

Frederickson, N., Frith, U., & Reason, R. (1997). *Phonological Assessment Battery.* Windsor: NFER-Nelson.

Gepner, B., & Mestre, D. R. (2002). Brief report: Postural reactivity to fast visual motion differentiates autistic children from children with Asperger syndrome. *Journal of Autism and Developmental Disorders, 32,* 231–238.

Hallett, M., Lebiedowska, M. K., Thomas, S. L., Stanhope, S. J., Denckla, M. B., & Rumsey, J. (1993). Locomotion of autistic adults. *Archives of Neurology, 50,* 1304–1308.

Hansen, P. C., Stein, J. F., Orde, S. R., Winter, J. L., & Talcott, J. B. (2001). Are dyslexics' visual deficits limited to measures of dorsal stream function? *Neuroreport, 12,* 1527–1530.

Henderson, S., & Sugden, D. (1992). *The Movement Assessment Battery for Children.* Sidcup, UK: The Psychological Corporation.

Hill, E. L. (1998). A dyspraxic deficit in specific language impairment and developmental coordination disorder? Evidence from hand and arm movements. *Developmental Medicine and Child Neurology, 40,* 388–395.

Hill, E. L. (2001). Non-specific nature of specific language impairment: A review of the literature with regard to concomitant motor impairments. *International Journal of Language and Communication Disorders, 36,* 149–171.

Jones, W., Hesselink, J., Courchesne, E., Duncan, T., Matsuda, K., & Bellugi, U. (2002). Cerebellar abnormalities in infants and toddlers with Williams syndrome. *Developmental Medicine and Child Neurology, 44,* 688–694.

McCandliss, B. D., & Noble, K. G. (2003). The development of reading impairment: A cognitive neuroscience model. *Mental Retardation in Developmental Disabilities Research Reviews, 9,* 196–204.

Milne, E., Swettenham, J., Hansen, P., Campbell, R., Jeffries, H., & Plaisted, K. (2002). High motion coherence thresholds in children with autism. *Journal of Child Psychology and Psychiatry, 43,* 255–263.

Milne, E., White, S., Campbell, R., Swettenham, J., Hansen, P., & Ramus, F. (in press). Motion and form coherence detection in autistic spectrum disorder: Relationship to motor control and 2:4 digit ratio. *Journal of Autism and Developmental Disorders.*

Nicolson, R. I., Fawcett, A. J., & Dean, P. (2001). Dyslexia, development and the cerebellum. *Trends in Neurosciences, 24,* 515–516.

Noterdaeme, M., Mildenberger, K., Minow, F., & Amorosa, H. (2002). Evaluation of neuromotor deficits in children with autism and children with a specific speech and language disorder. *European Child and Adolescent Psychiatry, 11,* 219–225.

Oram Cardy, J. E., Flagg, E. J., Roberts, W., Brian, J., & Roberts, T. P. L. (2005). Magnetoencephalography identifies rapid temporal processing deficit in autism and language impairment. *Neuroreport, 16,* 329–332.

Paterson, S. J., Brown, J. H., Gsödl, M. K., Johnson, M. H., & Karmiloff-Smith, A. (1999). Cognitive modularity and genetic disorders. *Science, 286,* 2355–2358.

Paulesu, E., Demonet, J. F., Fazio, F., McCrory, E., Chanoine, V., Brunswick, N. et al. (2001). Dyslexia: Cultural diversity and biological unity. *Science, 291,* 2165–2167.

Ramus, F. (2003). Developmental dyslexia: Specific phonological deficit or general sensorimotor dysfunction? *Current Opinion in Neurobiology, 13,* 212–218.

Ramus, F. (2004). Neurobiology of dyslexia: A reinterpretation of the data. *Trends in Neurosciences, 27,* 720–726.

Ramus, F., Rosen, S., Dakin, S., Day, B. L., Castellote, J. M., White, S. et al. (2003). Theories of developmental dyslexia: Insights from a multiple case study of dyslexic adults. *Brain, 126,* 841–865.

Raven, J., Court, J., & Raven, J. (1988). *Raven's Standard Progressive Matrices.* London: J. C. Raven Ltd.

Rosen, S., & Manganari, E. (2001). Is there a relationship between speech and nonspeech auditory processing in children with dyslexia? *Journal of Speech and Language Hearing Research, 44,* 720–736.

Shaywitz, S. E., Shaywitz, B. A., Pugh, K. R., Fulbright, R. K., Constable, R. T., Mencl, W. E. et al. (1998). Functional disruption in the organization of the brain for reading in dyslexia. *Proceedings of the National Academy of Sciences USA, 95,* 2636–2641.

Snowling, M. J. (2000). *Dyslexia* (2nd ed.). Oxford, UK: Blackwell.

Spencer, J., O'Brien, J., Riggs, K., Braddick, O., Atkinson, J., & Wattam-Bell, J. (2000). Motion processing in autism: Evidence for a dorsal stream deficiency. *Neuroreport, 11*, 2765–2767.

Stein, J. (2001). The magnocellular theory of developmental dyslexia. *Dyslexia, 7*, 12–36.

Stein, J., & Walsh, V. (1997). To see but not to read; the magnocellular theory of dyslexia. *Trends in Neurosciences, 20*, 147–152.

Tallal, P. (2004). Improving language and literacy is a matter of time. *Nature Reviews Neuroscience, 5*, 721–728.

Tallal, P., & Piercy, M. (1973). Defects in non-verbal auditory perception in children with developmental aphasia. *Nature, 241*, 468–469.

Vellutino, F. R. (1979). *Dyslexia: Theory and research.* Cambridge, MA: MIT Press.

White, S., Milne, E., Rosen, S., Hansen, P. C., Swettenham, J., Frith, U. et al. (2006). The role of sensorimotor processing in dyslexia: A multiple case study of dyslexic children. *Developmental Science, 9*, 237–269.

Whitehouse, D., & Harris, J. C. (1984). Hyperlexia in infantile autism. *Journal of Autism and Developmental Disorders, 14*, 281–289.

Wilkinson, G. S. (1993). *The Wide Range Achievement Test 3.* Wilmington, DE: Wide Range.

Witton, C., Talcott, J., Hansen, P., Richardson, A., Griffiths, T., Rees, A. et al. (1998). Sensitivity to dynamic auditory and visual stimuli predicts nonword reading ability in both dyslexic and normal readers. *Current Biology, 8*, 176–178.

Wright, B. A., Lombardino, L. J, King, W. M., Puranik, C. S., Leonard, C. M., & Merzenich, M. M. (1997). Deficits in auditory temporal and spectral resolution in language-impaired children. *Nature, 387*, 176–178.

COGNITIVE NEUROPSYCHOLOGY, 2006, 23 (5), 762–788

Psychology Press
Taylor & Francis Group

Developmental amnesia: Fractionation of developing memory systems

Christine M. Temple and Paul Richardson
University of Essex, Colchester, Essex, UK

Study of the developmental amnesias utilizing a cognitive neuropsychological methodology has highlighted the dissociations that may occur between the development of components of memory. M.M., a new case of developmental amnesia, was identified after screening from the normal population on cognitive and memory measures. Retrospective investigation found that he was of low birthweight. M.M. had impaired semantic memory for knowledge of facts and words. There was impaired episodic memory for words and stories but intact episodic memory for visual designs and features. This forms a double dissociation with Dr S. (Temple, 1992), who had intact verbal but impaired visual episodic memory. M.M. also had impaired autobiographical episodic memory. Nevertheless, learning over repeated trials occurred, consistent with previous theorizing that learning is not simply the effect of recurrent episodic memory. Nor is it the same as establishing semantic memory, since for M.M. semantic memory is also impaired. Within reading, there was an impaired lexico-semantic system, elevated levels of homophone confusion, but intact phonological reading, consistent with surface dyslexia and raising issues about the interrelationship of the semantic system and literacy development. The results are compatible with discrete semi-independent components within memory development, whereby deficits are associated with residual normality, but there may also be an explicit relationship between the semantic memory system and both vocabulary and reading acquisition.

INTRODUCTION

Cognitive neuropsychology and development

The application of cognitive neuropsychology to the study of developmental and acquired disorder of cognition in childhood provides a framework within which a number of theoretical questions can be addressed (Temple, 1997a, 1997b). These include the issue of whether development involves the unfolding of modular semi-independent structures, which then cross-communicate, or whether during development there is such intrinsic interdependency that the identification of component processes and modular subunits is not viable. If development does involve the emergence of component structures, a further issue concerns the commonality of these structures across children and also whether they are comparable or distinct from the functional architectures described for adult cognitive processes. Even in a system of semi-independent components, there may nevertheless be specific explicit interrelationships in childhood, which are less evident in adulthood.

Correspondence should be addressed to Christine M. Temple, Developmental Neuropsychology Unit, Department of Psychology, University of Essex, Wivenhoe Park, Colchester, Essex, CO4 3SQ, UK (Email: tempc@essex.ac.uk).

http://www.psypress.com/cogneuropsychology

DOI:10.1080/02643290500538315

For example, impairment of the semantic system may have impact upon both memory and emerging language (Temple & Richardson, 2004). There is a further issue of whether any distinct component processes have specific anatomical substrates and whether these substrates resemble those implicated in the study of adults or are distinct anatomical regions active during development.

These issues have implications for how we understand the nature of development. Traditionally, development has been described as a single pathway of emerging skills, with a series of invariant stages. In contrast, a functional architecture of semi-independent component processes, some developing in parallel, enables more than one independent route or system to develop, creating the potential for individual differences in the order of development of differing skills and different emergent patterns of relative strength and weakness. If there is disorder in a single pathway system or one in which there is pervasive inter dependency, then there would be pervasive impact of the disorder throughout the developing system (Thomas & Karmiloff-Smith, 2002). Alternatively, a compo-nential system incorporating parallel processes could allow residual normality, such that unaffected component skills are indistinguishable from normal performance (Bishop, 1997; Clahsen, Ring, & Temple, 2004; Clahsen & Temple, 2003; Temple, 1997a, 1997b; Temple & Clahsen, 2002). Understanding the nature of development is also relevant for understanding what limitations there are there to developmental plasticity and vice versa. Can the brain adapt to disorder or do identifiable selective impairments remain?

Knowledge of cognitive systems in older populations may inform the structure of the protocol of investigations, which may also be of interest in the study of children with neuropsychological abnormalities. The consequent identified patterns of performance may then inform the nature of more detailed investigations. The cognitive neuropsychological framework provides a means of characterizing skills and abilities at one point in time, thereby providing a baseline for follow-up or developmental investigations. It also provides a structure for cross-task comparisons, which may enable identification of focal areas of deficit. The approach has been successfully applied in the areas of the developmental dyslexias (e.g., Castles & Coltheart, 1996; Pitchford & Funnell, 1999; Samuelsson, 2000; Stuart & Howard, 1995), developmental dysgraphias (e.g., Clahsen & Temple, 2003; Temple, 1985a; Temple, 1986), developmental dyscalculias (e.g., Sokol, Macaruso, & Gollan, 1994; Temple, 1991; Temple & Marriott, 1998; Temple & Sherwood, 2002), developmental prosopagnosias (e.g., Campbell, 1992; De Haan & Campbell, 1991; Duchaine, 2000; Duchaine, Nieminen-von Wendt, New, & Kulomaki, 2003a; Duchaine, Parker, & Nakayama, 2003b; Temple, 1992), developmental disorders of spatial ability (e.g., McCloskey et al., 1995), developmental disorders of executive skill (e.g., Ozonoff & Jensen, 1999; Romans, Roeltgen, Kushner, & Ross, 1997; Temple, Carney, & Mullarkey, 1996; Temple & Martin Sanfilippo, 2003), and some developmental disorders of language (e.g., Clahsen & Temple, 2003; Temple, 2002b; Van Hout, 1993). This paper addresses the emergence of cognitive neuropsychological studies of the developmental amnesias, also called developmental dysmnesias in some studies.

The term developmental amnesia has been employed in relation both to a specific developmental disorder, in similar fashion to developmental dyslexia and developmental dyscalculia, with no known underlying explicit lesion of the central nervous system (e.g., Casalini, Brizzolara, Cavallaro, & Cipriani, 1999; De Renzi & Lucchelli, 1990), and to a very early acquired disorder following prenatal or perinatal anoxic episode or infective disease (Vargha-Khadem, Gadian, & Mishkin, 2002; Vargha-Khadem et al., 1997). The common feature is that the disorder of memory is evident from the outset of cognitivc development, and there is no prior memory competence that is subsequently lost. It should also be noted that the term developmental amnesia has been used to encompass a more broad range of memory disorders in children than the classical acquired amnesia label does in adulthood. In acquired adult amnesia, there is a chronic impairment in episodic memory in the absence of semantic memory deficit affecting language or knowledge about the world, although episodic memories from early in life may be preserved (Baddeley & Wilson, 1986; Wilson & Baddeley, 1988). Amongst the studies of developmental amnesia, a comparable dissociation has been reported between semantic and episodic memory (Vargha-Khadem et al., 2002; Vargha-Khadem et al., 1997) but there are also cases, as detailed below, in which both semantic and episodic memory are affected (De Renzi & Lucchelli, 1990; Temple, 1997b) and indeed cases in which semantic memory is impaired, and episodic memory is intact (Temple & Richardson, 2004).

This paper highlights fractionation within the developing memory system and the implications for the structure and organization of the development of normal memory skills. A new case is presented of developmental amnesia, in which there is material-specific dissociation within episodic memory and an episodic memory impairment, which affect both recall of new factual episodes and also personal autobiographical episodic memory. Despite these impairments, learning across trials is intact.

Components of memory

In studies of adulthood, there has been a broad differentiation between different forms of memory, despite ongoing discussion concerning the relationship between these forms. Semantic memory involves memory for factual knowledge such as *Paris is the capital of France. The Eiffel Tower is in Paris.* Semantic memory is also involved in knowledge of word meanings. There remains debate concerning whether there is a single semantic system or multiple semantic systems.

Episodic memory, in the traditional Tulving (1985, 1972) use of the term, involved the evocation of autobiographical memory for a specific personal event located in time and space. Nowadays, the term is often used for recall for a specific episode of presented material, with less emphasis on personal experience. Thus, episodic memory is involved in a student's memory for the content of a lecture that they have just attended or a story or picture that they have just seen or heard. In principle, personal autobiographical episodic memory as in Tulving and episodic memory for a recently presented episode of novel facts and stimuli could be distinct processes. In recognition of this, the term autonoetic is sometimes used for the autobiographical memories, though it is not exclusively used in this way and may be used for episodic memories more broadly. Conway (2002) has unusually suggested that the issue be addressed by removing autobiographical memory from the memories covered by the term episodic, thereby removing the group of memories for which the term was originally invoked. In the current paper, the term episodic is used more conventionally to encompass both Tulving's (1985, 1972) autobiographical episodic memories and memory for unique laboratory-based episodes of novel facts and stimuli. As is discussed below, episodic recall in studies of children with memory disorders have tended to emphasize laboratory-based memory for unique episodes of novel information. In contrast, the current paper addresses a case of developmental disorder in which both episodic memory for laboratory-based unique episodes of novel information and personal autobiographical episodic memory are impaired.

The issue of whether episodic memory is a single-component system or a multiple-component system has also been discussed in relation to recognition memory. Tulving's discussions (1985, 1972, 2002) emphasize an active recollective element to episodic memory, in which case recognition memory itself may not be a part of episodic memory. Indeed, since autobiographical events do not recur it is unclear what recognition memory would have meant in relation to an autobiographical episode in a prevideo era. In relation to current laboratory-based research exploring novel factual episodic memory, the paradigm of recognition memory has often been employed. Where recall is poor but recognition is good, interpretations in terms of retrieval difficulties within episodic memory have sometimes been discussed. However, recently the assignment of recognition memory as a form of episodic memory has been questioned.

Of significance in this discussion is the distinction between remembering and knowing. Remembering is seen as an active process like recall in which the event itself is remembered. Knowing may involve recognition without recollection of the specific event itself. In this sense since knowing does not involved the active recollection of a specific episode, it is not episodic as in the original Tulving formulation. According to Gardiner (2002), episodic memory is identified with autonoetic awareness, measured by a remember response, whereas semantic memory is identified with noetic awareness, measured by a know response. There is evidence of both of these processes contributing to recognition memory (Yonelinas, 2002). Further, it has been argued from animal studies that recognition memory need not depend upon episodic memory at all and may be based on a familiarity that is purely perceptual (Aggleton & Pearce, 2002; Morris, 2002). Tulving (2002) therefore suggests that successful performance on recognition memory may occur at episodic, semantic, or perceptual levels of memory. In the current study, recognition memory is therefore assessed separately from the assessment of semantic memory and the assessment of episodic memory.

It is important to emphasize that whilst an impairment in episodic memory is an impairment in memory for a unique novel event, whether autobiographical or laboratory based, it does not necessarily imply an impairment in learning new facts with repeated presentations. Tulving (2002) notes that considerable learning and memory can occur at a semantic (general knowledge) level without any intervention by episodic memory. Thus, young children can learn facts about the world long before they can recollect specific experiences from their past (Nelson, 1993; Perner & Ruffman, 1995). If learning was not possible in the face of episodic memory impairment, then there would not be cases of the capacity to learn new semantic knowledge in those with episodic impairment. Such cases have been described in both children and adults.

The acquisition of new semantic knowledge in terms of conceptual understanding of animals and birds is reported in two cases of severe episodic memory following a hippocampal tumour and in a case of craniopharyngioma (Guillery-Giraud, Martins, Parisot-Carbuccia, & Eustache, 2004). Acquisition of new semantic knowledge is also reported in a teenager with long-term episodic memory impairment following head injury (Maravita, Spadoni, Mazzuchi, & Parma, 1995). Broman, Rose, Hotson, and Casey (1997) also report learning of mathematical and logical skills in a child despite impairments of both semantic and episodic memory. As Tulving (2002) notes, adult-acquired amnesia patients with severely impaired or no functional episodic memory can also acquire new semantic information (Hamann & Squire, 1995; Kitchener, Hodges, & McCarthy, 1998; Tulving, Hayman, & Macdonald, 1991). Thus learning per se need not correlate with episodic memory ability. Multitrial learning may be possible despite impaired episodic memory. In the current paper, an exploration of such learning in the face of episodic impairment is included.

Procedural memory has received slightly varying definitions with a focus upon the delineation of the range of tasks that should be considered procedural. It includes memories for skills such as riding a bicycle, automated series such as reciting the number sequence or alphabet, and implicit memories for associations that cannot be explicitly recalled. Recent research has tended to focus on the explicit–implicit distinction more than skill acquisition. The term nondeclarative has also been employed for procedural processes encompassing skills, habits, and both classical and nonassociative learning (Squire, 1992a, 1992b).

Adult case descriptions of acquired memory impairments indicate the potential for dissociations between the memory systems discussed above following brain injury or disease. There is also an emerging picture in the developmental disorders of a range of developmental amnesias, within which these components may also be dissociable. Whilst acquired adult amnesia is a well-established syndrome, which has been investigated extensively, both acquired childhood amnesia and the developmental amnesias or dysmnesias have only become the focus of study relatively recently (Temple, 2002a). The total number of cases described in detail remains sufficiently limited, to enable listing individually. Yet the syndrome has considerable significance as a contribution to the debates concerning the extent of preformism, modularity, plasticity, and residual normality in the development of cognitive systems.

Impaired semantic memory and episodic memory

A series of cases of amnesia in children have been described in which both semantic and episodic memory were impaired. Acquired amnesia in childhood was reported by Ostergaard (1987) in a 10-year-old child, C.C., who had sustained an episode of anoxia following water intoxication in the treatment of diabetic ketoacidosis. This resulted in bilateral hippocampal damage with greater severity in the left hemisphere. Both semantic and episodic memory were impaired. The impairment in semantic memory encompassed both semantic memory for facts and vocabulary, with the latter reflected in slow lexical decision and impaired semantic classification and verbal fluency. Episodic memory was impaired on immediate and delayed story and design recall and delayed free recall of single words. Reading and spelling were also somewhat impaired. The amnesia did not appear to affect procedural memory, and the dissociation in memory skills was therefore similar to that observed in classical adult acquired amnesia.

A further case, T.C., had acquired amnesia following acute encephalopathy, possibly as a result of herpes simplex encephalitis (Wood, Brown, & Felton, 1989; Wood, Ebert, & Kinsbourne, 1982). T.C. also had severely impaired semantic and episodic memory but nevertheless made some scholastic progress, albeit slow. Brainerd and Reyna (1992) argued that logical and mathematical skills are independent of memory, and, consistent with this view, Broman, Rose, Hotson, and Casey (1997) reported a case of acquired amnesia in childhood in which there was impaired semantic and episodic memory, yet mathematical and logical skills had developed. Receptive vocabulary, naming, and literacy were, however, impaired in this case. There was loss of volume in bilateral hippocampal and medial temporal areas, with no evidence of amygdala atrophy. Broman et al. (1997) argued that where there was impairment of the hippocampus and its circuitry, language development and skills would be affected in addition to memory.

Changes in the pattern of acquired amnesia in childhood with recovery were reported in a 15-year-old girl, V.T., who had a mild head injury (Maravita et al., 1995). Initially, there was impaired semantic memory and impaired episodic memory, but when reassessed 23 months later V.T. continued to have impaired episodic memory but semantic memory had improved. It appeared that she had partially recovered previously learnt material, as her acquisition of semantic knowledge was easier for material that she had been studying prior to her injury. Even so, her performance never reached the previous level of proficiency.

The first detailed case report of developmental amnesia was that of De Renzi and Lucchelli (1990) in a 22- year-old man, M.S., who had had memory difficulties since early childhood. M.S. was born early at 7 months of gestation with a birthweight of 2,500 g. The computerized tomographic (CT) scan was normal but an electroencephalogram (EEG) showed bilateral bursts of theta and delta waves with a left frontotemporal prevalence. Intelligence was good with a verbal IQ of 110 and a performance IQ of 111. Semantic memory and episodic memory were both impaired. Semantic memory for words, as reflected in vocabulary level, was normal, though difficulty was reported with complex names. There had been severe difficulty with the acquisition of reading and spelling, with reading remaining slow and laborious in adulthood. Procedural memory as reflected by knowledge of automated series such as the alphabet or months of the year was also impaired. A further case of developmental amnesia was reported by Maurer (1992). N.S. had a CT scan when she was 9 years old that revealed low-density areas in both temporal fossa indicating absence of the left temporal lobe and the pole and medial parts of the right temporal lobe (Maurer, 1992). The aetiology of the abnormality was thought to be a prenatal stroke. Semantic and episodic memory were impaired but procedural memory was intact.

In the case of developmental amnesia reported by Temple (1997b), the issue of potential linked effects in language was discussed. Julia, a 12-year-old girl, had memory difficulties and delayed language development early in preschool years. At the age of 6 years, temporal lobe epilepsy developed but the CT scan was normal. Intelligence assessment indicated that half of subtest scores were in the normal range but there was severe impairment in semantic memory for facts on the Information subtest of the Wechsler Intelligence Scale for Children–Revised (WISC-R; Wechsler, 1974) and in semantic knowledge of words on the Vocabulary subtest of the WISC-R (Wechsler, 1974). There was also severe anomia with naming skills at a 5-year-old level, which reflected impaired establishment of knowledge about words—that is, a semantic-representation anomia rather than merely retrieval difficulties (Temple, 1997b; Van Hout, 1993). Episodic memory for both verbal recall of stories and nonverbal recall of designs was impaired. Procedural memory as reflected by the recall of automated sequences such as the alphabet, days of the week, months of the year, and numbers 1–30 was intact.

Impaired episodic memory but intact semantic memory

In all of the cases of acquired childhood amnesia and developmental amnesia discussed above both semantic and episodic memory were impaired. The possibility of a dissociation between the development of these two systems has been raised in a series of papers, reporting cases where episodic memory is impaired but semantic memory is intact (Baddeley, Vargha-Khadem, & Mishkin, 2001; Gadian et al., 2000; Vargha-Khadem et al., 2002; Vargha-Khadem et al., 1997). These studies describe cases of amnesia following hypoxic-ischaemic episodes at or shortly after birth, causing bilateral hippocampal pathology with some extension to the putamen and thalamus, and a subsequent amnesia characterized by relatively intact semantic memory, language, and literacy skills but impaired episodic memory. The cases are significant as they indicate that the development of semantic memory is not dependent upon intact episodic memory. The cases also indicate, in contrast to the views of Broman et al. (1997), that hippocampal pathology need not impact upon the development of vocabulary and literacy skills. Vargha-Khadem et al. (1997) proposed that the sensory memory functions of the perirhinal and entorhinal cortices might be sufficient to support context-free semantic memories but not context-rich episodic memories for which hippocampal circuitry would be required. They proposed that for both semantic and episodic memory to be affected severely, the hippocampi and underlying cortices would both have to be damaged.

Brizzolara, Casalina, Montanaro, and Posteraro (2003) also described impairment of episodic memory and preservation of semantic memory following encephalopathy at the age of 6 years, with consequent bilateral hippocampal, insula, thalamus, ponto-mesencephalic, and temporal lobe pathology. Guillery-Girard et al. (2004) described a similar dissociation in a case of craniopharyngioma and in a case of hippocampal tumour. As noted above, they successfully demonstrated that despite the severe impairment in episodic memory, the children not only recalled established semantic facts but were also able to learn new semantic knowledge in terms of conceptual understanding of animals and birds.

Isaacs et al. (2003) compared children at the age of 8–9 years, who had been preterm babies and who had hippocampal atrophy of up to 23%, and cases of developmental amnesia who had had birth hypoxia and had hippocampal atrophy of 27–56%. Whereas those with developmental amnesia were broadly impaired on episodic measures and were impaired on all delayed-recall measures, the preterm children were impaired only on immediate story recall and delayed route recall. Isaacs et al. (2003) suggested that the degree of hippocampal atrophy may be relevant to the extent of the episodic memory impairment.

Baddeley et al. (2001) investigated one of the cases of birth anoxia and episodic memory impairment in more detail. Significantly, they found that whilst the active recollective and recall processes of episodic memory were significantly impaired, recognition memory was not impaired. The child being studied did not "remember" but "knew". This indicated that a record of the memories was being encoded and stored but retrieval processes were significantly impaired. It was these retrieval processes for which it was suggested that the hippocampus is significant.

Intact episodic memory but impaired semantic memory

Recently, we have described a case of developmental amnesia in an 8-year-old child, C.L. (Temple & Richardson, 2004). C.L. was detected following screening in the normal school population, suggesting that developmental amnesia may be more pervasive than has been recognized previously (Temple & Richardson, 2004). C.L. had impaired semantic memory for both knowledge of facts and knowledge of words, including general world knowledge, knowledge of word meanings and superordinate knowledge of words. In contrast to the deficits in semantic memory, there were no impairments in episodic memory for verbal or visual material. The double dissociation between this case and the cases of Vargha-Khadem et al. (1997, 2002) suggested that semantic and episodic memory have the capacity to develop independently and supported both arguments for modularity in cognitive development (Temple, 1997a, 1997b) and arguments for residual normality in developmental disorders (Temple & Clahsen, 2002).

Reading for C.L. was characterized by poor lexico-semantic reading skills but intact phonological reading skills, indicating surface dyslexia (Coltheart, Masterson, Byng, Prior, & Riddoch, 1983; Coltheart, Rastle, Perry, Langdon, & Ziegler, 2001; Temple 1984, 1985b) and suggesting that semantic impairments may sometimes have pervasive effects upon semantic knowledge, vocabulary knowledge, and lexico-semantic processes in reading. Procedural memory was also impaired in this case. Knowledge of arithmetical facts was spared, consistent with adult studies suggesting that this form of semantic knowledge is distinct from other semantic facts (Butterworth, Cappelletti, & Kopelman, 2001; Cappelletti, Butterworth, & Kopelman, 2001) and indicating a material-specific effect to the intact semantic skills.

Dissociations between episodic memory and procedural memory

C.L. had intact episodic memory but had impaired procedural memory, on a mirror drawing task of a star (Temple & Richardson, 2004). The reverse dissociation has been described in pediatric cancer patients who have been given midazolam for conscious sedation during unpleasant procedures (Pringle, Dahlquist, & Eskenazi, 2003). The children were shown degraded pictures whilst under sedation. Subsequently they were shown further degraded pictures and asked either (a) whether they had they seen it before, an episodic question, or (b) what it was, with a number of increasingly less degraded versions to look at. The children demonstrated no memory for the episodic event of having seen the pictures before but did show evidence of implicit/procedural memory, taking fewer trials than before to recognize the stimulus.

Impaired visual episodic memory but intact verbal episodic memory

The case of Dr S. was described by Temple (1992). Dr S. had no known pathology and no explicit focal abnormality on magnetic resonance imaging (MRI) but had experienced difficulty with memory for visual material and faces, for as long as she could remember. Dr S. was highly intelligent with a verbal IQ of 136 and a performance IQ of 147. She had degrees in both medicine and psychology. Her semantic knowledge was extensive with no evidence of impairment. She also had a large vocabulary and thereby semantic knowledge of words. Her episodic memory for verbal material was also very good with detailed recall of new stories. Her visual perception was intact yet her episodic visual recall for designs was severely impaired. Recall of the Figure of Rey after a 3-min delay was at a severely impaired level on norms for a 30-min delay. Thus, Dr S. had severely impaired visual episodic memory but strongly developed episodic verbal memory.

Impaired verbal episodic memory but intact visual episodic memory

Material-specific effects within episodic memory are also evident in the case of developmental amnesia in a 9-year-old girl, O.N. (Casalini et al., 1999). O.N. had no neurological symptoms, but her father had similar difficulties. She had poor semantic memory for facts and words and had difficulties in naming, which affected her spontaneous speech. Her verbal episodic memory was also poor, with difficulty in learning new verbal material; however, nonverbal memory and learning were relatively good, indicating a modality-specific episodic impairment.

The number of case reports of developmental amnesia is expanding but to date is relatively limited (Temple, 2002a). This may be because the syndrome is rare. Another possibility is that there are larger numbers of children with developmental amnesia who fail to be identified. In pursuit of this issue, normal children attending normal schools were screened to determine whether unidentified children of normal intelligence with specific impairments of memory could be detected. One case identified by this means, with impairment of semantic but not episodic memory, was reported by Temple and Richardson (2004). A second case with impairment of both semantic and episodic memory is reported below.

The study aimed to address the development of semantic and episodic memory as well as learning and literacy in the screened case of amnesia to determine whether there was pervasive impairment of semantic and episodic memory or whether there were dissociations within the development of semantic and episodic memory systems, supporting multiple components within these systems and the degree of interdependence between these systems and vocabulary, literacy, and learning.

The study explored semantic memory for general knowledge facts, knowledge of words, and personal autobiographical semantic facts. It also explored episodic memory, in terms of verbal recall of unique episodes of words and stories, visual recall of unique episodes of patterns and visual features of pictures, and personal autobiographical episodic memory. It explored recognition memory, for which there may be semantic, episodic, and perceptual bases (Tulving, 2002). The study reports impaired semantic memory. There is also impaired memory for unique episodes of words and stories, impaired personal autobiographical episodic memory, and impaired behavioural day-to day episodic memory. In contrast, episodic memory for unique episodes of visually presented information is intact. The study also addressed the pattern of development of vocabulary knowledge and literacy skills in a child who develops such linguistic skills in the context of semantic and verbal episodic memory impairment. Finally, it addressed learning with repeated presentations of both visual and verbal material. The results are relevant to current debates concerning modularity in skill development, the organization of memory systems in development, and the structure of memory more broadly.

METHOD

Participants

The screened children were 239 eight- to nine-year-old children. Details of the screening and selection criteria are given in Temple and Richardson (2004). A summary is provided here. The screening battery involved three tasks. An estimate of general intelligence was derived from administering alternate items from Ravens Standard Progressive Matrices, from which a prorated score was calculated (Raven, 1998). A measure of semantic memory for established facts was derived from the Information subtest of the Wechsler Intelligence Scales for Children (WISC-III UK; Wechsler, 1992). A measure of episodic memory for recently encoded information was derived from a modification of the Rey Auditory–Verbal Learning Task (Rey, 1964). Parental consent was obtained. Children were administered the screening battery at their schools, with group testing within classes. Within each age group, for each task, impaired performance was defined as performance below the 5th centile, and normal average performance was defined as being between one standard deviation above and one standard deviation below the mean. Specific memory impairment was defined as normal average intelligence with impaired performance on at least one of the two memory tasks. One such child, M.M., with specific memory impairment was selected for further study.

M.M.: Case history

Retrospective examination of medical notes indicated that birth was early at 32 weeks, and birthweight was 2.29 kg. M.M. had Apgars at birth of 7 at 1 minute and 10 at 5 minutes; however, oxygen was required for 24 hours. There was also mild hyaline membrane disease. Developmental milestones were generally achieved slowly: walking at 18 months and talking at around 2 years.

M.M. attended a mainstream primary school. Grades tended to be below the class average, and parents noted some problems with reading and writing. He had previously been assessed for extra teaching assistance in the classroom but his parents were informed that his difficulties were not sufficient to warrant this support.

M.M. was 9 years 8 months at the time of investigation. He had normal average intelligence, with a prorated IQ from Ravens Progressive Matrices (Raven, 1998) of 103.

Typically developing controls

The typically developing control group (TD) was selected from age-matched, screened children of normal intelligence whose memory screening scores were normal and whose parents agreed that they could participate in a more detailed study. There were 11 eight- to nine-year-old children in the TD group. All of the TD children were reported by parents to have reached developmental milestones within normal limits. Parents reported no significant difficulties in school in relation to reading, writing, or memory. None had extra classroom assistance. The TD group had a mean age of 8.98 years ($SD = 0.35$) and a mean prorated IQ from Ravens Progressive Matrices (Raven, 1998) of 105.45 ($SD = 6.50$).

Semantic memory tasks

Semantic knowledge of facts

General knowledge of semantic facts

1. The Information subtest of the Wechsler Intelligence Scales for Children (WISC-III UK; Wechsler, 1992) consists of a series of general knowledge questions of increasing difficulty. Scores were scaled for age. This task formed one of the population screening measures.
2. A series of 75 general knowledge questions was adapted from the Trivia Quiz book (Henderson Publishing, 1995). If the correct answer was not given, then the child was asked to select the correct answer from three forced-choice alternatives.

Knowledge of arithmetical facts. The digits 2, 3, and 5 were paired with the numbers 1–10. Each of the pairs was randomly presented orally to the child as an addition, subtraction, and multiplication question, with 30 questions for each procedure. For division, the digits 2, 3, and 5 were paired with those numbers 1–10 that could be divided exactly by these digits to generate 10 questions. Thus, there were 100 questions in total.

Semantic knowledge of words

Lexical decision. The Spot-the-Word test from the Speed and Comprehension of Language Processing Test (SCOLP; Baddeley, Emslie, & Nimmo-Smith, 1993a, 1993b) requires the child to make a lexical decision for 40 spoken pairs of word and nonwords.

Receptive vocabulary. In a subtest of the Psycholinguistic Assessment of Language Processing and Aphasia (PALPA; Kay, Lesser, & Coltheart, 1992) the child heard a series of 40 spoken names and for each item had to select the matching picture from an array of five items. The distractor items were closely or distantly semantically related to the target.

Conceptual organization. Forty items based on the PALPA (Kay et al., 1992) were divided into six categories of which three were living things (animals, fruit, and vegetables), and three were nonliving things (tools, furniture, and vehicles). The task was based on a questionnaire designed by Laiacona, Barbarotto, and Capitani (1993). Items were presented in a standardized random order. The name of the item was spoken aloud, and then the child was asked six questions relating to superordinate classes or subordinate features. For each question, the child had to select the correct response from three alternatives. For example, for the item apple, the General Superordinate question was "Is it an object, an animal, or a plant?" The Subordinate: Comparison of Perceptual Attributes question was "Is it bigger, smaller or the same size as a cherry?" Further examples are given in Temple and Richardson (2004).

Semantic verification. This task is from the SCOLP (Baddeley et al., 1993a, 1993b). Participants judged the truth of verbally presented statements—for example, "Figs are people", "Lettuce can be eaten". The responses were recorded for accuracy within a 120-s time limit. There were 90 items in total.

Oral fluency. Two conditions were used: semantic and phonemic. In the first, the child was given a designated category and had to generate items from that category, within a 60-s time limit. This was repeated for three categories: animals, musical instruments, and food (Isaacs & Kennie, 1973)

For comparison, a nonsemantic task of phonemic fluency was also given. In the phonemic condition, the child was given a letter and had to generate words beginning with that letter within a 60-s time limit. They were not allowed to provide derivatives of words previously given. This was repeated for three letters: F, A, and S (Gaddes & Crockett, 1975).

Episodic memory tasks

Recall of a specific verbal event

Single-word recall

1. The Rey Auditory–Verbal Learning Task (Rey, 1964) was given in a modified form, in which 20 words were read once to the child for immediate written recall. This task formed one of the population screening measures.
2. The 16 words from the initial trial of the verbal learning subtest of the Wide Range Assessment of Memory and Learning (WRAML; Sheslow & Adams, 1990) were read aloud for immediate oral recall.
3. At least one month after (1), The Rey Auditory–Verbal Learning Task (Rey, 1964) was given again in a modified form in which 20 words were read aloud once as a distractor item. The children were told not to learn the words. Ten minutes later they were asked as a surprise to recall orally as many of the words as possible.

Story recall. The Story Memory subtest from the WRAML was used (Sheslow & Adams, 1990). Story B was read to the child who then had to repeat back as much as they could remember, trying to use the same phrases. Delayed recall of both Story B and Story C was requested after half an hour.

Recall of a specific visual event

Design recall. The Design Memory subtest from the WRAML was used (Sheslow & Adams, 1990). The child was shown one of four line drawings of a design for 5 s. The drawing was then removed, followed by a 10-s delay, and then the child had to draw the design. The procedure was repeated for the three further designs.

Picture feature recall. The Picture Memory subtest from the WRAML was used (Sheslow & Adams, 1990). The child was shown a picture of a scene for 10 s and was then shown a picture of a similar scene but with multiple small changes, involving addition of features, deletion of features, or substitution of features. The child had to spot the changes and identify with a circle the areas of the picture where something had disappeared, altered, or been added to. Each child was tested with four scenes. This task did not require the child to draw and therefore did not have the overt constructional component that was required in the design section. On the other hand, it did not require the child simply to recognize the original stimulus but to identify where changes had taken place within the original picture. Thus, overt recall of features of the design was required for successful execution of the task.

Personal semantic and episodic autobiographical memory

Recall of episodes in earlier life. The Autobiographical Memory Interview (AMI; Kopelman, Wilson, & Baddeley, 1989) is a semi-structured interview that objectively measures the "personal semantic" and "autobiographical" episodic knowledge of participants. The first component assesses the recall of facts from personal history (e.g., "What was the name of your first school?"); the latter assesses recall of specific events and incidents from their own history (e.g., "Tell me about your first day at school"). Each component from the AMI assesses personal memories across three broad time bands: childhood, early adult life, and recent events.

The "Childhood" section of the AMI test was given, which addresses two stages of childhood: infancy (0 to 5 years) and later childhood (5 to 11 years). In order to prevent a ceiling effect on scores, the AMI was modified with additional questions being added to both stages. The potential scores for personal semantic and autobiographical questions were raised from 13 to 24 and 6 to 18, respectively. The veracity of answers was corroborated against those of parents/guardians.

Behavioural episodic memory. Sunderland, Harris, and Baddeley's (1983) questionnaire-based assessment of memory performance is based on a list of different types of error: errors that are wide ranging, those that are likely to occur, and those that are suggestive of cognitive difficulties. It was presented in the form of an interview to a parent and was scored in the standard way. Each item was read aloud and was rated by the parent for frequency of occurrence over the past few weeks. The answers were rated on a 5-point scale, ranging from "several times a day" to "never". Some items relied more on the participants having been exposed to irregularly occurring events (such as meeting someone for the first time). For these items, another 5-point scale was used, indicating the proportion of situations that had resulted in a memory failure ranging from "on every occasion" to "never".

A total of 20 items within the questionnaire were identified that addressed episodic memory: for example, "Forgets something told yesterday or a couple of days ago", "Forgets to pass on important message/information", "Forgets what they did yesterday/confuses events", "Unable to remember name of someone met for first time recently". A behavioural episodic memory score was calculated for these 20 items alone.

The full questionnaire is based on a list of 35 different types of error. This list of items was additionally categorized into five headings relating to the context of the difficulty—verbal, reading and writing, faces and places, activities, and learning new things—which were then analysed individually.

Recognition memory

Verbal recognition memory
Immediate single word recognition. The Recognition Memory Test was used (Warrington, 1984). The child was shown 50 written words at a rate of approximately one per 3 s and for each had to say whether it was pleasant or unpleasant. The child was then immediately presented with 50 pairs of words and had to select from each pair the word that had been seen before.

Delayed story recognition. The Story Memory Recognition subtest from the WRAML was used in assessing immediate and delayed recall as previously (Sheslow & Adams, 1990). After the delayed recall, which occurred half an hour after initial presentation, the child was asked forced-choice, recognition memory questions about details of the story. There were 30 questions, with three alternative answers given for each.

Visual recognition memory
Immediate face recognition. The Warrington Recognition Memory Battery was used (WRMB, Warrington, 1984). The child was shown 50 black and white photographs of faces at a rate of approximately one per 3 s and for each had to say whether it was pleasant or unpleasant. The child was then immediately presented with 50 pairs of faces and had to select from each pair the face that had been seen before.

Procedural memory

Mirror drawing
A mirror drawing task was used in which the child saw a picture of a star inside another star and had to draw a line between the two stars. They were only able to draw the line via the stars' reflections in a mirror. Three trials were given in each of two test sessions. The error score was the number of times the child's pen crossed one of the stars in the picture.

Behavioural procedural memory
Sunderland et al.'s (1983) questionnaire contained a question that related to behavioural procedural memory: "Unable to pick up a new skill/game/gadget after one or two practices." M.M.'s parent's rating of this item was compared to rating of this item by the parents of children in the TD group.

Reading

A series of items were presented in written form for reading aloud:

1. The Schonell Graded Word Reading Test (Schonell & Schonell, 1956).
2. The Graded Nonword Reading Test (Snowling, Stothard, & McLean, 1996).
3. The stimulus list of Behrmann and Bub (1992), consisting of 60 regular and 60 irregular words, each composed of 10 items from six frequency bands.
4. A homophonic word list composed of 20 pairs of homophones (Temple, 1984). The 40 items were randomly ordered. After trying to read each word aloud the child was asked what each word meant.
5. Marshall's Morphological List (unpublished), containing 96 items, which were base lexical items or derived or inflectional forms.
6. As a measure of text reading, the Neale Analysis of Reading Ability was also given (Neale, Christophers, & Whetton, 1989).

Learning with repeated presentation

Visual learning of locations
The Visual Learning subtest from the WRAML was used (Sheslow & Adams, 1990). The child was shown the locations of 14 coloured designs on a board, which were then hidden under covers. They were then shown a picture of a design and asked to point to its location on the board. If the child was correct, the cover was removed and if the child was incorrect the correct location was shown. There were four trials.

Verbal learning of a set of words
In the Selective Reminding Memory Test, adapted from the Rey Auditory–Verbal Learning test, the child was read a list of 15 words and then had to remember as many as possible (Rey, 1964). After each trial, the child was told the words that they had missed in that trial. There were five trials.

Visual learning of paired associates
This subtest is from the old Wechsler Memory Scale-R (WMS-R; Wechsler, 1987). It is not in the more recent revised WMS-III (Wechsler, 1997). Six abstract line drawings were each paired with a colour. Each pair was shown to the child. Then the drawings were shown without their colour pair, and the child had to indicate the associated colour. There were six trials.

Verbal learning of paired associates
This subtest is also from the WMS-R (Wechsler, 1987), and it is retained within the WMS-III (Wechsler, 1997). There were four pairs of words for which there was an established semantic relationship and four pairs that were unrelated. The child was read the series of pairs and was then presented with one word from each pair and was asked to produce the associated word. There were six trials.

RESULTS

The data were analysed using the t tests designed by Crawford and Howell (1998) for the analysis of single case studies in neuropsychology. Performance was classified as impaired if it differed significantly from the TD group on these tests or if it was below the TD group range. Given the predicted direction of inferior performance by M.M., tests were one-tailed.

Semantic memory

The means and standard deviations for results in this section are given in Table 1.

Semantic knowledge of facts
General knowledge of facts. M.M. was significantly impaired in comparison to the TD group in general knowledge of facts on the Information subtest of the WISC-III, $t = 5.67$, $p < .0001$. M.M. was also significantly impaired in the recall of general knowledge of facts on the Quiz, $t = 1.97$, $p < .04$, on which he also scored below the TD range. On the combined total for free recall and forced-choice recall on the Quiz, M.M. was again significantly poorer than controls, $t = 3.90$, $p < .002$, and below the control range.

Table 1. *Semantic memory results: Knowledge of facts and knowledge of words*

Test	*M.M.*	*TD*[a]	*Memory*
Semantic knowledge of facts			
Information subtest (WISC-III)	3*	10.64 (1.29)	impaired
Quiz—recall correct	17*	33.18 (7.86)	impaired
Quiz—recall + forced choice correct	35*	54.73 (4.84)	impaired
Total arithmetical facts	75*	96.4 (3.28)	impaired
Semantic knowledge of words			impaired
Lexical decision	14*	29.73 (3.52)	impaired
Receptive vocabulary	37*	39 (0.89)	impaired
Conceptual organization	29.6*	35.43 (3.18)	impaired
Semantic verification	26	33.9 (4.86)	$t = 1.56$; $p = .07$
Semantic fluency	26*	45.63 (6.15)	impaired
Comparison task			
Phonemic fluency	21	18.01 (3.86)	intact

[a]Mean (standard deviations in parentheses).
*Statistically significant, see text.

Arithmetical facts. M.M. was significantly impaired in comparison to controls on knowledge of arithmetical facts for addition, subtraction, multiplication, and division, and he was significantly impaired on the total number of items correct out of 100, $t = 6.25$, $p < .0001$. His scores were also below the control range.

Semantic knowledge of words

Lexical decision. The scores indicate how many words, out of 50 pairings of words and nonwords, were identified correctly. M.M. identified significantly fewer correctly than the TD group, $t = 4.28$, $p < .001$, and performed below the control range.

Receptive vocabulary. The scores indicate the number of correctly identified target pictures in response to the spoken words. M.M. was significantly impaired in comparison to the TD group, $t = 2.15$, $p < .03$.

Conceptual organization. M.M. scored below the control level on each of the six types of question relating to superordinates or subordinates. Performance averaged across the categories revealed significantly poorer performance by M.M. than by the TD group, $t = 1.78$, $p < .05$.

Semantic verification. The scores indicate how many statements were correctly identified as either true or not within the time limit of 2 min. M.M.'s performance was nonsignificant but with a trend towards significant impairment, $t = 1.56$, $p = .07$.

Semantic fluency. M.M.'s performance on the oral fluency tasks is illustrated in Figure 1. M.M. generated significantly fewer items than the TD group on the total of the three semantic categories, $t = 3.06$, $p < .006$, and performed below the TD range; however, performance did not differ from the TD group on the comparison task of phonemic fluency. The total performance on phonemic fluency across the three trials was at a normal level, $t = 0.74$, $p = .24$.

Given that there were 10 comparisons in this section, for the tasks whose data are presented in Table 1, a single significant result might have

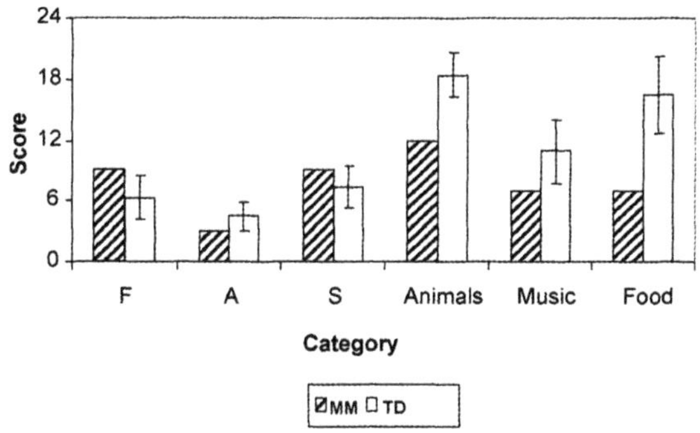

Figure 1. *Phonemic and semantic oral fluency scores.*

been attributable to a chance occurrence; however, there were 9 comparisons related to semantic memory scores of which 8 were significant, and 1 was borderline. The only task, relating to the data in Table 1, that was robustly nonsignificant was also the only task for which semantic knowledge was not required—that is, phonemic fluency.

Summary of semantic memory

The results indicate that M.M. had significantly impaired knowledge of semantic facts for both general knowledge and arithmetic. M.M. also demonstrated significantly impaired semantic knowledge of words as reflected by lexical decision, receptive vocabulary, ability to make conceptual judgements about words, and capacity to generate words from semantic cues. In contrast, the ability to generate words from phonemic cues was unimpaired.

Episodic memory

Recall of a unique verbal event

Table 2 gives the scores for the number of items correctly recalled on the verbal episodic measures. On single word recall, M.M. was significantly poorer than the TD group on the three tasks of immediate written recall of the modified Rey task, $t = 3.09$, $p < .006$, immediate oral recall of the WRAML list, $t = 2.50$, $p < .016$, and the delayed recall surprise oral Rey task, $t = 2.79$, $p < .009$. On immediate story recall, M.M. was significantly worse than the TD group on both

Table 2. *Episodic memory results: Verbal recall and visual recall*

Test		*M.M.*	*TD*[a]	*Memory*
Verbal episodic recall				
Immediate single-word recall	Written Rey	3*	8.00 (1.55)	impaired
	Oral WRAML	3*	5.82 (1.08)	impaired
Delayed single-word recall	Surprise oral Rey	1*	3.36 (0.81)	impaired
Immediate story recall	WRAML Story B	13*	17.20 (2.14)	impaired
	WRAML Story C	3*	14.40 (5.30)	impaired
	WRAML total	16*	31.60 (7.11)	impaired
Delayed story recall	WRAML Story B	9*	15.80 (2.89)	impaired
	WRAML Story C	0*	14.50 (5.81)	impaired
	WRAML total	9*	30.30 (8.49)	impaired
Visual episodic recall				
Design memory recall	WRAML 1	7	11.20 (3.76)	intact
	WRAML 2	14	10.20 (2.44)	intact
	WRAML 3	6	6.00 (3.68)	intact
	WRAML 4	9	7.40 (2.50)	intact
	Total	36	34.80 (7.00)	intact
Picture feature recall	Classroom	5	4.30 (0.95)	intact
	Beach	6	5.90 (1.73)	intact
	Farm	5	6.60 (2.27)	intact
	Store	7	6.70 (3.27)	intact
	Total	23	23.36 (5.18)	intact

Note: WRAML = Wide Range Assessment of Memory and Learning.
[a]Mean (standard deviations in parentheses).
*Statistically significant, see text.

WRAML Story B, $t = 1.88$, $p < .045$, and WRAML Story C, $t = 2.06$, $p < .033$. On delayed story recall, M.M. was also significantly worse than the TD group on both WRAML Story B, $t = 2.25$, $p < .024$, and WRAML Story C, $t = 2.39$, $p < .019$.

Recall of a unique visual event

The scores in Table 2 indicate a consistent pattern of performance on tasks of visual episodic recall. M.M. did not differ significantly from the TD group on design recall for any of the four WRAML designs. M.M. also did not differ significantly from the TD group on the recall of visual features on any of the WRAML pictures.

Personal autobiographical episodic memory

Recall of episodes earlier in life. Performance on the expanded AMI is illustrated in Figure 2, with overall scores given in Table 3. The scores refers to the mean correct number of answers, as judged to be correct by parents. M.M. differed significantly from the TD group on both personal autobiographical semantic memory, $t = 4.23$, $p < .001$, and personal autobiographical episodic memory, $t = 1.80$, $p < .05$.

Behavioural episodic memory. On Sunderland et al.'s (1983) questionnaire, high scores indicated poorer

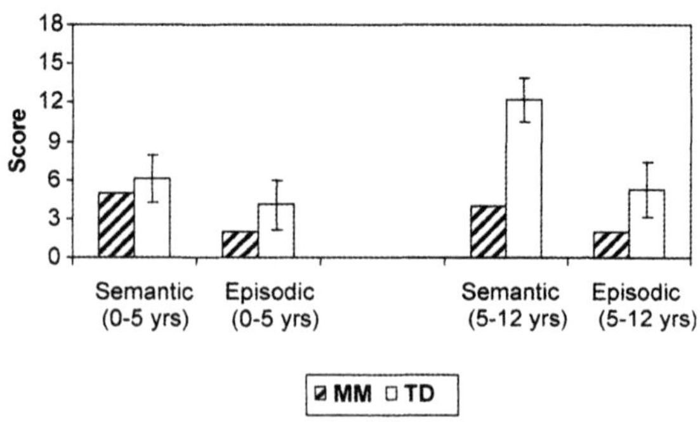

Figure 2. *Autobiographical semantic and episodic memory scores.*

Table 3. *Personal autobiographical episodic memory results*

Test	*M.M.*	*TD*[a]	*Memory*
Personal autobiographical episodic memory	4*	9.36 (3.14)	impaired
Personal autobiographical semantic memory	9*	18.27 (2.10)	impaired

[a]Mean (standard deviations in parentheses).
*Statistically significant, see text.

memory than low scores. On the behavioural episodic memory questions, within the questionnaire, M.M. attained a score of 72 as rated by a parent, indicating that episodic memory difficulties were occurring with considerable frequency in day-to-day life. The parents of the TD group rated their children in a way that corresponded to a mean score of 9.45 (3.96). Thus M.M. was significantly impaired in behavioural episodic memory in comparison to the TD group as rated by parents, $t = 14.16$, $p < .0001$. Performance on the full questionnaire as rated by parents is illustrated in Figure 3. M.M. was rated overall as having significantly more difficulty than the TD group, having a mean overall score of 110 compared to the control mean of 17.82 ($SD = 6.08$), $t = 14.52, p < .0001$.

Summary of episodic memory
The results indicate that M.M. has a severe impairment of verbal episodic memory. The impairment was pervasive across tasks. Both personal autobiographical episodic memory and behavioural episodic memory are also significantly impaired for M.M., in comparison to the TD group. In contrast to these deficits, visual episodic memory is intact.

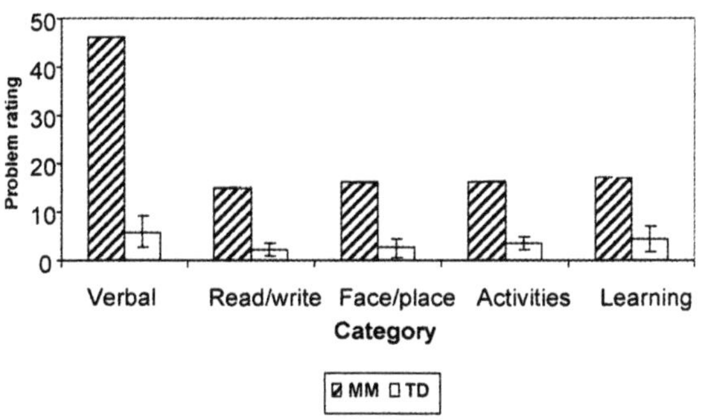

Figure 3. *Results for behavioural episodic memory difficulties.*

Recognition memory

Recognition memory scores are reported in Table 4. On the WRMB recognition memory for words, which occurred immediately after the stimuli were presented, M.M.'s score was weak but not significantly worse than the TD group, $t = 1.32$, $p = 0.10$. Verbal recognition memory after a thirty minute delay was significantly impaired on both the WRAML story B, $t = 7.66$, $p < .0001$ and the WRAML story C, $t = 3.39$, $p < .003$. Thus, verbal recognition memory was adequate for single words but significantly impaired for delayed story recall. WRMB recognition memory for faces was unimpaired at a level just above the TD mean, $t = 0.042$, $p = .48$.

Procedural memory

Mirror star tracing
M.M. exhibited a normal learning trend on the star-drawing task, making fewer errors over consecutive trials. Performance is illustrated in Figure 4. Performance across trials did not differ significantly from that of the TD group. Accuracy on the final trial was also at a level close to the control mean. Thus, procedural memory for M.M. is intact for this measure.

Behavioural procedural memory

On the Sunderland et al.'s (1983) questionnaire, there is an item that related to behavioural procedural memory: "Unable to pick up a new skill/game/gadget after one or two practices." M.M.'s parent rated him as "very rarely" having this difficulty, a better rating for M.M. in terms of behaviour than that on any other item on the questionnaire (except for the visual memory measure "Fails to recognize someone met for the first time recently", on which she also rated him as very rarely having difficulty). The rating of 1 on each of these measures did not differ

Table 4. *Recognition memory results*

Test		*M.M.*	*TD*[a]	*Memory*
Verbal recognition				
Story facts recognition (delayed)	WRAML Story B	7*	12.60 (0.70)	impaired
	WRAML Story C	6*	11.6 (1.58)	impaired
	WRAML total	13*	24.2 (2.04)	impaired
Word recognition (immediate)	WRMB	30	35 (3.63)	$t = 1.32$; $p = .10$
Visual recognition				
Face recognition (immediate)	WRMB	38	37.82 (4.12)	intact

Note: WRAML = Wide Range Assessment of Memory and Learning. WRMB = Warrington Recognition Memory Battery.
[a]Mean (standard deviations in parentheses).
*Statistically significant, see text.

significantly from average TD ratings on each of these items. M.M.'s class teacher also completed the Sunderland et al. (1983) questionnaire. Too few of the teachers of the TD children returned the questionnaire for valid statistical analysis but it may be worth noting that M.M.'s teacher, whilst rating M.M. as having many memory difficulties in the classroom, also rated him as "very rarely" having difficulty on the behavioural procedural memory item.

Reading

The means and standard deviations for the results in this section are given in Table 5. Accuracy scores refer to the number of items read correctly for the single-item lists and the text reading ages on the Neale. M.M.'s ability to read single words on the Schonell was significantly poorer than that of the TD group, $t = 2.76$, $p < .01$. M.M. was also significantly poorer than the TD group at text reading, in relation to accuracy, $t = 2.81$, $p < .01$, rate, $t = 2.58$, $p < .02$, and comprehension, $t = 1.80$, $p < .05$. These reading scores were all below the TD range, with reading ages for M.M. of 6–7 years. M.M. also made significantly more errors on morphological list, $t = 11.84$, $p < .0001$, and made significantly more homophonic errors than the TD group, $t = 1.94$, $p < .04$. Performance on both these lists was below the TD range. Despite the severe impairment in single-word and text reading evident from these scores, M.M.'s ability to read nonwords did not differ from that of the TD group, $t = 1.23$, $p > .13$, and was within the TD range. Nonword reading was therefore unimpaired, indicating well-developed phonological reading skills.

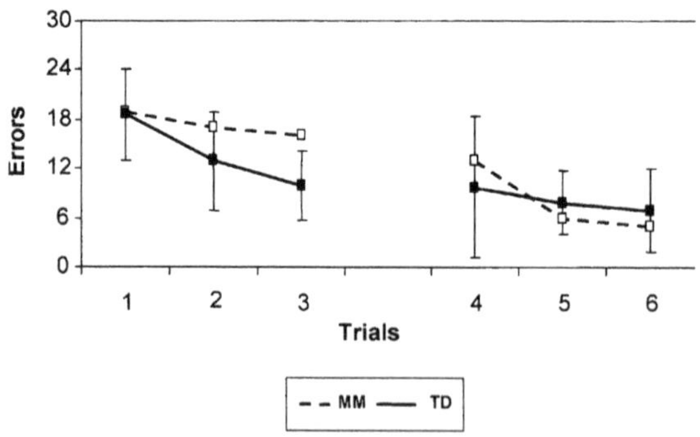

Figure 4. *Errors scores for the mirror star-drawing task.*

Regular and irregular words

M.M. showed a frequency effect on the Behrmann and Bub (1992) list, reading regular words of high frequency more easily than those of low

Table 5. *Results for reading*

Test	*M.M.*	*TD*[a]	*Memory*
Single words accuracy	19*	60.55 (14.39)	impaired
Text accuracy	6*	10.08 (1.52)	impaired
Text rate	6.5*	10.37 (1.43)	impaired
Text comprehension	7.17*	9.58 (1.28)	impaired
Nonwords accuracy	18	21.64 (2.84)	intact
Morphological accuracy	34*	89.27 (4.47)	impaired
Homophonic errors	11*	4 (3.46)	impaired

[a]Mean (standard deviations in parentheses).
*Statistically significant, see text.

frequency. His performance was significantly worse than that of the TD group at reading regular words averaged across all frequencies, $t = 7.83, p < .001$, and irregular words across all frequencies, $t = 4.56, p < .001$. Overall M.M. demonstrated a significant regularity effect, reading regular words significantly better than irregular words, $\chi^2 = 5.87, p < .02$.

Reading skills summary

M.M. was significantly impaired in word recognition skills in comparison to controls. There was impaired reading of both regular and irregular words, though there was also a significant regularity effect, with regular words being read more easily than irregular words. There was also a significantly elevated level of homophone confusion. However nonword reading was normal. The lexico-semantic reading route is impaired in development but phonological reading skills are intact. This pattern of reading performance is that of surface dyslexia.

Learning with repeated presentation

Visual learning of locations

M.M. exhibited a learning curve in both modalities, cumulatively acquiring more correct responses over each successive trial. The results are illustrated in Figures 5a and 5b. For M.M., performance on the first visual trial, reflecting initial memory for location, was significantly lower than that for the TD group, $t = 2.12, p < .03$, but across all trials,

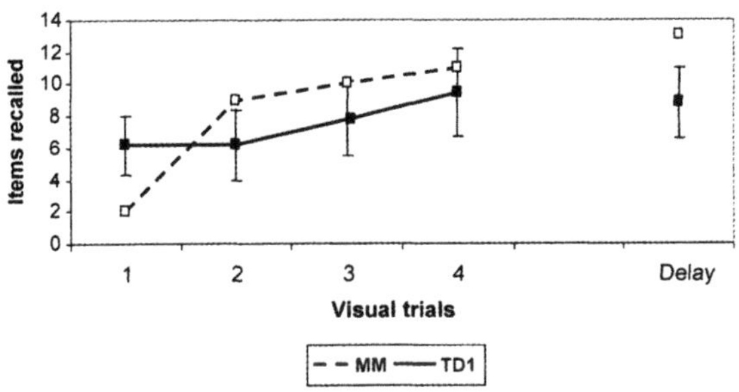

Figure 5a. *Results for learning visual material with repeated presentation.*

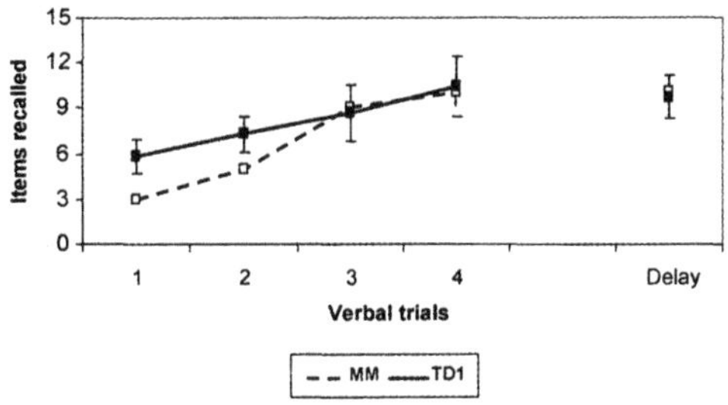

Figure 5b. *Results for learning verbal material with repeated presentation.*

visual learning of the positions was normal. Delayed visual recall for M.M. was high.

Verbal learning of a set of words

Performance on the first verbal trial was significantly lower for M.M. than for the TD group, $t = 2.50, p < .016$; however, across verbal trials, learning was normal for M.M. Delayed verbal recall was also normal for M.M.

Verbal and visual learning of paired associates

On the initial trial, M.M.'s performance was poor, $t(\text{visual}) = 1.84, p < .05$; $t(\text{verbal}) = 1.57, p < .07$. However, learning across visual and verbal trials was normal. Delayed recall was also normal for both visual and verbal pairs. These results indicate normal paired-associate learning for M.M.

Discussion

Developmental amnesia

Children with developmental amnesia constitute a population whose performance provides evidence relevant to debates concerning normal development. Such evidence addresses issues of the relative interdependence and independence of component skills within cognitive systems, which are also important for the modelling of adult cognitive systems. Specifically, children with developmental amnesia provide evidence about the degree of interrelationship or independence of memory systems in development, the pervasiveness of a componential modular organization within memory development, and the relationships between memory systems and other cognitive domains such as language and literacy. Cases in the literature to date encompass those with impairments of the following: both episodic and semantic memory; episodic but not semantic memory; semantic but not episodic memory; procedural but not episodic memory; episodic but not procedural memory; visual episodic but not verbal episodic memory; and verbal episodic but not visual episodic memory. This paper has reported a new case of developmental amnesia, M.M., who has significant memory impairment, despite normal intelligence. M.M. was identified following the screening of normal children attending normal schools. The case indicates that amongst the normal school population there are previously unidentified children with memory impairments, raising an issue about the pervasiveness of developmental amnesia.

Semantic memory

M.M. had a memory impairment that was not generalized across all aspects of memory but that did affect semantic memory. The semantic memory impairment was pervasive across both semantic knowledge of facts and semantic knowledge of words (see Table 1). The results were consistent across multiple tasks, including general knowledge, knowledge of multiplication facts, knowledge of words as assessed by lexical decision, knowledge of word meanings as assessed by receptive vocabulary, and access to known words from semantic cues on oral fluency. This semantic memory disorder and its extension to an impairment in semantic knowledge of words was comparable to the previously reported case C.L. (Temple & Richardson, 2004), who was also identified following screening from the normal population, and also to the case of Julia (Temple, 1997b) and the case of Casalini et al. (1999). In the case of C.L. (Temple & Richardson, 2004), despite the semantic memory impairment for facts about the world and for knowledge of words, there was normal development of semantic knowledge about arithmetical facts. For M.M., there was no such selective preservation of arithmetical factual knowledge. Knowledge of arithmetical facts was also impaired for M.M. For C.L., there had also been intact development of autobiographical semantic knowledge, but for M.M. the semantic memory disorder extended to autobiographical semantic knowledge. Thus for M.M. the semantic memory impairment was generalized with no evidence of any preserved skills.

The fact that M.M. had a semantic memory impairment, which extended to an impairment in semantic knowledge of words, raises the possibility that some cases of developmental amnesia may initially present as children with language difficulties, particularly with anomias. This was a feature of the initial referral of Julia (Temple, 1997b), where her anomic difficulties were more immediately conspicuous than her memory problems. On closer analysis, such cases, like Julia, would demonstrate absence of knowledge of the words rather than simple failure to retrieve the lexical labels associated with items. They would be expected to have semantic representation anomias rather than semantic access anomias (Temple, 1997b; Van Hout, 1993).

Of note, in relation to vocabulary development, although semantic fluency was impaired for M.M., phonemic fluency was intact. This suggests that it is not that vocabulary has failed to develop but rather that it is semantic knowledge of that vocabulary that is problematic. The phonemic knowledge of the vocabulary, which would enable word access from a phonemic cue, is normal, and vocabulary levels are sufficient to enable normal performance on the cued phonemic retrieval task. Nevertheless, there may also be some degradation of vocabulary levels as lexical decision, which in principle does not require semantic activation, is also impaired for M.M.

For M.M., there was also impairment to those components of literacy systems that are dependent upon semantic representations. Thus, there was impaired lexico-semantic reading, reflected in poor reading of all words but particularly impaired reading of irregular words with consequently significant regularity effects in reading. Irregular words violate phonological reading rules and are therefore particularly dependent upon word-specific semantic knowledge in order to be read accurately.

Weak semantic skills within literacy systems were also evident from the elevated level of homophone confusion. To distinguish homophones, phonological reading skills are again inadequate as the words have the same phonological pattern. Lexico-semantic skills concerning the meaning of the words are required for their differentiation. Thus, elevated homophone confusion is taken as evidence of impaired ability to use semantic knowledge in reading. Such difficulties are characteristic of surface dyslexia (Coltheart et al., 1983; Temple, 1984, 1985b).

Despite the lexico-semantic difficulties within reading for M.M., phonological reading skills were intact, with normal ability to read nonwords, which is also a further characteristic of surface dyslexia. This pattern of reading difficulties in a child with semantic memory difficulties is similar to that demonstrated by both C.L. (Temple & Richardson, 2004) and Julia (Temple, 1997b). In each case, semantic memory disorder co-occurs with impaired lexico-semantic reading systems. The distinction between impairment of the reading route, which utilizes semantic knowledge but intact phonological reading skills, is consistent with many studies that have argued for the modularity of these two reading processes (Coltheart et al., 2001).

There is ongoing debate concerning whether we have a unitary semantic system that underlies all tasks or whether there are multiple semantic systems dedicated to distinct tasks. M.M., C.L., and Julia all have a semantic memory disorder, which affects knowledge of facts but also affects semantic knowledge of language and semantic skills within reading. Such a pattern argues either for a common semantic system in development, which has impact upon memory, language, and literacy, or for an impairment that has comparable impact upon the semantic systems that underlie memory, language, and literacy. The former is more parsimonious in relation to the current study. Evidence in support of the latter would be found if cases of developmental amnesia were described within which there was semantic memory disorder but no difficulties with word knowledge or literacy.

A common semantic system in development, which has impact upon memory, language, and literacy, argues that whatever the "modular" structure of developing systems, they would have to incorporate intercommunication, cross-connections, and dependence from the semantic "module" to memory, language, and literacy. In the strictest Fodorian (Fodor, 1983) terms, this would actually render the semantic system nonmodular. Alternatively in the more contemporary use of this terminology, it may create a specification of how some of the connections from a semantic "module" must flow in development. It also suggests that the influence and interdependencies of the semantic system within development may be similar to the influence and interdependencies of the semantic system in adulthood, which become most evident during the progress of semantic dementia (Hodges, Graham, & Patterson, 1995; Patterson & Hodges, 1992, 2000). In semantic dementia, semantic memory impairment is also associated with loss of the knowledge of the meanings of words in vocabulary and with the development of surface dyslexia in reading.

Whatever the arguments concerning the implications for the concept of modularity of the links between the semantic system and the other systems it appears to influence, this does not mean that memory itself is not composed of discrete semi-independent components. As is discussed below, sharp dissociation within memory skills characterizes episodic memory for M.M.

Episodic memory

As discussed earlier, there is current debate concerning whether episodic memory is a single system or whether it may have distinct subcomponents. One candidate division has been between episodic memory for unique episodes of novel information and episodic memory for autobiographical knowledge. Another potential division is in relation to whether the content of the episodic memory is visual or verbal. For M.M., verbal episodic memory for a unique episode of novel information was impaired but visual episodic memory for a unique episode of novel information was intact. M.M. failed to remember stories and word lists but could remember designs and visual features of pictures. This indicated a material-specific impairment of episodic memory. The dissociation within episodic memory, demonstrated by M.M., with fractionation between impaired verbal episodic memory for stories and words and intact visual episodic memory for designs and visual features, is similar to that described by Casalini et al. (1999) for O.N. O.N. was impaired in both semantic and episodic memory but there was a material-specific effect to the episodic impairment with verbal episodic memory impaired but preserved visual episodic memory for the structure of patterns and designs. These dissociations, within episodic memory, for M.M. and ON form a double dissociation with the case of Dr S. (Temple, 1992). Dr S. was a lady of high intelligence who had strong verbal episodic memory skills, reflected, for example, in excellent story recall but very weak visual episodic memory skills, with severely impaired memory for patterns and designs. The double dissociation between the cases of M.M. and O.N. compared to Dr S. suggests that verbal and visual episodic memory, for unique episodes of novel information, have relatively independent developmental paths and argues for material-specific modularity within episodic memory systems. This potential distinction within episodic memory systems also receives support from studies of temporal lobe epilepsy and temporal lobectomy cases in childhood. It leaves open the issue of whether the mechanism is the same for both types of material and what is impaired is management of a particular type of data set, or whether the underlying mechanisms for the different types of stimuli are themselves distinct.

For M.M., a further dissociation within episodic memory concerns the good episodic recall for unique events involving visual patterns and visual features of pictures but yet the significantly impaired recall of visual locations on the initial trial of the visual learning tasks. An initial trial is still a unique episode of novel information, as it has not yet been repeated. This suggests that the intact visual episodic memory applies to memory for identity and structure rather than memory for locations. It is already known that in development the two visual channels for visual recognition and visual location knowledge can be selectively impaired (Ariel & Sadeh, 1996; McCloskey et al., 1995). The episodic memory data here suggest a single dissociation for M.M. with impaired episodic memory for locations but intact episodic memory for structure and identity of designs.

The investigation of episodic memory for M.M., included analyses of both autobiographical episodic memory and day-to-day behavioural episodic memory. In both areas, episodic memory was impaired. Thus, the episodic disorder is not simply an abstracted condition evident in the laboratory, it is a disorder with explicit impact in the outside world. The data from M.M. do not provide any evidence to support a distinction between the episodic memory systems underlying personal autobiographical episodic memory and episodic memory for unique novel events.

As discussed above, Tulving (2002) has suggested that successful performance on recognition memory may occur at episodic, semantic, or perceptual levels of memory. For M.M., verbal recognition memory was adequate for single words but significantly impaired for delayed story recall whilst recognition memory for faces was unimpaired. The content-specific nature of these difficulties is similar to the content-specific results for episodic recall but provides no definitive evidence relating to the issue of the relationship of recognition memory to other memory systems.

Procedural memory

Despite impairment, for M.M., in semantic memory, verbal episodic memory, visual episodic memory for locations, and personal autobiographical episodic memory, procedural memory was intact, at least as assessed on a mirror drawing task and on parental and teacher assessment of behaviour. Thus, at least in relation to the tasks assessed here, the development of procedural memory is not dependent upon semantic memory or those components of episodic memory that are impaired for M.M. In adult amnesia, procedural memory is also intact despite pervasive episodic impairment.

Learning
Hintzman (1986) argued that semantic memory is an emergent property of episodic memory, with the common elements of repeated episodic memories forming a semantic memory over time. The context of the memory becomes obsolete. Squire (1992a, 1992b; Squire & Zola, 1998) also argued that independence of limbic-diencephalic systems is achieved through consolidation. If this were true, then semantic memory problems could exist independently of the functioning of episodic memory, but difficulties in episodic memory would always copresent with poor semantic memory skills. As seen for the cases of Vargha-Khadem (Baddeley et al., 2001; Gadian et al., 2000; Vargha-Khadem et al., 1997, 2002) impaired episodic memory does not require semantic memory to be impaired. Rather, the double dissociation between the Vargha-Khadem cases and C.L. (Temple & Richardson, 2004) suggests that semantic knowledge and episodic memory develop separately from each other. This raises the further issue of what happens during learning. If the development of semantic memory can be independent of episodic memory, can learning itself be independent of episodic memory? As discussed above, there is some evidence from previous studies of both adults and children that learning is possible in the face of episodic impairment (Broman et al., 1997; Guillery-Girard et al., 2004; Hamann & Squire, 1995; Kitchener et al., 1998; Maravita, et al., 1995; Tulving et al., 1991). Further evidence derives from the data here. Despite weak initial skills, M.M. had normal learning across trials, with repeated presentations. The evidence in both verbal and nonverbal domains from learning with repeated presentations indicated that despite his episodic impairment, learning takes place if there are repeated presentations.

In the case of M.M., the data further highlight that this learning with repeated presentations is not the same as the acquisition of established semantic knowledge. For whilst M.M. appears to demonstrate normal learning in the laboratory when there are repeated presentations of stimuli or stimuli pairings, he nevertheless has an extensive semantic memory impairment. One possibility is that there is abnormality in longer term processes of memory consolidation. Another possibility is that learning that takes place with repeated trials is a distinct process to semantic memory acquisition. This would mean not only that learning with repeated presentations is distinct from episodic memory but also that it is distinct from the acquisition of semantic memory. We know that the idea of semantic memories being derived from repeated episodic exposures or repetition across learning trials is in any case inadequate, as in semantic memory acquisition, single-trial acquisition is not uncommon. If it was uncommon there would be severe limitations in the pedagogical processes of attending lectures and reading books. Whilst the emphasis is often upon what is forgotten, it is also clear that we have the capacity to establish extensive semantic memories from such single-trial exposures. Learning with repeated presentations may be relevant to the acquisition of particular forms of knowledge—for example, those for which semantic content is more limited. A possible candidate in this domain is knowledge of arithmetical facts, which appears from both studies of adults and children to be dissociable from other forms of semantic knowledge (Butterworth et al., 2002; Cappalletti et al., 2001) and for which the need for repeated presentation in the acquisition process is evident in children trying to learn their tables. Even here though, M.M., who appears able to learn across repeated presentations, has difficulty. Investigation over longer delays and in relation to different types of material would enable differentiation of these alternative possibilities.

Etiology
The case O.N., whose characteristics resemble those of M.M., was reported as having a family history of similar difficulties (Casalini et al., 1999). No relevant family history was established for M.M. but possibly pertinent background was revealed from retrospective examination of medical notes. Although identified from the

normal school sample, M.M. was found retrospectively to have been born at 32 weeks with a birthweight of 2,290 g, which fits the World Health Organization (WHO) classification for both preterm birth (<37 weeks) and low birthweight (<2,500 g). Thus, although not selected on this basis, this new case of developmental amnesias was subsequently found to be both preterm and of low birthweight. M.S., the early case of developmental amnesia detailed by De Renzi and Lucchelli (1990), was also of low birthweight, at 2,500 g with birth at 28 weeks.

After preterm birth, the most common medical complication is hyaline membrane disease, which M.M. displayed. Also known as respiratory distress syndrome, it results from immaturity in the lungs associated with surfactant deficiency. In M.M.'s case the condition was mild, and oxygen was given for just 24 hours. No further explicit details are available.

Gadian et al. (2000) link the episodic memory impairment that they report to the effects of the birth hypoxia, in particular upon the hippocampus. In common with these cases, M.M. has verbal episodic memory impairment but M.M. also has semantic memory impairment, and visual episodic memory is unimpaired. Thus, whilst the case resembles those of Gadian et al. (2000) in terms of a verbal episodic memory impairment it differs in terms of the additional semantic memory impairment and also in terms of the material-specific nature of the episodic impairment.

Hippocampal abnormality is reported in low-birthweight, preterm children who are similar to M.M. (Isaacs et al., 2000). Isaacs et al. (2000) studied memory development in preterm children and found that parents noted significantly increased everyday memory problems on the Rivermead Behavioural Memory Test. The children were also impaired in episodic recall of both stories and designs from the Wechsler Memory Scales. Isaacs et al. (2000) also reported reduced hippocampal volume in an MRI analysis of the children but to a less severe degree than that reported by Gadian et al. (2000). Isaacs et al. (2003) found that 8–9-year-old preterm children were impaired on immediate story recall and delayed route recall. In contrast, Briscoe, Gathercole, and Marlow (2001) found only 3/20 preterm children had impaired scores on the Rivermead, and their groups did not differ significantly from controls. Visual memory impairment has not been reported in preterm children on recall of the Figure of Rey (Isaacs et al., 2000; Rushe et al., 2001). Rushe et al. (2001) also failed to find impairment in preterm children in immediate or delayed story recall from the Rivermead. The composition of the children in these group analyses is unclear but consistent effects across all preterm children have not yet been established, although a link between prematurity and memory difficulties remains probable in some cases. The characterization of such difficulties may vary across cases. In the absence of further case-by-case analyses, in these group preterm studies, the etiological issue remains unresolved.

CONCLUDING COMMENTS

M.M. is a further case of developmental amnesia who illustrates the variable forms of the syndromes that are subsumed within this label. He provides further evidence that such memory disorders need not be generalized and may have impact upon some forms of memory and not others. Similarly, they may have impact upon some components of linked cognitive systems but not others. Impairments are specific to particular forms of memory and particular aspects of literacy or language with residual normality in each domain. This is not consistent with recent theorizing suggesting that within developmental disorders impairments are necessarily pervasive in all domains (Thomas & Karmiloff-Smith, 2002). The results are consistent with more modular theories of cognitive development, within which there are discrete components of cognitive skills, which can have independent trajectories.

PrEview proof published online 30 March 2006

REFERENCES

Aggleton, J. P., & Pearce, J. M. (2002). Neural systems underlying episodic memory: Insights from animal research. In A. Baddeley, M. Conway, & J. Aggleton (Eds.), *Episodic memory* (pp. 204–231). Oxford, UK: Oxford University Press.

Ariel, R., & Sadeh, M. (1996). Congenital visual agnosia and prosopagnosia in a child: A case report. *Cortex, 32*, 221–240.

Baddeley, A. D., Emslie, H., & Nimmo-Smith, I. (1993a). *Speed and capacity of language processing*. Bury-St-Edmunds, UK: Thames Valley Test Company.

Baddeley, A., Emslie, H., & Nimmo-Smith, I. (1993b). The Spot-the-Word Test: A robust estimate of verbal intelligence based on lexical decision. *British Journal of Clinical Psychology, 32*, 55–65.

Baddeley, A., Vargha-Khadem, F., & Mishkin, M. (2001). Preserved recognition in a case of developmental amnesia: Implications for the acquisition of semantic memory? *Journal of Cognitive Neuroscience, 13*, 357–369.

Baddeley, A. D., & Wilson, B. (1986). Amnesia, autobiographical memory and confabulation. In D.C. Ruben (Ed.), *Autobiographical memory.* Cambridge, UK: Cambridge University Press.

Behrmann, M., & Bub, D. (1992). Surface dyslexia and dysgraphia: Dual routes, single lexicon. *Cognitive Neuropsychology, 9*, 209–251.

Bishop, D. V. M. (1997). Cognitive neuropsychology and developmental disorders: Uncomfortable bedfellows. *Quarterly Journal of Experimental Psychology, 50A*, 899–923.

Brainerd, C. J., & Reyna, V. F. (1992). Explaining "memory free" reasoning. *Psychological Science, 3*, 332–339.

Briscoe, J., Gathercole, S. E., & Marlow, N. (2001). Everyday memory and cognitive ability in children born very prematurely. *Journal of Child Psychology and Psychiatry, 42*, 749–754.

Brizzolara, D., Casalini, C., Montanaro, D., & Posteraro, F. (2003). A case of amnesia at an early age. *Cortex, 39*, 605–625.

Broman, M., Rose, A. L., Hotson, G., & Casey, C. M. (1997). Severe anterograde amnesia with onset in childhood as a result of anoxic encephalopathy. *Brain, 120*, 417–433.

Butterworth, B., Cappelletti, M., & Kopelman, M. (2001). Category specificity in reading and writing: The case of number words. *Nature Neuroscience, 4*, 784–786.

Campbell, R. (1992). Face to face: Interpreting a case of developmental prosopagnosia. In R. Campbell (Ed.), *Mental lives: Case studies in cognition*. Oxford, UK: Basil Blackwell.

Cappelletti, M., Butterworth, B., & Kopelman, M. (2001). Spared numerical abilities in a case of semantic dementia. *Neuropsychologia, 39*, 1224–1239.

Casalini, C., Brizzolara, D., Cavallaro, M. C., & Cipriani, P. (1999). "Developmental dysmnesia": A case report. *Cortex, 35*, 713–727.

Castles, A., & Coltheart, M. (1996). Cognitive correlates of developmental surface dyslexia: A single case study. *Cognitive Neuropsychology, 13*, 25–50.

Clahsen, H., Ring, M., & Temple, C. M. (2004). Lexical and morphological skills in English-speaking children with Williams syndrome. In S. Bartke & J. Siegmueller (Eds.), *Williams syndrome across languages* (Vol. 36, pp. 221–244). Amsterdam: John Benjamins.

Clahsen, H., & Temple, C. M. (2003). Words and rules in children with Williams syndrome. In Y. Levy & J. Schaeffer (Eds.), *Language competence across populations*. Hillsdale, NJ: Lawrence Erlbaum Associates, Inc.

Coltheart, M., Masterson, J., Byng, S., Prior, M., & Riddoch, J. (1983). Surface dyslexia. *Quarterly Journal of Experimental Psychology, 35*, 469–496.

Coltheart, M., Rastle, K., Perry, C., Langdon, R., & Ziegler, J. (2001). DRC: A dual route cascaded model of visual word recognition and reading aloud. *Psychological Review, 108*, 204–256.

Conway, M. A. (2002). Sensory-perceptual episodic memory and its context: Autobiographical memory. In A. Baddeley, M. Conway, & J. Aggleton (Eds.), *Episodic memory* (pp. 53–70). Oxford, UK: Oxford University Press.

Crawford, J. R., & Howell, D. C. (1998). Comparing an individual's test score against norms derived from small samples. *The Clinical Neuropsychologist, 12*, 482–486.

De Haan, E., & Campbell, R. (1991). A fifteen year follow-up of a case of developmental prosopagnosia. *Cortex, 27*, 489–509.

De Renzi, E., & Lucchelli, F. (1990). Developmental dysmnesia in a poor reader. *Brain, 113*, 1337–1345.

Duchaine, B. C. (2000). Developmental prosopagnosia with normal configural processing. *Neuroreport, 11*, 79–83.

Duchaine, B. C., Nieminen-von Wendt, T., New, J., & Kulomaki, T. (2003a). Dissociations of visual recognition in a developmental agnosic: Evidence for separate developmental processes. *Neurocase, 9*, 380–389.

Duchaine, B. C., Parker, H., & Nakayama, K. (2003b). Normal recognition of emotion in a prosopagnosic. *Perception, 32*, 827–838.

Fodor, J. A. (1983). *The modularity of mind.* Cambridge, MA: MIT Press.

Gaddes, W. H., & Crockett, D. J. (1975). The Spreen–Benton aphasia tests: Normative data as a measure of normal language development. *Brain and Language, 2*, 257–280.

Gadian, D. G., Aicardi, J., Watkins, K. E., Porter, D. A., Mishkin, M., & Vargha-Khadem, F. (2000). Developmental amnesia associated with early hypoxic-ischaemic injury. *Brain, 123*, 499–507.

Gardiner, J. M. (2002). Episodic memory and autonoetic consciousness: A first-person approach. In A. Baddeley, M. Conway, & J. Aggleton (Eds.), *Episodic memory* (pp. 11–30). Oxford, UK: Oxford University Press.

Guillery-Girard, B., Martins, S., Parisot-Carbuccia, D., & Eustache, F. (2004). Semantic acquisition in childhood amnesic syndrome: A prospective study. *Cognitive Neuroscience and Neuropsychology, 15*, 377–381.

Hamann, S. B., & Squire, L. R. (1995). On the acquisition of new declarative knowledge in amnesia. *Behavioural Neuroscience, 109*, 1027–1044.

Henderson Publishing Ltd. (1995). *Trivia quiz.* Woodbridge, UK: Author.

Hintzman, D. L. (1986). Schema abstraction in a multiple trace memory model. *Psychological Review, 93*, 411–428.

Hodges, J. R., Graham, N., & Patterson, K. (1995). Charting the progression in semantic dementia: Implications for the organisation of semantic memory. *Memory, 3*, 463–495.

Isaacs, B., & Kennie, A. T. (1973). *The Set Test as an aid to the detection of dementia in old people.* London: Royal College of Psychiatrists.

Isaacs, E. B., Lucas, A., Chong, W. K., Wood, S. J., Johnson, C. L., Marshall, C. et al. (2000). Hippocampal volume and everyday memory in children of very low birth weight. *Pediatric Research, 47*, 713–720.

Isaacs, E. B., Vargha-Khadem, F., Watkins, K. E., Lucas, A., Mishkin, M., & Gadian, D. G. (2003). Developmental amnesia and its relationship to degree of hippocampal atrophy. *Proceedings of the National Academy of Sciences, 100*, 13060–13063.

Kay, J., Lesser, R., & Coltheart, M. (1992). *PALPA: Psycholinguistic Assessments of Language Processing in Aphasia.* Hove, UK: Psychology Press.

Kitchener, E. G., Hodges, J. R., & McCarthy, R. (1998) Acquisition of post-morbid vocabulary and semantic facts in the absence of episodic memory. *Brain, 121*, 1313–1327.

Kopelman, M. D., Wilson, B. A., & Baddeley, A. D. (1989). The autobiographical memory interview: A new assessment of autobiographical and personal semantic memory in amnesic patients. *Journal of Clinical and Experimental Neuropsychology, 11*, 724–744.

Laiacona, M., Barbarotto, R., & Capitani, E. (1993). Perceptual and associative knowledge in category specific impairment of semantic memory: A study of two cases. *Cortex, 29*, 727–740.

Maravita, A., Spadoni, M., Mazzucchi, A., & Parma, M. (1995). A new case of retrograde amnesia with abnormal forgetting rate. *Cortex, 31*, 653–667.

Maurer, R. G. (1992). Disorders of memory and learning. In F. Boller & J. Grafman (Series Eds.) & S. J. Segalowitz & I. Rapin (Vol. Ed.), *Handbook of neuropsychology: Vol. 7. Child Neuropsychology* (pp. 241–259). North Holland: Elsevier Science Publishers.

McCloskey, M., Rapp, B., Yantis, S., Rubin, G., Bacon, W. F., Dagnelie, G. et al. (1995). A developmental deficit in localising objects from vision. *Psychological Science, 6*, 112–117.

Morris, R. G. M. (2002). Episodic-like memory in animals: Psychological criteria, neural mechanisms and the value of episodic-like tasks to investigate animal models of neurodegenerative disease. In A. Baddeley, M. Conway, & J. Aggleton (Eds.), *Episodic memory* (pp. 181–203). Oxford, UK: Oxford University Press.

Neale, M. D., Christophers, U., & Whetton, C. (1989). *Neale analysis of reading ability–revised British edition.* Windsor, UK: NFER-Nelson.

Nelson, K. (1993) The psychological and social origins of autobiographical memory. *Psychological Science, 4*, 7–14.

Ostergaard, A. L. (1987). Episodic, semantic and procedural memory in a case of amnesia at an early age. *Neuropsychologia, 25*, 341–357.

Ozonoff, S., & Jensen, J. (1999). Brief report: Specific executive function profiles in three neurodevelopmental disorders. *Journal of Autism and Developmental Disorders, 29*, 171–177.

Patterson, K., & Hodges, J. R. (1992). Deterioration of word meaning: Implications for reading. *Neuropsychologia, 12,* 1025–1040.

Patterson, K., & Hodges, J. R. (2000). Semantic dementia: One window on the structure and organisation of semantic memory. In L. S. Cermak (Ed.), *Handbook of neuropsychology: Memory and its disorders.* Amsterdam: Elsevier.

Perner, J., & Ruffman, T. (1995) Episodic memory and autonoetic consciousness: Developmental evidence and a theory of childhood amnesia. *Journal of Experimental Child Psychology, 59,* 516–548.

Pitchford, N. J., & Funnell, E. (1999). An acquired form of developmental phonological dyslexia. *Cognitive Neuropsychology, 16,* 573–587.

Pringle, B., Dahlquist, L. M., & Eskenazi, A. (2003). Memory in pediatric patients undergoing conscious sedation for aversive medical procedures. *Health Psychology, 22,* 263–269.

Raven, J. C. (1998). *Raven's Progressive Matrices.* Windsor, UK: NFER-Nelson.

Rey, A. (1964). *L'examen clinique en psychologie.* Paris: Presses Universitaires de France.

Romans, S., Roeltgen, D., Kushner, H., & Ross, J. (1997). Executive function in girls with Turner's syndrome. *Developmental Neuropsychology, 13,* 23–40.

Rushe, T. M., Rifkin, L., Stewart, A. L., Townsend, J. P., Roth, S. C., Wyatt, J. S. et al. (2001). Neuropsychological outcome of adolescence of very preterm birth and its relation to brain structure. *Developmental Medicine and Child Neurology, 43,* 226–233.

Samuelsson, S. (2000). Converging evidence for the role of occipital regions in orthographic processing: A case of developmental surface dyslexia. *Neuropsychologia, 38,* 351–362.

Schonell, F. J., & Schonell, E. F. (1956). *Schonell reading and spelling: Diagnostic and attainment testing.* Edinburgh, UK: Oliver and Boyd.

Sheslow, D., & Adams, W. (1990). *Wide Range Assessment of Memory and Learning WRAML.* London, UK: The Psychological Corporation.

Snowling, M., Stothard, S., & McLean, J. (1996). *Graded Nonword Reading Test.* Bury St Edmunds, UK: Thames Valley Test Company.

Sokol, S. M., Macaruso, P., & Gollan, T. H. (1994). Developmental dyscalculia and cognitive neuropsychology. *Developmental Neuropsychology, 10,* 413–441.

Squire, L. R. (1992a). Declarative and non-declarative memory: Multiple brain systems supporting learning and memory. *Journal of Cognitive Neuroscience, 4,* 232–243.

Squire, L. R. (1992b). Memory and the hippocampus: A synthesis from findings with rats, monkeys and humans. *Psychological Review, 99,* 195–231.

Squire, L. R., & Zola, S. M. (1998) Episodic memory, semantic memory and amnesia. *Hippocampus, 8,* 205–211.

Stuart, M., & Howard, D. (1995). KJ: A developmental deep dyslexic. *Cognitive Neuropsychology, 12*(8), 793–824.

Sunderland, A., Harris, J. E., & Baddeley, A. D. (1983). Do laboratory tests predict everyday memory? *Journal of Verbal Learning and Verbal Behaviour, 22,* 341–357.

Temple, C. M. (1984). Surface dyslexia in a child with epilepsy. *Neuropsychologia, 22,* 569–576.

Temple, C. M. (1985a). Developmental surface dysgraphia: A case report. *Applied Psycholinguistics, 6,* 391–406.

Temple, C. M. (1985b). Surface dyslexia: Variation within a syndrome. In K. Patterson, J. C. Marshall, & M. Coltheart (Eds.), *Surface dyslexia* (pp. 269–288). Hove, UK: Lawrence Erlbaum Associates Ltd.

Temple, C. M. (1986). Developmental dysgraphias. *Quarterly Journal of Experimental Psychology, 38A,* 77–110.

Temple, C. M. (1991). Procedural dyscalculia and number fact dyscalculia: Double dissociation in developmental dyscalculia. *Cognitive Neuropsychology, 8,* 155–176.

Temple, C. M. (1992). Developmental memory impairment: Faces and patterns. In R. Campbell (Ed.), *Mental lives: Case studies in cognition* (pp. 199–215). Oxford, UK: Blackwell.

Temple, C. M. (1997a). Cognitive neuropsychology and its application to children. *Journal of Child Psychology and Psychiatry, 38,* 27–52.

Temple, C. M. (1997b). *Developmental cognitive neuropsychology.* Hove, UK: Psychology Press.

Temple, C. M. (2002a). Developmental amnesias and acquired amnesias of childhood. In A. D. Baddeley, M. D. Kopelman, & B. A. Wilson (Eds.), *The handbook of memory disorders* (2nd ed., pp. 521–542). Chichester, UK: John Wiley and Sons.

Temple, C. M. (2002b). Oral fluency and narrative production in children with Turners syndrome. *Neuropsychologia, 40,* 1419–1427.

Temple, C. M., Carney, R. C., & Mullarkey, S. (1996). Frontal lobe function and executive skills in children with Turner's syndrome. *Developmental Neuropsychology, 12*, 343–363.

Temple, C. M., & Clahsen, H. (2002). How connectionist simulations fail to account for developmental disorders in children. *Behavioral and Brain Sciences, 25*, 769–770.

Temple, C. M., & Marriott, A. J. (1998). Arithmetical ability and disability in Turner's syndrome: A cognitive neuropsychological analysis. *Developmental Neuropsychology, 14*, 47–67.

Temple, C. M., & Martin Sanfilippo, P. (2003). Executive skills in Kleinfelter's syndrome. *Neuropsychologia, 41*, 1547–1559.

Temple, C. M., & Richardson, P. (2004). Developmental amnesia: A new pattern of dissociation with intact episodic memory. *Neuropsychologia, 42*, 764–781.

Temple, C. M., & Sherwood, S. (2002). Representation and retrieval of arithmetical facts: Developmental difficulties. *Quarterly Journal of Experimental Psychology, 55A*, 733–752.

Thomas, M., & Karmiloff-Smith, A. (2002). Are developmental disorders like cases of adult brain damage? Implications from connectionist modelling. *Behavioral and Brain Sciences, 25*, 727–788.

Tulving, E. (1972). Episodic and semantic memory. In E. Tulving & W. Donaldson (Eds.), *Organisation of memory* (pp. 381–403). New York: Academic Press.

Tulving, E. (1985). Memory and consciousness. *Canadian Psychologist, 26*, 1–12.

Tulving, E. (2002). Episodic memory and common sense: How far apart? In A. Baddeley, M. Conway, & J. Aggleton (Eds.), *Episodic memory* (pp. 269–288). Oxford, UK: Oxford University Press.

Tulving, E., Hayman, C. A. G., & Macdonald, C. A. (1991). Long-lasting perceptual priming and semantic learning in amnesia: A case experiment. *Journal of Experimental Psychology: Learning, Memory, and Cognition, 17*, 595–617.

Van Hout, A. (1993). Acquired aphasia in childhood and developmental dysphasias: Are the errors similar? Analysis of errors made in confrontation naming tasks. *Aphasiology, 7*, 525–531.

Vargha-Khadem, F., Gadian, D. G., & Mishkin, M. (2002). Dissociations in cognitive memory: The syndrome of developmental amnesia. In A. Baddeley, M. Conway, & J. Aggleton (Eds.), *Episodic memory: New directions in research* (pp. 153–163). London: Oxford University Press.

Vargha-Khadem, F., Gadian, D. G., Watkins, K. E., Connelly, A., Van Paesschen, W. V., & Mishkin, M. (1997). Differential effects of early hippocampal pathology on episodic and semantic memory. *Science, 277*, 376–380.

Warrington, E. K. (1984). *Recognition Memory Battery.* Windsor, UK: NFER-Nelson.

Wechsler, D. (1974). *The Wechsler Intelligence Scale for Children–Revised.* New York: The Psychological Corporation.

Wechsler, D. (1987). *Wechsler Memory Scale–Revised manual.* San Antonio, TX: The Psychological Corporation.

Wechsler, D. (1992). *The Wechsler Intelligence Scale for Children–III.* New York/London: The Psychological Corporation.

Wechsler, D. (1997). *Wechsler Memory Scale* (3rd ed.). London, UK: The Psychological Corporation.

Wilson, B. A., & Baddeley, A. D. (1988). Semantic, episodic and autobiographical memory in a post-meningitis patient. *Brain and Cognition, 8*, 31–46.

Wood, F. B., Brown, I. S., & Felton, R. H. (1989). Long-term follow-up of a childhood amnesic syndrome. *Brain and Cognition, 10*, 76–86.

Wood, F. B., Ebert, V., & Kinsbourne, M. (1982). The episodic–semantic memory distinction in memory and amnesia: Clinical and experimental observations. In L. S. Cermak (Ed.), *Human memory and amnesia.* Hillsdale, NJ: Lawrence Erlbaum Associates, Inc.

Yonelinas, A. P. (2002). Components of episodic memory: The contribution of recollection and familiarity. In A. Baddeley, M. Conway, & J. Aggleton (Eds.), *Episodic memory* (pp. 31–52). Oxford, UK: Oxford University Press.

COGNITIVE NEUROPSYCHOLOGY

Manuscripts are invited for submission. Please note that authors are encouraged to submit papers electronically to expedite the peer review process. Please email your paper, saved in a standard document format type such as Word (in PC format), Rich Text Format, or PDF to **reviews@psypress.co.uk**

COGNITIVE NEUROPSYCHOLOGY NOTES FOR CONTRIBUTORS

METHODOLOGICAL CONSIDERATIONS

Papers should in general satisfy methodological standards expected of publications on normal cognitive processes in such journals as the *Journal of Experimental Psychology* or *Cognitive Psychology*, as well as satisfying requirements appropriate for neuropsychological publications in journals such as *Brain* (e.g., where studies of neuropsychological patients are reported, efforts should be made to provide a clear background description of the general neurological and neuropsychological status of the patient).

The importance of single case studies for the resolution of theoretical issues is acknowledged, and methodologically adequate single case studies are welcomed. In reports of such studies, the nature of a patient's deficits should be documented in quantitative terms (a simple syndrome label is insufficient). The level of detail required here depends upon the specific hypothesis being tested. Essentially what is needed is documentation of the presence of specified deficits and preserved capacities as these are related to particular hypotheses.

In reports of group studies, criteria for selecting and for grouping patients must be detailed and explicit, and related to the particular hypotheses being tested. The designation of a group of patients simply as "Broca's aphasics", for example, would not be sufficient. A set of patients classified as Broca's aphasics can be extremely heterogeneous, and any conclusions reached in such a study may, in fact, be true for only a few of the patients in this group. One way around this problem is to treat each patient as an individual, i.e., carry out single case studies. Another is to provide explicit evidence of homogeneity of the group in a group study.

FORMAT OF SUBMISSIONS

Submission of an article is taken as acceptance by the author that the publisher will hold copyright on all material published in the journal, including printed, electronic, and other publication formats, in all languages. It is the author's responsibility to ensure that the article contains nothing that is libellous or infringes copyright.

1. Manuscripts are invited for submission. Please note that authors are encouraged to submit papers electronically to expedite the peer review process. Please email your paper, saved in a standard document format type such as Word, Rich Text Format, or PDF, to **reviews@psypress.co.uk**. Alternatively, if you wish to submit a hard copy, please send one copy of the manuscript AND a disk version to: Journals Editorial Assistant, Psychology Press Ltd, 27 Church Road, Hove, East Sussex, BN3 2FA, UK. Tel: (0)20 7017 7724; Fax: (0)20 7017 6717 Your covering email/letter must include full contact details (including email), the title of the journal to which you are submitting, and the title of your article.
2. All manuscripts should be prepared and submitted in American Psychological Association (APA) format following the latest edition of the *Publication Manual of the APA* (currently 5th edition), or any recent issue of an APA journal such as the *Journal of Experimental Psychology: General.* The citation of unpublished reports of empirical investigations is strongly discouraged.
3. Authors may request blind refereeing. In this case, it is the responsibility of the author to prepare his or her manuscript such that after detachment of the title page no clues remain as to authorial identities.
4. Each paper submitted to the Editor will be assigned to an Action Editor, who will thenceforth have full editorial responsibility for the paper, and will obtain and transmit to authors reviews from at least two independent reviewers.
5. The publishers require the submission of final, accepted manuscripts on disk (accompanied by matching hard copy). Guidelines for preparation of text and artwork for final electronic submission are available from the Editor or by email from **reviews@psypress.co.uk**
6. Specified corresponding authors will receive their article by email as a complete PDF. This allows the author to print up to 50 copies, free of charge, and disseminate them to colleagues. In many cases, this facility will be available up to two weeks prior to print publication of the article. One copy of the journal issue in which their paper appears will be sent by post to all specified corresponding authors free after print publication. Paper offprints can still be *purchased* by authors on request.

www.ingramcontent.com/pod-product-compliance
Ingram Content Group UK Ltd.
Pitfield, Milton Keynes, MK11 3LW, UK
UKHW052024060326
468742UK00012B/3384
* 9 7 8 1 8 4 1 6 9 8 1 3 7 *